Postmodern

Series
edited by
Theo D'haen
and
Hans Bertens

‘I’m telling you stories’: Jeanette Winterson and the Politics of Reading

Postmodern Studies 25

‘I’m telling you stories’: Jeanette Winterson and the Politics of Reading

Edited by
Helena Grice
and Tim Woods

Amsterdam - Atlanta, GA 1998

The paper on which this book is printed meets the requirements of 'ISO 9706: 1994, Information and documentation - Paper for documents - Requirements for permanence'.

ISBN: 90-420-0340-5

Transferred to digital printing 2003
Printed in The Netherlands

CONTENTS

LIST OF ABBREVIATIONS

All references to Jeanette Winterson's work will be to the following editions. Citations will be made to the following abbreviations accompanied by a page number within the text. Specific details of each edition are to be found in the Select Bibliography.

AL Jeanette Winterson, *Art And Lies*

AO Jeanette Winterson, *Art Objects: Essays on Ecstasy and Effrontery*

GS Jeanette Winterson, *Gut Symmetries*

O Jeanette Winterson, *Oranges Are Not The Only Fruit*

P Jeanette Winterson, *The Passion*

SC Jeanette Winterson, *Sexing The Cherry*

WB Jeanette Winterson, *Written On The Body*

READING JEANETTE WINTERSON WRITING

HELENA GRICE AND TIM WOODS

> Matter, that thing the most solid and well-known, which you are holding in your hands and which makes up your own body, is now known to be mostly empty space. Empty space and points of light. What does this say about the reality of the world? (*SC* 8)

REALITY or 'reality'? Reference in narratives has always been a thorny issue. The extent to which there is an extralinguistic dimension which can be tangibly known without recourse to textual representation, is one of the key areas of debate within the contemporary philosophical and aesthetic currents of postmodernism. Within literary production in Britain during the past decade, Jeanette Winterson has gradually risen to prominence as a writer who self-consciously explores the equivocal status of an objective reality. Her fiction frequently calls into question assumptions about narratorial identity, fictional artifice, and objective reality. Her novels may be described as 'historiographic metafictions',[1] narratives which appear to possess a recognition that narrative is not objective and that any representation of history is always an ideologically-laden discourse. Indeed, many of Winterson's fictions are engaged in an ironic re-thinking of history. In *The Passion*, Henri's narrative is punctuated with a distrust of stories that he relates to the reader. When Patrick tells of seeing a man's skin lifted off his back, Henri warns 'Don't believe that one' (*P* 23). Winterson constantly foregrounds the fictionality of history. In one interview, she has said: 'People have an enormous need ... to separate history, which is fact, from storytelling, which is not fact ... and the whole push of my work has been to say, you cannot know which is which'.[2] Winterson's telling refrain throughout *The Passion* — 'I'm telling you stories. Trust me' — fits her fiction squarely within historiographic metafiction's assertion 'that its world is both resolutely fictive and yet undeniably historical, and that what both realms share is their constitution in and as discourse' (Hutcheon, 142). It is this paradoxical assertion that fiction embodies and connects lies and truths, stories and trust, a relationship upon which Winterson preys, that has provided this book with much of its conceptual structure, as well as its title.

Jeanette Winterson's recent high profile in the media — with newspaper articles, magazine, radio, and television interviews, and the highly acclaimed broadcast of her novel rewritten as a television script, *Oranges Are Not the Only Fruit* — has gradually opened the path for her work to figure prominently on many British school syllabi and university curricula. This collection of essays partly reflects contemporary popular media attention and increased academic interest. Jeanette Winterson has now published several highly acclaimed novels: an early novel (which she regrets writing) *Boating for Beginners*; a substantial body of mature fiction in *The Passion*, *Oranges Are Not the Only Fruit*, *Sexing the Cherry*, *Written on the*

Body, and *Art and Lies*; and, very recently, her latest novel entitled *Gut Symmetries*. She has also published a wide-ranging book of essays of literary and cultural criticism entitled *Art Objects*. Furthermore, in addition to the television script of *Oranges*, she has also published another film script, entitled *Great Moments in Aviation*. Much of this output actively raises issues of significant interest within contemporary debates on literary and cultural studies: it interrogates the dominant contemporary models of history; it re-assesses power relations between the sexes, and actively seeks to represent and inscribe new female experiences; it explores the relations between language, 'truth' and representation; it explores the power relationship between the reader and text; it demonstrates a clear desire to use fictional experimentation to explore 'other' states of consciousness and repressed 'narratives', in what are frequently thought of as 'postmodern' styles. Winterson's fiction opens up the sites of literature, sexual politics, and history, in ways which have been considered by many as innovative, exciting and stimulating. Yet the reception of her work has not been without its detractors and critics. Some have found her work derivative, contradictory, sometimes offensive, and even old-fashioned. Consequently, Jeanette Winterson's rise has not been without its pitfalls, her literary trajectory reading like a game of snakes and ladders.

Despite the equivocal reception accorded to her work, we think that this substantial body of writing warrants serious and sustained attention, and that the current lack of any book-length study available to people interested in her work might be rectified by this collection. Given such a dearth of material on her writing, and the extensive teaching of her fiction as part of literature courses both at schools and at universities, we hope that such a book will provide an exciting opportunity to initiate a broader discussion about the merits, affiliations and preoccupations of Winterson's fiction. The intention of this book is to draw together a number of essays by acknowledged readers and prominent academics, which explore the cultural context of Winterson's writing to date. The essays are comparative in their attention to Winterson and other contemporary writers, theoretically and methodologically informed, and deal with topical cultural issues. The book contains both essays which are directly focused on individual novels, and some which are more general in their focus on Winterson's writing and the context of her feminist, lesbian, historical and philosophical concerns.

We have chosen to separate the essays into two broad sections which reflect the principal foci of Winterson's fiction and the methodologies which have been adopted by the essays. Clearly, any categorisation sets false boundaries. Such a grouping as 'The Politics of Reading and Writing' may potentially encompass all the pieces found within these pages. By the same token, the essays set out in 'Sexing the Text' recognise that Winterson's lesbian politics coincide with but are not subsumed by the feminist, philosophical or historical interests in her work. Our intention in sectionalising the essays in this way, is to allow the pieces to productively engage and complement each other: no doubt the reader will be able to perceive other connections across the sections. Winterson's difficulty as a writer sometimes engenders non-standard modes of response to her work, or what might be termed 'dialogic responses', strategies which will be discussed below.

The Politics of Reading and Writing

It is something of a banality to speak of the politics of this, that, or the other in literary studies these days. For better or worse, the shock effect has disappeared. However, Jeanette Winterson's writing does bring the politics of reading gendered narratives to the foreground once again. It is one of the principal purposes of this book to investigate this politics of reading, especially in the context of the way sexual identities of the narrator are challenged by

Winterson's fiction. A politics of reading is concerned with reading as a process of interpretation 'by which meanings and experiences are produced through a dialectical encounter between reader and text in a context or a set of interlocking contexts'.[3] Reading theory reading texts in this way opens up a pathway for abstract theory to be seen as a part and parcel of a dialogical activity, in which fiction harbours theories, just as theory harbours fictions. It explores the interaction of the reader's ideology and the context of the text's production. These essays effectively interrogate texts through theoretically informed positions, seeking to summarise, contextualise and *interrogate* the key debates informing contemporary theories about gender, lesbian identity, postmodernity and history; and, most importantly, assess and demonstrate the *effectiveness* of the different approaches in the reading of Winterson's fiction. The essays allow readers to see how theory and text can *interact*, rather than remaining on parallel but unmeeting lines. The fiction is always performing and enacting a theoretical position; whilst theory is always offering a practical position from which to act. However, in focusing on the politics of reading, one must not be tempted to view interpretation as a private reading experience which only concerns an independent text and an individual reader. These essays offer reading as interpretation, but interpretation as an engagement in a process by which meanings and experiences are produced through a dialectical encounter between reader and text in a context, or a set of interlocking contexts.

The act of interpretation is a search for a language adequate to the intimate experience of reading. Yet the interpretative act can also obscure the emotional experience of reading. Ute Kauer argues that Winterson's *Written on the Body* is a text which seeks to deconstruct the conventional clichés of gender in a search for a new language of love, passion and gendered codes of behaviour. Indeed, since language is an imprecise tool, clichés hide or disguise emotions, rather than describing them. Lynne Pearce is equally concerned with how to relate to texts at an emotional level and how interpretative actions can obscure the emotional experience of reading. In her disarmingly honest account of how her heavy ideological investment in Winterson's fiction acted counter-theoretically, Pearce compellingly argues that the reading process frequently causes the reader to employ all sorts of mechanisms and guile to protect and propagate her or his particular allegiances to a writer. Rather than a reader-power which controls texts through critical terminology, the critical apparatus brought to bear on texts is often a mark of a reader's frustrated efforts to stay in touch with his or her construction of an author. Consequently, Pearce states that 'what presents itself as critical and political judgement and discrimination is often concealing a far more messy and desperate struggle between text and reader'. So whilst we may think of reading as a process of naturalising strangeness through the need to make meaning, and as a search for a ground to support one's own identity, in Pearce's terms, reading as interpretation becomes a way of displacing and disfiguring a prior emotional investment with an author. Interpretation leads to a cover-up, an emotional betrayal, which is not always self-consciously performed.

The complexity of Winterson's texts constantly invites a number of alternative interpretations. These essays seek to demonstrate some of the different ways of reading that single texts can initiate. Indeed, all texts can produce and be approached from, vastly different ideological and methodological positions. Even the same text can elicit widely varying responses: for example, in her essay, Paulina Palmer reads *The Passion* in relation to the politics of lesbian desire; whereas Scott Wilson reads the same novel from within a much more overtly masculinist philosophical reading tradition in relation to the politics of history. Texts are therefore not single entities which may be easily assimilable by a single reader; as 'intertexts', they open themselves to a plurality of readings and positions; and this collection of essays may serve in part to demonstrate how different critical readings may be enacted.

The manner in which Winterson's novels form an intertextual web with other texts and stories, is a feature upon which a number of these essays comment. One can distinguish between two sorts of intertextuality, which may be termed 'weak' and 'strong' intertextuality. *Weak* intertextuality can be conceived of more readily as 'textual influence': where one writer has *consciously* borrowed words, phrases, ideas, images or structures from another writer, either as a gesture of acknowledging the other writer's importance, or in a gesture of ironic comment or textual subversion. *Strong* intertextuality, on the other hand, can be conceived of as a practice of imitation, quotation or borrowing which takes place *unconsciously*, because of the deep structural situation of certain ideas within a particular culture, much like ideological, gender, or racial structures. This *strong* version of intertextuality is described by Michel Foucault as follows:

> The frontiers of a book are never clear-cut: beyond the title, the first line and the last full-stop, beyond its internal configuration, its autonomous form, it is caught up in a system of references to other books, other texts, other sentences: it is a node within a network ... The book is simply not the object that one holds in one's hands; and it cannot remain within the relative parallelepiped that contains it: its unity is variable and relative. As soon as one questions that unity it loses its self-evidence: it indicates itself, constructs itself, only on the basis of a complex field of discourse.[4]

The fact that meaning is *activated* by a productive engagement between reader and various texts and discourses, suggests that no author has control over the delimitation of any meaning within his or her text. The fact of intertextuality as an unconscious reading and writing activity is described by Roland Barthes in another context, where he argues that intertextuality ought to be conceived of as:

> a passage, an overcrossing: thus it answers not to an interpretation, even a liberal one, but to an explosion, a dissemination. The plural of the Text depends, that is, not on the ambiguity of its contents but on what might be called the *stereographic plurality* of its weave of signifiers (etymologically, the text is a tissue, a woven fabric) ... The intertextual in which every text is held, it itself being the text-between of another text, is not to be confused with some origin of the text: to try to find the 'sources', the 'influences' of a work, is to fall in with the myth of filiation; the citations which go to make up a text are anonymous, untraceable, and yet *already read*: they are quotations without inverted commas.[5]

The purposes of textual appropriation for a feminist politics is one of the main areas of debate in Tess Cosslett's essay. The intertextuality of Winterson's *Oranges* with Cynthia Ozick's *Ruth*, versions of Malory's narratives, the Bible and *Jane Eyre*, is considered within the context of how stories from different texts can be manipulated, altered, and reformed to signify alternative things; indeed, how the establishment of 'symbolic identities' between texts, or 'parallels-with-differences', cater for different kinds of feminist aims. Within this intertextual matrix, Cosslett aims to consider what function religion has for Winterson; but more importantly, asks how can women relate to Christianity, one of the most patriarchal systems and institutions we have in our society?

Lynne Pearce has structured her essay as a sophisticated internal dialogue with Jeanette Winterson's fiction, partly in an attempt to come to terms with her shifting writing strategies. Scott Wilson adopts a similar 'dialogic response' to elaborate upon Winterson's intertextual strategies in his essay, enacting an intricate intertextual dialogue with her characters in *The Passion*. In his case, intertextualist appropriation appears as a strategy for resisting the closure of history. Wilson's essay acts as an imaginative dramatic dialogue which begins by situating itself in the mind of Johanna Burckhardt, Hegel's landlady and pregnant with Hegel's illegitimate son. Arguing that Hegel's dialectical philosophical system cannot account for chance — cannot account for a fourth term — Wilson perceives Henri's narrative as a recognition of 'those areas of the heterogeneous forces that escape or are excluded from the Hegelian state of universal recognition'. Giving a 'postmodern turn' to Hegel, Henri emerges in Wilson's intertextual dialogue as a Bataillean figure who maintains the indeterminacy of history. In a quantum leap, Ludwig Fischer is Wilson's second voice, saved as a consciousness in cyberspace, who returns as a literary critic studying Winterson's novel *The Passion*. Wilson's multiply voiced essay mimics the postmodern strategies which he is discussing, and offers Winterson's novel as a riposte to Hegel's cul-de-sac logic of a transcendent universal history.

In view of Wilson's critical reading strategy, it is probably just as well that Winterson has acknowledged that 'you can't hold onto your work once it's in the public domain and there is no such thing as a fixed text ... it's always changing under your hands and people find all sorts of things you didn't know were there'.[6] Yet paradoxically, whilst Winterson's *writing practice* would seem to concur with such views, her *private practice* would seem to suggest the opposite. For example, in eschewing her early novel *Boating for Beginners*, and in openly lambasting and criticising various academic readers for their opinions about her work, Winterson has sought to place boundaries on the slippage of meaning in her texts. In commenting upon her own life and work, she has edited out references to *Boating for Beginners*, as well as unglamorous early occupations and romantic involvements. She is also accustomed to making some very high claims for her work. She has described *Oranges* as 'experimental' and 'threatening'; and when, at the end of 1992 she was asked by *The Daily Telegraph* to name her rave read of the year, she chose her own. She has openly sought to prevent dissemination, and to offer herself as an *author*-ity concerning the meaning and value of her texts within British literary culture.

Contradictions may be detected, too, between Winterson's writing practice in different texts. Although a self-declared experimentally self-conscious writer, a reading of some of her work places her at times further from the cutting edge of fictional experimentation. Winterson's realist impulse is most obviously evident in her autobiographical novel, *Oranges Are Not the Only Fruit*. In common with many other twentieth century women writers, Winterson chooses to render her life story in a narrative mode which straddles the generic divide between fiction and autobiography, in the production of an autobiographical fiction, with an accompanying alter ego, 'Jeanette'. The autobiographical impetus, as Shari Benstock notes, arises out of the desire to 'know the self', to 'recapture the self'.[7] It necessarily assumes that there is a locatable self and that this 'self' is knowable, beliefs rather at odds with the slippery subjectivities evident elsewhere in Winterson's work. Some theorists of women's autobiography have argued that the deployment of a fictional/autobiographical mode self-consciously acknowledges the inevitable fictionality of autobiography, perhaps also evident in Winterson's own answer to the question of the autobiographical mode in *Oranges*: 'Is Oranges an autobiographical novel? No not at all and yes of course' (*O* xiv). Yet it remains that the autobiographical impulse *per se* often betrays realist/liberal humanist leanings. *Oranges* exhibits few of the self-conscious literary devices common to other more experimental women's autobiographies (although Winterson herself asserts otherwise), like Audre Lorde's *Zami: A New Spelling of My Name* or Maxine Hong Kingston's *The Woman Warrior*, which partly 'temper' this latent realism and which are indeed a feature of the rest of Winterson's oeuvre. The foregrounding of narrative devices stresses the constructed nature of the textual self: its absence in *Oranges* masks this and instead works to affirm the authority of the author over her own story. Shari Benstock describes this process:

> gaps in the temporal and spatial dimensions of the text itself are often successfully hidden ... so that the fabric of the narrative appears seamless, spun of whole cloth. The effect is magical — the self appears organic, the present the sum total of the past, the past an accurate predictor of the future. This conception of the autobiographical rests on a firm belief in the *conscious* control of the artist over subject matter; this view of the life history is grounded in authority (Benstock, 19).

Rather than an 'experimental' text, as Winterson herself describes it in the introduction, or 'innovative' text, as it is described in the jacket blurb of the Vintage edition, *Oranges* is a largely traditional developmental narrative in the vein of the *bildungsroman*, starting with the author's early trials and tribulations, and culminating in her triumph in the face of adversity (if only evident in the fact that she survived a horrendous upbringing to tell the tale). This is particularly apparent in her use of biblical books as an organising framework for her text: never shy of appropriating high cultural references, Winterson uses a supremely patriarchal text to organise her own story.

It might be argued that Winterson's refusal to write her life story in an experimental form relates to her own view of her position in twentieth-century letters. It is recognisable (as Lyn Pykett notes) that Winterson locates herself and her work as part of an on-going modernist tradition, but the writers with whom she identifies most frequently are not mainly those women who wrote their autobiographies in new and experimental ways, like Stein's *Everybody's Autobiography*, Woolf's *Moments of Being* or H.D.'s *End to Torment*, but male writers like Eliot, Joyce and Lawrence. Winterson is commonly associated with discourses concerning postmodernist philosophies and aesthetics. Some of the essays in this volume explicitly associate her with novelists like Italo Calvino, Salman Rushdie and William Gibson. Indeed, many of these essays respond to and enlarge upon her anti-essentialist views on gender, subjectivity and language. Nevertheless, Winterson's postmodernist credentials remain a vexed issue. As Lyn Pykett argues in her essay, Jeanette Winterson is also engaged in 'a collaborative dialogue with Modernism'. After charting the postmodernist characteristics in her fiction, such as the fictive basis for knowledge and representation, Pykett argues that Winterson manifests an anti-materialism in her affirmation of art as a means of transcending and escaping the confines of history. The modernist matrix within which Pykett situates Winterson's intertextuality — Eliot, Joyce, Woolf — construes Winterson's fictional strategies as a form of aesthetic renewal for a dilapidated and sagging culture.

However, Winterson's work may also be located within a tradition of British women writers who employ fantasy and the fabulous in their fictions, which also coincides with so many postmodernist stylistic interests. Like Angela Carter or Sara Maitland, Winterson fills her novels with a society of outsiders, grotesque misfits and marginals. These include characters of excess: *Sexing the Cherry*'s voluminous Dog Woman, the wasted lover Louise in *Written on the Body*, the viscid and mercurial Villanelle and the diminutive servant Domino in *The Passion*; characters with bodily differences: Villanelle's webbed feet and missing heart and Patrick's telescopic eye in *The Passion*; and characters with extraordinary powers: weightlessness, the power to walk upon water, to see for miles, to predict the future. These fantastic elements, as Lorna Sage has discussed, are a means of writing 'against the patriarchal grain'.[8] It is not merely that the presence of these eccentrics is in itself subversive, but, with the exception of Louise, it is precisely these characters' abilities in excess of their roles within patriarchy that facilitate their successful manipulation of patriarchal structures to their advantage.

Within the same tradition, Winterson exhibits the concern to use — and abuse — representations of women inherited from older and other narrative modes like mythology, folklore and fairy-tale. This is analogous to Gilbert and Gubar's discussion of women writers' concern with the revision of images of women in *The Madwoman in the Attic*.[9] This is most explicit (albeit most rudimentary) in *Boating for Beginners*, where she revises biblical stories, but is also evident more recently in the 'Sappho' sections of *Art and Lies*. Elements of the world of fairy tale also frequently feature: tales are embedded within tales; magic and magical acts abound; metaphors are literalised, as the Queen of Spades steals hearts, women walk on water and dancers are literally so light they float. Incidentally, with the exception of Patrick and his telescopic eye, it is only women in Winterson's texts who possess supernatural powers. Winterson arms her women well when she revisits the war of the sexes in her work.

Despite the many differences between Winterson's texts, they return repeatedly to certain issues: love and desire; identity and subjectivity; artifice and aesthetic self-reflexivity; lesbian and gendered perspectives; the difficulty of forging a language suitable for the discussion of non-heterosexual love; and the relationships between narrative and reference. These common critical reference points are explored within the essays in this volume, and they testify to the manner in which Winterson's complex texts evoke a common bond of associations. Nevertheless, Winterson's fiction appears to resist simple categorisation such as realist, postmodernist, or fantasy, and the multiplicity of approaches to her fiction within the essays included within this volume attest to this resistance. For instance, in *The Passion*, as with so much of her fiction, Winterson frequently uses fantasy to destabilise any notion of the transparency of language. As we have noted, a frequent device is the literalisation of metaphor. When Villanelle asks Henri to help her to rescue the heart that she has lost, Henri believes that she had 'been talking figuratively' (*P* 115). However, she insists that 'In that house, you will find my heart. You must break in, Henri, and get it back for me' (*P* 115). We are later told that he finds her heart, and that Villanelle swallows it again. Henri echoes our realist distrust: 'Not possible' (*P* 121). But the postmodern text replies, 'I tell you her heart was beating' (*P* 121).

However, behind this apparent radical aesthetic practice of mixing genres, there lurks a fiercely traditional recuperation of aesthetic practices and categories. For example, in *Sexing the Cherry*, one of Winterson's more interesting experiments with different modes of fiction, and arguably displaying 'postmodern' techniques in its refusal to fit the narrative traits of realism, Winterson presents this representation of the artist:

> our inward life of pure time is sluggish or fast-flowing depending on our rate of conductivity ... Artists and gurus are, in the language of science, superconductors.
>
> Our rate of conductivity is probably determined by an ability, learned or innate, to make the foreground into the background, so that the distractions of the everyday no longer take up our energy. Monks and contemplatives have tried to achieve this by withdrawing from the world — utter concentration, trance-like concentration, is what is needed. Passion, delirium, meditation, even out-of-body, are words we use to describe the heightened condition of superconductivity. It is certainly true that a criterion for true art, as opposed to its cunning counterfeit, is its ability to take us where the artist has been, to this other different place where we are free from the problems of gravity. When we are drawn into art we are drawn out of ourselves. We are no longer bound by matter, matter has become what is: empty space and light (*SC* 91).

Despite Winterson's stated resistance to the Romantic idea of the artist as a lone figure wrapped up in isolated contemplation of the world,[10] the description of the artist here is deeply indebted to romantic notions of the artist as genius, seer and prophet. The artist is depicted as a person who is somehow specially endowed to describe the world to other humans, possessing a secret and magic power of communication. This is Pykett's description of the Winterson artist as transcending and escaping the confines of history. From the Greek 'to manifest, to show', the term 'epiphany' has traditionally been used to designate the revelation of some divine or superhuman being, although it has recently acquired currency as a figurative or secularised equivalent to account for moments of striking perception. When speech fails, the visionary person may find himself caught up in the flames of ecstasy, a word which resonates with the subtitle of *Art Objects: Essays in Ecstasy and Effrontery*. It is perhaps not surprising then that Winterson should elsewhere position herself within the Romantic tradition: in the introduction to *Oranges*, she compares her writerly sensibilities to those of Keats and Byron. Yet this visionary dimension to Winterson's conception of aesthetic practice, nevertheless maintains her writing within a *utopian* aesthetic practice, a practice which wishes to make its production politically effective.

Sexing the Text

At the beginning of an essay entitled 'The Semiotics of Sex', Winterson recounts the following meeting:

> I was in a bookshop recently when a young woman approached me.
> She told me she was writing an essay on my work and that of Radclyffe Hall. Could I help?
> 'Yes.' I said. 'Our work has nothing in common.'
> 'I thought you were a lesbian,' she said (*AO* 103).

This acts as a springboard for a discussion of the way in which the identification of the 'wells of loneliness' of queer subjectivity elides any rigorous attention to aesthetic criteria and obscures critical judgement. In other words, despite the publication of *Oranges*, Winterson wishes to separate the autobiography of a writer from the activity of writing: 'Forcing the work back into autobiography is a way of trying to contain it, of making what has become unlike anything else into what is just like anything else' (*AO* 106). In sectionalising some of the essays in this volume under the heading 'Sexing the Text', there is no intention to 'cauterise' the impact of Winterson's work by placing her work within the context of queer politics, against which Winterson cautions. For whilst we might acknowledge that 'The straight world is wilful in its pursuit of queers' (*AO* 104), nevertheless, Winterson's frank and explicit discussion and exploration of sexuality and gender has often surrounded her fiction in controversy and debate. This has largely arisen within a context in the late 1980s and 1990s of an increasing public debate (albeit frequently truncated and policed) about the centrality of sex and sexuality within many different fields of inquiry and life, as well as an intense scrutiny of the cultural production, dissemination, and vicissitudes of sexual meanings and differences.

The introduction to a book on Jeanette Winterson's fiction is not the place to rehearse in great detail the subtleties and nuances of recent transformations that have taken place in analysing a phenomenon as complex as sexuality. Indeed, much of this history is supplied by the essays included herein. Nevertheless, Monique Wittig, a theorist to whom several of these essays link Jeanette Winterson's fiction, has set out the position of sexual difference as a social construct, produced by the heterosexual hegemony of 'the straight mind':

> A materialist feminist approach shows that what we take for the cause or the origin of oppression is in fact only the *mark* imposed by the oppressor ... what we believe to be a physical and direct perception is only a sophisticated and mythic construction. an 'imaginary formation' which reinterprets physical features ... through the network of relationships in which they are perceived. (They are seen *black*. therefore they *are* black: they are seen as *women*. therefore they *are* women. But before being *seen* that way. they had first to be *made* that way).[11]

'Lesbians are not women', is Wittig's provocative conclusion to this essay, meaning that they are not dependent on men, which is the heterosexual definition of femininity. Citing Wittig's startling phrase, Patricia Duncker describes how lesbian identity deliberately throws a spanner into the production works of heterosexual definitions of sexuality. Tracing what she perceives to be the historical trajectory of 1970s and 1980s feminist theory as it 'grew up' into lesbian and queer politics in the 1990s, Duncker tries to situate Jeanette Winterson's writing within this wider perspective of the feminist and lesbian writing which preceded her fiction. 'Queer calls attention to the instability of gender' writes Duncker, as she charts the increasingly acknowledged instability of sexual and gender identities, an instability and fluidity which manifests itself throughout Winterson's fiction.

This interest in the fluidity of identity is borne out by her fictions which are populated, in Carteresque fashion, with performers, mistresses and purveyors of artifice: the weightless dancing princesses in *Sexing the Cherry*; Villanelle, the cross-dressing card-dealer in *The Passion*, who 'performs' acrobatic sexual acts with her partner, the Queen of Spades, as well as the gravity-defying feat of walking upon water. Gendered identity, as Ute Kauer, Patricia Duncker and Paulina Palmer make clear, is particularly flexible in Winterson's work. Several characters change their gender, either actually (Marlene in *Boating for Beginners*), or temporarily (Villanelle), or their gender remains ambiguous (Lothario in *Written on the Body*). In *Boating for Beginners*, the reader even comes across a shop of gender 'spares', the rejects of which reappear as sausages in the butcher's, Meaty Big and Bouncy. One is literally the sum of one's parts, or, at least, the parts one chooses. In a gesture curiously both essentialist and anti-essentialist, the literalisation of linguistic metaphors works to undo gender roles. Paulina Palmer suggests in her essay that Winterson's acrobats and trapeze artists evoke images of vitality and transgressive jouissance. Indeed, contrary to Duncker's pessimism about a potential liberatory sexual politics in the 1990s, this transgression and jouissance is ultimately conceived of by Palmer as empowering and liberatory. In attempting to discuss the problematics of the shifting definitions of lesbian narrative in relation to *The Passion*, Palmer argues that lesbian narrative, quoting Teresa de Lauretis, seeks to subvert the traditional representations of women by 'rewriting the [female] body beyond its pre-coded, conventional representations', creating a new economy of desire. This new 'lesbian narrative space', in going beyond conventional models of women, proposes the lesbian woman as an 'excess' 'erupting in a plenitudinous display of baroque imagery, episodes of magic realism, and competing genres and narrative-lines'.

The image of lesbian sexuality erupting, or exploding, is also deployed in both Duncker's and Stowers's essays. Stowers, also anxious not to blunt Winterson's 'dissidence', attempts to consider Winterson's oeuvre as a whole as a consistent lesbian aesthetic. Overlapping with Palmer's work, Stowers also regards Winterson's increasing interest in the multi-faceted dimension of female sexuality as a problematisation of the conventional heterosexual definitions of masculinity and activity and femininity and passivity. For Stowers, as for Palmer, the lesbian body is an 'excess' that exceeds the hegemonic gendered logic, which offers 'new configurations of narrative practice and textuality', liberating male and female sexuality from rigid categorisation.

In many respects, Winterson appears to regard the strangeness of language as a disruption of the phenomenological world; it renders the 'I' of personal experience problematic and uncertain, rather than eliminating it altogether. Strangeness — or should one say queerness — is a borderline position that *deconstructs* the representation of identity; and as Winterson herself states, 'complexity leads to perplexity' (*AO* 113). Perplexity exists because counter to easily categorised discourses and objects, with determinate sequences of cause and effect, one has to negotiate a series of complications and implications which transgress 'disciplinary' boundaries which have abstractly compartmentalised knowledge to such a degree, that the objects of study have been 'emptied out', separated into closed systems or bracketed off from one another. Winterson's fiction forces the reader to work at reading; to reconsider the relationships of things and people in the world, and to recognise the multiplicities in things rather than their singularities. Although Winterson acknowledges that art is about communication, her writing is a frontal assault on the straightforward exchange of communication and the easy assimilation of identity. Ute Kauer addresses the problem of the sexual ambiguity in the first person narrator in *Written on the Body*, where Winterson constantly ironises the role of the narrator by infamously disguising the gender of the narrator. For Kauer, the text eventually emerges as a mockery of male and female assumptions concerning narratorial subjectivity, during which 'the very fact that the gender is undeclared shows a typical postmodern tendency to deconstruct the trust in the medium of narration'.

Winterson's most recent novel *Gut Symmetries* (which was published after most of these essays were written), also attempts a disruption of conventional gender boundaries, through a deconstruction of the binary structure of heterosexual relations by involving a third party. Maintaining her suspicions of ontological security and epistemological stability, Winterson establishes elaborate parallels between the uncertainties of matter theorised by quantum physics, the slippages of poststructuralist theory, and the aleatorical patterns of the Tarot and the Jewish Kabbalah. The final essay in this volume analyses the way Winterson sets about undermining and subverting orthodox sexual patterns, by creating a complex yet disjunctive interplay of a variety of different discourses; although we suggest that ultimately Winterson leaves certain gendered stereotypes in place, despite her self-consciousness about the gender politics of the binary love-plot.

Together, the two sections of this book contribute to a material reading of Jeanette Winterson's fiction, as well as an understanding of the politics of reading, writing and sexuality. While there is not necessarily agreement between authors as to what this means or should involve, all of them address these issues, whether implicitly or explicitly, at some point in their work. It is hoped that this book will act as an initiative for serious discussion of Winterson's contribution to writing, rather than sneaking up to harass her by the backdoor. From the moment of its conception, this project has taken a long time to see daylight: and we would like to thank the contributors for their patience and support in awaiting the completion of this volume. We are grateful to Alison Coleman, Andrew Hadfield and Brean Hammond, of the University of Wales, Aberystwyth, for their advice, help and support in the preparation of this project. Finally, we would also like to thank Fred van der Zee at Editions Rodopi, and the series editors, Theo D'haen and Hans Bertens, for their help with the editing of the manuscript in the concluding stages.

Notes

1. Linda Hutcheon. *A Poetics of Postmodernism* (London: Routledge. 1989) 5. All further page references will be given after quotations in the text.
2. Jeanette Winterson in conversation with Rosemary Harthill. 'Writers Revealed'. Radio 4. Autumn. 1990.

3. Jeremy Hawthorn. *Cunning Passages: New Historicism, Cultural Materialism and Marxism in the Contemporary Literary Debate* (London: Edward Arnold. 1996) 23.
4. Michel Foucault. *The Archaeology of Knowledge* (New York: Pantheon. 1972) 23.
5. Roland Barthes. 'From Work to Text'. in *Image-Music-Text* (1977: London: Fontana. 1984) 159-60.
6. Jeanette Winterson in interview with Felicity Goody. 'Profile'. Radio 4. 23rd August. 1989.
7. Shari Benstock. *The Private Self: The Theory and Practice of Women's Autobiographical Writings* (Chapel Hill: University of North Carolina Press. 1988) 11. All further page references will be given after quotations in the text.
8. Lorna Sage. *Women in the House of Fiction: Post-war Women Novelists* (Basingstoke: Macmillan. 1992) 168.
9. Sandra Gilbert and Susan Gubar. *The Madwoman in the Attic: The Woman Writer and the Nineteenth-Century Literary Imagination* (New Haven: Yale University Press. 1979) 73-76.
10. Jeanette Winterson in interview with Felicity Goody. 'Profile'. Radio 4. 23rd August. 1989.
11. Monique Wittig. *The Straight Mind and Other Essays* (Hemel Hempstead: Harvester Wheatsheaf. 1992) 11-12.

PART I

The Politics of Reading and Writing

INTERTEXTUALITY IN ORANGES ARE NOT THE ONLY FRUIT: THE BIBLE, MALORY, AND JANE EYRE

TESS COSSLETT

THE concept of intertextuality is two-faced. It encompasses both 'texts entering via authors (who are, first, readers) and texts entering via readers (co-producers)'.[1] The text is full of (even composed of) echoes and reworkings of other texts; and the reader brings to her interpretation all the texts she has encountered. In particular, the reader may use knowledge not only of earlier texts which are being responded to or incorporated, but also of contemporary texts that respond to these same earlier texts in different ways. A complex conversation between texts can thus take place. It is this process that I am interested in pursuing in this article: the dialogues between *Oranges Are Not the Only Fruit* and three of its intertexts — the Bible, Malory's *Morte D'Arthur*, and Charlotte Brontë's *Jane Eyre* — and between Oranges and three contemporary reworkings of these same intertexts: Cynthia Ozick's *Ruth*, Marion Zimmer Bradley's *The Mists of Avalon*, and Jean Rhys's *Wide Sargasso Sea*.[2] It is not just that I happen to have read these contemporary texts: by drawing them into these dialogues, I hope to address the related questions of how women/feminist writers can appropriate well-established canonical texts of great cultural power, and how a concept of intertextuality can be used in feminist readings.

My three canonical intertexts have what Norman Fairclough calls a 'manifest' intertextual relationship with *Oranges*: they are all named or referred to in the text.[3] In an interview for *The English Review*, Winterson is quoted as saying that 'when I was very young we had only six books in the house, two of them were the bible and a third was Cruden's complete concordance to the bible ... Of the other three, one was, astonishingly, Malory's Morte D'Arthur and this is what I read over and over again'.[4] *Oranges* both is and is not autobiographical: in the fictional household in the text, there is a another book, the mother's 'favourite non-Bible book', *Jane Eyre*, 'and she read it to me over and over again, when I was very small' (*O* 73). The repetition of 'over and over again' emphasises that this is another story that 'embedded itself in my consciousness', as Malory did for the real Jeanette.[5] Both texts are also embedded in the novel, *Oranges*. The Bible, the *Morte D'Arthur*, and *Jane Eyre* can be used to stand for the three main components that, in my reading, make up *Oranges*: the religious fundamentalism of the heroine's family, and her vocation as missionary and then 'prophet'; the 'fantasy' sections, which rework the plot in terms of fairy story and medieval romance; and the romance plot — Jeanette's discovery of love with Melanie, and her continuing quest for romance. Of course, the three intertwine: in one of the book's climaxes, Winterson mingles the language of religion and romance to describe her heroine's continuing ıe all-consuming relationship: images of 'tablets of stone' (the Bible) and the [illegible]lalory) mix in a definition of 'romantic love' (*Jane Eyre*) (*O* 165).

This kind of pirating and combining of different kinds of narrative is central to Winterson's art. In the chapter called 'Deuteronomy', discussing 'history', she refuses to accept any one version of the truth: instead, she puts together different accounts to produce not 'a seamless wonder', but 'a sandwich laced with mustard of my own'. She goes on to advise the reader to 'make your own sandwiches' — advice I have taken as a license to put together the plate of sandwiches which is this article (*O* 93). Her insistent relativism is set against, and disrupts, the unbending fundamentalism of her mother's religion: Malory is a counterweight to the Bible, a different reality; and so is *Jane Eyre*, at least in its unexpurgated version. While we learn in the text that Jeanette's mother has adapted *Jane Eyre* to fit her beliefs, the Jeanette who writes the book is able to adapt and appropriate the Bible. So all three texts take part in the novel's liberating project.

Each, however, is present in the novel in a different way. Not only is the Bible present as subject matter, as the ground of belief and source of language and imagery for the members of Jeanette's community, but the chapters of the novel are given the titles of books from the Old Testament. On one level, this is comic parody: 'Genesis' recounts the heroine's family background, her adoption by her mother; 'Exodus' contains her escape to school; 'Joshua' her blowing her own trumpet, standing up against the community in defence of her lesbian sexuality. The stories of the world's creation, and a nation's survival, are applied to the events of an individual life. Winterson is sending up the community's habit of seeing their mundane lives in these cosmic terms. At the same time, she is claiming for herself the language of her adversaries: school, according to her mother, is a 'breeding ground', not a liberation from captivity; and Jeanette's refusal to give up her lesbianism is demonic possession, not Joshuan trumpet-blowing. The chapter titles are both parodic send-up, and deeply serious appropriation.

But what is the precise relation of these chapter titles to their contents? There is a sense in which they are just vague general labels, indicating a mood and a few aspects of a story. Material from elsewhere in the Bible comes into them: 'Genesis' contains parodic references to the New Testament, in Jeanette's mother's ambition to emulate the Virgin Mary and adopt a Messiah, without Wise Men, but with sheep. 'Numbers' (in *Oranges*) refers back seriously to Genesis (in the Bible), sanctifying Jeanette's and Melanie's lovemaking: 'And it was evening and it was morning; another day' (*O* 86). There is not a fixed, given Biblical story to be retold in each chapter: here, *Oranges* is unlike the texts by Ozick, Bradley and Rhys, which all have an inescapable given story, however much it may be told from different points of view, or with more sympathetic insight. Nevertheless, the chapter titles have resonance beyond their limited reference. It would be impossible to look at all of them in the space of a short article: I have chosen the last chapter of the novel, entitled 'Ruth', to look at in more detail.

The immediate relevance of the chapter title 'Ruth' to Winterson's story is the exile of the heroine, from mother, home, religion. One of my first associations with the figure of Ruth is Keats's lines about 'the sad heart of Ruth, when, sick for home, / She stood in tears amid the alien corn'.[6] Keats is referred to familiarly as a role model in Winterson's Introduction to the Vintage edition of *Oranges* (he put on a clean shirt when depressed): perhaps these lines were in her mind too. While there are also more positive connotations to the Ruth story, this sense of painful separation should not be lost sight of. It also informs the Perceval story as it appears in *Oranges*. Jeanette, as a lesbian, has set off into a difficult exile. There are also, however, more positive aspects to the story. Some feminist commentators want to appropriate the Book of Ruth as woman-authored, and, as evidence, cite the centrality and agency of the women characters.[7] Here, Winterson's reference to Ruth could indicate a liberation from patriarchal structures, as Jeanette finally takes charge of her own, woman-centred story. Other commentators point out that Ruth has made the break with her past because of her bond with another woman, Naomi, her mother-in-law.[8] As Mieke Bal comments, '"And Ruth clave unto her" (1.14). Now, this verb is a very strong one. It is exclusively used with a male subject, in reference to the matrimonial bond'.[9] The parallel with Jeanette's lesbianism is clear.[10] Yet there is a difficulty in making this the central and closest parallel. By this time, the relationship with Melanie is broken, and there is no female character to whom Jeanette can 'cleave' as she breaks with her past. Betrayal, by Melanie, by her mother, by the Church, is a major theme of this last chapter. Obviously, Jeanette is committed to lesbianism, but the loneliness of Perceval and Jane here cuts across and revises the female companionship of Ruth.

Here it would seem that Winterson is veering away from a close parallel with Ruth, using the name only to refer generally to strong themes of loneliness and woman-identification. But there are other, more complicated resonances. At the beginning of the biblical story, Naomi tells her daughters-in-law, after the deaths of their husbands, not to follow her back to her own country, but to return to their 'mother's house'. This is a highly unusual way to refer to their homes ('father's house' would be more usual), and is used by feminist scholars to argue for the female authorship of the text.[11] It is obviously a close parallel to Winterson's text, as Jeanette, like Ruth, leaves her mother's house (her father is just a cipher; her mother has turned her out). But, in a turn that has disappointed some readers, the book ends with a visit back to the mother. The Book of Ruth is also a story of exile and return, though it is Naomi, rather than Ruth, who is returning back to her native land. In so far as Ruth partakes of this return, and finds a new home, it is because of her bond to Naomi, the woman who becomes in effect her adoptive mother. Jeanette's mother of course is also her adoptive mother, not her birth mother. Putting the two stories side by side, both the separation from the mother and the subsequent return to the (adoptive) mother are emphasised. These 'mothers' are two different people in the biblical story — in *Oranges*, they are two readings of the same person. We will find that the Perceval story also provides contradictory alternative readings of the mother. Here, the depth of Jeanette's problematic bond to her mother, the 'thread' that still binds them, is stressed. At the same time, the theme of continuing exile is emphasised at the end of *Oranges*: 'Families, real ones, are chairs and tables and the right number of cups, but I had no means of joining one, and no means of dismissing my own; she had tied a thread around my button, to tug when she pleased' (*O* 171).

Winterson's text uses the material of Ruth to produce richly multiple effects — a 'sandwich of her own', that has provoked further sandwich-making on my part, including my reading of the original text and of feminist commentators on it. Apparently, rabbinic interpretations cast Ruth 'into a stereotypic ideal of submissive, obedient femininity'.[12] Both Winterson and the feminist commentators are going in for radical reinterpretation and re-reading. But while feminist theologians are stuck with the whole story, Winterson can ignore the parts that do not speak to her themes: that is, Ruth's wooing of and marriage to Boaz, and the birth of her son, who will ensure the lineage of David. Winterson's story instead circles round themes of exile and return, female bonding, mother/daughter relations, loss and loneliness, female autonomy, in a non-linear order, to produce an ambiguous, open ending. As Linda Hutcheon says of modern parody, 'another context can be invoked and then inverted, without a step-by-step pedestrian signalling of the entire form and spirit'.[13] Looking at what Winterson has left out, emphasises the effect that her lesbianism has on the stereotypical feminine story of marriage and motherhood: a sense of loss, a sense of hope, an absence of closure: 'I knew a woman in another place. Perhaps she would save me. But what if she were asleep?' (*O* 171).

Cynthia Ozick's essay 'Ruth', appears as the last piece in *A Feminist Companion to Ruth*, along with the commentaries of feminist theologians. It is in this context that I want to look at it: labelled, at least by the editor, as a feminist piece, part of the work of feminist re-interpretation of the Bible. At the same time, the editor explains its presence in the volume by arguing that 'works of art which are inspired by biblical passages' are on the same level as 'theological exegesis and literary criticism'.[14] In her Introduction to the volume in which the essay first appeared in book form, Ozick argues for undoing the dividing line between essays and fiction: an essay can also be 'a bewitched contraption', like a story.[15] So we can also read 'Ruth' as a fiction like *Oranges*. The essay is partly autobiographical, partly descriptive, partly a re-telling of the Ruth story, partly didactic.

Ozick begins by telling us 'there were only two pictures on the walls of the house I grew up in'. One is a photograph of her grandfather, a Jewish scholar, one is a reproduction — perhaps torn from a calendar — of a painting of a young woman in a field. This second picture was 'in those spare days, all I knew of "art"'. The parallel with Winterson's household, with only six books, two of them the Bible, is striking. Both women grew up under the shadow of a limited number of powerful cultural icons. What do they make of their cultural inheritances, how do they escape or re-inflect them? At first it seems as if the painting, which Ozick's mother calls 'Ruth', is, like Malory for Winterson, a way into an alternative world of 'art', fantasy, imagination, unfixedness. The picture, entitled 'The Song of the Lark', turns out to have been painted by Breton, not Millet, as Ozick had thought, and the original faces the opposite way: 'A calendar reversal! — but of course it seems to me that the original is in sullen error'. Ozick prefers her own version, her own 'sandwich'; she elaborates it further, quoting from Tolstoy to evoke the flowers in the painted field. All this contrasts with the fixedness of the picture of the grandfather: 'I will not learn anything new about him. He will not acquire a different maker. Nothing in his view will be reversed' (Ozick 1993, 192).

But the project of the essay is to bring Ruth and the grandfather together, to make her the necessary forerunner of him, to place them both in a historical lineage. For Ozick, the imaginative evocation of the scent of the flowers in Ruth's field is a way into the truth of what really happened: 'without the smell of the flowers, we cannot pass through the frame of history into that long ago'. Winterson, of course, has a very different view of history, as a matter of stories and 'string full of knots', that can be rearranged infinitely. In contrast, Ozick turns to the Bible to find out 'what the story tells us she [Ruth] really did say'. Ozick is one of a group of 'new' American Jewish writers, whose 'interest is not in the sociological or even the psychological legacy of a Jewish background, but in the national design and religious destiny of Judaism, in its workable myths'.[16] While both women often take on a 'prophetic' role, Winterson in her 'Ruth' chapter is losing her religious faith, while Ozick interprets Ruth as finding hers. Ozick grants that love for Naomi is part of the reason for Ruth's going with her, but she emphasises as the overriding reason Ruth's declaration for monotheism, 'your God shall be my God', which makes 'her act far, far more than a ringing embrace of Naomi, and far, far more than the simple acculturation it resembles' (Ozick 1993, 208).

In fixing on this as the central meaning of the Ruth story, Ozick then has to hurry though the rest of the story in a brief summary — her reading is as selective as Winterson's, though her faith means she can't completely ignore what is given. While Winterson justifies what she is doing as relativistic sandwich making, Ozick takes as her 'Muses' the rabbis, who 'are not cultural relativists', and whose commentary, however far-fetched and without a seeming basis in the text, is 'not the current sort of exegesis that ushers insights out of a tale by scattering a thousand brilliant fragments, but rather the kind that ushers things toward: a guide toward principle' (Ozick 1993, 200). Principle, moral values, and belief, give validity to Ozick's idiosyncratic interpretation, just as it is God, the 'Lord of History', who unites myth, history and destiny for her. Fragments and unity; relativism and monotheism; fiction and history; these oppositions seem to characterise the differences between Winterson and Ozick in their readings of Ruth. Yet there are also similarities, one being the idiosyncrasy, the selectivity of their readings.

Is feminism another meeting-point? I have been presenting Ozick as a writer whose first allegiance is to Jewishness, not feminism. But her essay is included in the *Feminist Companion to Ruth*, and her one direct remark about feminism in the essay is not hostile: 'What we nowadays call feminism is of course as old as the oldest society imaginable: there have always been feminists: women (including the unsung) who will allow no element of themselves — gift, capacity, natural authority — to go unexpressed, whatever the weight of the mores' (Ozick 1993, 201). Naomi partakes of this quality when she takes the decision to return home; so does Ruth, when she declares her faith. But, as one critic puts it: 'How, I found myself wondering, does she square her commitment to sexual egalitarianism with her passionately traditional Judaism ...?'[17] Ozick could remind us of Jeanette's mother, another strong, idiosyncratic, dogmatic woman, putting her strength to the service of an ultimately patriarchal institution.

In this particular essay, the question Pollitt asks would seem to turn on the relationship of Ruth to the grandfather, and of Ozick to the rabbis. As I said, Ozick's interpretation of the 'Ruth' painting at first leads away from Judaism, but then she asserts that 'if the woman had not been in the field, my grandfather, three-thousand years afterward, would not have been in the study-house ... The track her naked toes make through spice and sweetness, through dodder, vetch, rape, and scabious, is the very track his forefinger follows across the letter-speckled page'. Nature/woman is contrasted very obviously with culture/man here, but is also made primary and necessary. But further on, when Ruth declares for monotheism, she is compared to the male prophet Abraham, one of the founders of Jewish culture, and her deviance from the usual female role is stressed: 'Ruth marries into Israel, yes; but her mind is vaster than the private or social facts of marriage and inculcation; vaster than the merely familial' (Ozick 1993, 195, 209-210). Ruth takes over the best of both feminine and masculine roles. The role of Ruth is by implication the role of Ozick, her interpreter. Ozick's 'reversed', personal, imaginative, 'feminine' reading of the story both supersedes and precedes her grandfather's rigidities; and she also takes over from the male rabbis (first making their interpretations look rather trivial and off the point), and provides a female-centred interpretation. Both Ruth and Ozick gain status as female prophets of Israel: there is no sense of the grandfather, or the rabbis, having the ultimate religious authority. That belongs to God, who has often provided women with an excuse for authority and autonomy.[18] Interestingly, Jeanette in *Oranges* also sees herself as a prophet, and she claims to 'miss God', blaming his 'servants' for the narrow-mindedness of the Church.

Obviously, the texts by Winterson and Ozick are from vastly different cultures, and have different agendas: sexuality, for instance, is not on Ozick's; the destiny of the Jewish people is not on Winterson's. Difference is rightly a key word these days; but I am also interested in what Nancy Miller has called 'connection across the grain of cultural difference'.[19] In the context of this chapter, and of my interests here, what is significant is the freedom both writers show in their handling of given cultural materials, freedom to reinterpret, to ignore, to appropriate, to construct female heroines and role-models. That freedom is greatly enabled by the autobiographical mode used by both writers: an interpreting, prophetic 'I' is present, who recognises and enables readers to recognise the 'given' material as separate, malleable. Those writers like Bradley and Rhys who enter into their given stories, who take them as the 'reality' of their fictions, run the danger of becoming entrapped by them.

Winterson's appropriations from Malory are as selective and ambiguous as her references to the Bible. The main difference is that Perceval's story is not just alluded to, but appears in four separate short sections, interleaved with Jeanette's contemporary story, in the chapters 'Judges' and 'Ruth'. The juxtapositions of the two stories are, however, as suggestive and oblique as those between Ruth and 'Ruth': sometimes the Perceval story seems to be a direct parallel to events in the main story; sometimes an opposing version, how things could have been different; sometimes a story of what is hidden or cannot be said. So, in 'Judges', as the church makes its final attempt to exorcise Jeanette's lesbianism, and her mother appears as chief persecutor, the Perceval segments dwell on Arthur's and Perceval's grief at their having parted, and Perceval's uncertainty about the Grail that he is compelled to pursue. The Perceval story here moves forward to a point beyond the present upheavals and agonies, accepting Jeanette's leaving as already accomplished; it suggests (or wishes for?) a deep emotional bond between her and her mother; like the Ruth reference, it stresses the loneliness of Jeanette's choice, but also its inevitability.

The other two Perceval segments, in 'Ruth', occur as Jeanette is revisiting her mother: Perceval is homesick in a temporary stopping place; and he ends by dreaming that the thread attaching him to Arthur is broken. The 'thread' image is also prominent in the main story, as an irremovable attachment between Jeanette and her mother. Here, the Perceval story suggests a different possible outcome: the thread can be broken, and the mother can be just a temporary 'host' in a strange castle, not the familiar Arthur. In all cases, the Arthurian world provides a relief from the pressures and persecutions and hypocrisies of the biblical fundamentalist world, a transposition into a simpler realm of longing and searching. This is ironic, as in Malory it is with the Grail legend that a sense of sin and guilt intrudes into his chivalric world, and the religious is superimposed on the secular.[20] But Winterson inverts this pattern: the quest is, by implication, for lesbian romance; the Round Table is the companionship of her mother and the fundamentalists.

Commentators agree that Malory was not particularly interested in the Grail legend, but put it in 'because it was there'.[21] Winterson's reworking goes beyond Malory to some other tellings of the 'Parzifal' story — perhaps by Wagner, who is present in *Oranges* in the egg competition as a shared delight between Jeanette and Elsie. It is Elsie who also refers to Yeats, as a poet of the imagination — another way out of the prison of fundamentalist literalism. What Winterson adds to Malory, from other sources, is the characterisation of Perceval as the 'young fool'. In the sources, this means he is a holy innocent, who will finally ask the right, naïve, question to reveal the Grail. Winterson picks on and stresses his youth, and casts him almost as a Shakespearean fool, amusing Arthur with childlike tricks. By stressing his youth like this, his position as the darling of Arthur's court, she can set up a father/son (mother/daughter?) relationship between them. The overriding theme of her Perceval story is Perceval's homesickness for Arthur and his court, and Arthur's missing of Perceval. This forms an obvious parallel with Jeanette's leaving her mother and the church.

In the 'Parzival' stories, a lot is made of Parzival's upbringing by his *mother*, with whom he has a very close bond. In Malory, we learn that Perceval has transferred this bond to Arthur and the Round Table: 'for synes ye departed from your modir ye wolde never se her, ye founde such felyship at the Table Rounde';[22] Winterson takes this a step further by setting up a symbolic identity between Arthur and the mother: the simple polarities in the originals between mother/male companionship are unsettled. Startlingly, Perceval's aunt, in Malory, first accosts him by asking 'whan herde you tydynges of youre modir?'[23] The return to the mother at the end of Winterson's book is ushered in by 'someone' who asks her 'when did you last see your mother?', a parodic reference to a Victorian painting ('When did you last see your father?'), but also perhaps to Malory. Also perhaps suggested by Malory is the intensity of Arthur's grief at Perceval's departure, though in Malory it is a general lament for the breakup of the Round Table and the departure of the knights in search of the Grail: 'ye have nogh slayne me for the avow that ye have mayde ..., ye have beraufte me the fayryst and the trewyst of knighthode that ever was seen ... for I have loved them as well as my lyf'.[24]

The intensity of the male companionship here might bring up the question of homosexuality (a hint taken up by Bradley, in her retelling of the Arthur legend), as a parallel to Jeanette's lesbianism. But by stressing Perceval's youth, and by the strong parallel between Arthur and the mother, Winterson occludes this possibility. Nevertheless, it is there for the reader to pick up; and the first Perceval segment in *Oranges* occurs just after Winterson's narrator has pronounced rather dogmatically on male homosexuality: 'At that point I had no notion of sexual politics, but I knew that a homosexual is further away from a woman than a rhinoceros. Now that I do have a number of notions about sexual politics, this early observation holds good'. This is said to rebut her mother's idea that Jeanette, in being a lesbian, is 'aping men', while of a homosexual church member the mother says 'Should have been a woman that one' (*O* 125-6). A homosexual man is not a failed woman; nor is a lesbian a failed man; but nevertheless the novel is intent on making parallels-with-differences, and in swapping round the genders of its main story. So when Jeanette's story is retold in the fantasy world of Winnet Stonejar, the mother becomes a male enchanter, Melanie a male lover; and in the Perceval story the gender of both Jeanette and her mother becomes male.

This switching to different but analogous stories relates to what Winterson says about the novel in the Introduction to the Vintage edition of 1991, where she claims a liberal humanist generality for her story: 'Superficially, it seems specific: an evangelical household and a young girl whose world is overturned because she falls in love with another young girl. In fact, *Oranges* deals absolutely with emotions and confrontations that none of us can avoid' (*O* xiv). More recently, in *Written on the Body*, she has again been involved in obscuring gender differences. Whether this is advanced queer theory, or old-hat liberal humanism, is an open question. But in *Oranges*, the separation of the parallel stories, the insistent, proliferating relativism, keeps specificity and generality in a productive and non-oppressive 'impossible tension' (*O* xiv). By setting up a partial identification with a male hero in her Arthurian sections, Winterson neatly avoids whatever restrictions were placed on Malory's female characters.[25] On the other hand, the 'male' hero is to some degree 'feminised': 'a warrior who longed to grow herbs'.[26] Gender boundaries are crossed and blurred, though not abolished.

In dealing with the Arthurian material Winterson, as with 'Ruth', ignores the parts of the story that do not interest her. So, in Winterson's version, it is the Grail quest alone that breaks up the Round Table: the adultery between Lancelot and Guinevere that finalises the process in Malory is left out. Winterson's Arthurian world is without sin and without sex, except in so far as lesbian romance is symbolically present, transposed into the Grail itself. Perceval's final vision of the Grail is also left out: we see him only in the process of questing. This is similar to the omission of the end of Ruth's story, and once again emphasises the unclosed nature of Winterson's ending. In *Merlin's Daughters*, Charlotte Spivack remarks that contemporary women writers of fantasy (including Bradley), tend to stress the later parts of the hero's quest, especially the return, in narratives that are circular rather than linear. The stages of the quest she identifies as 'miraculous birth and inspired childhood through a period of meditation, the undertaking of a quest, a literal or symbolic death, journey to the underworld, and ultimately rebirth and apotheosis'.[27] Most of these stages can be identified in *Oranges*, but not necessarily in this order. The ending is both a return, and the middle of an unfulfilled quest.

Bradley's *The Mists of Avalon*, unlike Winterson's pick-and-mix way with Malory, works doggedly through the whole story. As Spivack says, 'Bradley includes virtually the entire career of Arthur, and minor as well as major characters'.[28] Bradley does in fact leave out Perceval, who appears only as a name; his role is taken by Galahad. But the Grail legend is very important to her conception, and is drastically re-interpreted. In retelling the Arthurian story from the perspective of the women characters, and rehabilitating Morgaine-le-Fay (the chief narrator) from her role as wicked enchantress, *Mists* operates as a classic feminist 'revision', in a similar way to Jean Rhys's *Wide Sargasso Sea*. In contrast, Winterson does not seem to be 'revising' her originals as such, but appropriating and changing bits of them as she wants. Bradley's project demands that the story should stay more or less as it is, but that its motivations and values should be seen quite differently once the neglected female perspective is given. The exhaustive treatment of the entire story has its own feminist purpose: Bradley (or Morgaine) is seen to have an explanation for *all* of it, nothing can escape the women's perspective.

The Arthurian legend is placed by Bradley within a longer and wider interpretation of history, in which Celtic and pre-Celtic mother goddesses and matriarchal societies are displaced by a narrow, patriarchal Christianity. Here, the Grail legend plays a significant part: the Grail is rewritten as the Cauldron of Ceridwen, a mother goddess. The Christians attempt to appropriate it; the way it operates for the knights who seek it seems to be as an intuition of what their religion leaves out. The Grail itself has an obvious female symbolism, used both by Bradley and by Winterson for their own different purposes. At the end of Bradley's novel, the heroine learns that the mother goddess still survives within Christianity (as Mary), and the implication is that her religion is now returning, allowing Bradley to write the story, and the readers to appreciate it.

Bradley is providing her feminist readers with a history, and an explanation for their present state. Here, her project intersects with Ozick's, in this sense of history and destiny, the need for legitimating stories. By placing the story in this wider framework, Bradley gains power over it, puts it in its place as a regrettable phase; but she is also in thrall to it, she gives it status as history, and she is stuck with a plot that is necessarily tragic, that must end with the dispossession of the women.[29] Unlike Ozick, Bradley does claim to be a relativist. Morgaine, speaking at the beginning of the story, maintains that her version is only one of many, and that the big mistake of the Christians was to insist on the truth of their single version: 'For this is one thing the priests do not know, with their One God and One Truth: that there is no such thing as a true tale'.[30] But this disclaimer does not stop the novel reading like the 'true' version, the redressing of the balance; there are no competing versions within the novel itself.

Some remarks by Linda Anderson about women and history and the contemporary novel are very relevant here. Anderson attacks a movement towards 'realist' texts that try to recreate women's roles in history; such texts merely reinscribe women's historical oppression, and conceal the constructedness of 'history'. Instead, she valorises Toni Morrison's *Beloved* as a text that both deals with a 'real' historical period, but also, through the use of fantasy, problematises memory and truth, and allows for the presence/absence of the unrecorded and unrecordable.[31] This contrast could apply to the differences between Bradley and Winterson in their treatment of the Arthurian material, except that I have no wish to elevate Winterson at Bradley's expense, but only to point out the different strategies they use, with their advantages and drawbacks. Bradley is obviously writing a different kind of novel, a popular blockbuster with overtones of Mills and Boon. Like a Mills and Boon novel, it is very well researched and informative: its recreation of Celtic beliefs has especially been praised.[32] In this sense, it is working as a 'realist' novel, trying to recreate both beliefs and conditions of the time. We learn a lot about the material circumstances of the women's lives. This is very different from the dream-world inhabited by Winterson's medieval characters.

Like a Mills and Boon novel, it is also full of torrid heterosexual sex-scenes. Bradley has been praised for a feminist attitude to women's sexuality, presenting it as empowering and guilt free (at least for the adherents of the matriarchal religion).[33] But the emphasis on sex, and on heterosexuality, works to confirm a very conventional picture of women and femininity. Though the women are shown as passionately interested in 'male' ideas like the future of the kingdom, the succession to the throne, the religion of the state, their efforts to affect these matters amount to an endless preoccupation with who couples with whom to provide which possible ruler. Heterosex and pregnancy are their main concerns. This is an effect both of the historical 'accuracy', and of the value that the story places on patriarchal ideas of descent and inheritance — again, perhaps historically accurate, and also inevitable if the Arthurian story is to be taken as a given framework (would it be possible to imagine a 'revision' in which Arthur would turn out to be some totally insignificant bit-player, and the real drama to be about something quite different?).

Bradley does imagine a homosexual attraction between Lancelot and Arthur, but presents this very negatively, in a way that has been read as homophobic.[34] There is also a scene in which Morgaine sleeps with Raven, one of the other priestesses: this is presented very positively, but it is unclear whether sex is involved. As Spivack puts it, approvingly, 'to read this novel is to imbibe the nature of womanhood, of being a mother, of loving a man, of being violated, of being adored, of being both a victim and a beneficiary of that very nature of femaleness'.[35] The novel presents this highly questionable definition of 'woman' not just as something constructed by the period, but as a natural and spiritual essence, connected to the nature of the Mother Goddess herself. Here we come to some more important differences between Bradley and Winterson: not just that Winterson is a constructivist, Bradley an essentialist, but that Winterson, leaving Christianity, has no use for a substitute, 'feminist' religion of mother goddesses. She misses God, but has to do without Him.

The three women writers I have looked at so far are each very differently placed in relation to traditional belief systems: Winterson is freeing herself from a narrow, literalist fundamentalism, for which she substitutes relativism and uncertainty. Ozick returns to and re-appropriates her traditional faith. Bradley opposes Christian patriarchal monotheism with a polytheistic matriarchal paganism. In all cases, their methods of dealing with their intertexts reflect these positions. Very crudely, they could be divided according to Kristeva's three 'generations' of feminists, as explained by Toril Moi:

1. Women demand equal access to the symbolic order. Liberal feminism. Equality. [Ozick?]
2. Women reject the male symbolic order in the name of difference. Radical feminism. Femininity extolled. [Bradley?]
3. (This is Kristeva's own position.) Women reject the dichotomy between masculine and feminine as metaphysical. [Winterson?][36]

As we have seen, Winterson doesn't totally subscribe to position three in *Oranges*: genders are different but analogous. But her haphazard appropriation of intertexts both 'female' (Ruth) and 'male' (Malory), and her rejection of 'metaphysical' certainty, contrast with Ozick's and Bradley's negotiation with or opposition to strong male-centred belief systems.

The relationship of *Jane Eyre* to *Oranges* is different again to those of the other two intertexts. The book itself is mentioned in the text, as read by both Jeanette and her mother. The mother's suppression of the romantic ending, and Jeanette's discovery of this truth, shadows the unfolding of the plot, and fits into a debate about romance, which is first debunked (Pierre and the stomach ulcer) and then reclaimed for lesbians (the Holy Grail). *Jane Eyre* can in fact be seen as a powerful hidden presence throughout *Oranges*. Like Jane, Jeanette is maltreated by a false mother-figure; she suffers at school; she battles against loveless fundamentalist religion; she has a demonic alter-ego; she is parted from her love by religious prohibitions.

Putting the three intertexts together, a kind of composite heroine emerges in the last chapter: Jeanette/Winnet/Ruth/Perceval/Jane, all united in exile and questing. At the same time, they all represent slightly different versions of the same story: Winterson suggests many possible outcomes. *Jane Eyre* appears to add to and share in the relativity and uncertainty of Winterson's project. But while, as we have seen, Winterson blithely suppresses or ignores the parts of her intertexts that do not fit her purposes, especially endings which involve heterosexual romance (Ruth and Boaz; Lancelot and Guinevere), here the reverse happens. It is Jeanette's mother who suppresses the 'real' ending of *Jane Eyre*: Jane is one of her heroines, but in the version she tells Jeanette, the story ends with Jane agreeing to a loveless marriage with St. John Rivers, so that they can go to India together as missionaries.

This of course fits in with the mother's attitudes to sex, her fundamentalism, and her proposed destiny for Jeanette as a missionary. In the book as written by Charlotte Brontë, however, Jane refuses St. John's proposal, helped by a supernatural call from Rochester. Brontë's story can be read as Jane's escape from the puritan pressures of religion, represented at first by the hateful Brocklehurst (Pastor Spratt?) and later, more insidiously, by the persuasive St. John. Instead, she opts for romance with Rochester: but it is a tempered and redefined romance, that can only happen when Rochester is disabled (or castrated, as some critics have argued). Jeanette's rediscovery of what her mother has suppressed parallels her quest for lesbian romance instead of fundamentalist religion. For her too, it is a redefined romance, between women rather than between woman and disabled man, though some critics have argued that what happens at the end of *Jane Eyre* is a feminisation, not a castration, of Rochester.[37]

But what is striking here is that Winterson is implicitly appealing to a 'real', 'true' version of the intertext, which her mother is presented as illegitimately truncating. The omission of the 'true' ending says something about the mother's one-sidedness, dogmatism, and propensity to paint 'the white roses red' (*O* 134). Winterson provides the missing pieces, by including romance, and the Malory-world of fantasy and desire, and by reading the Bible differently. And yet she, as much as her mother, rewrites and truncates the stories she uses. The only difference is that Winterson's narrator recognises what she is doing, admits to her sandwich making, while her mother claims to be in possession of the truth. The novel reveals the constructed, arbitrary, desire-led nature of the mother's world too. At the same time, there is a sense of the similarity of these two strong women, both powerful story tellers and revisionists. Jeanette takes her mother's virtues, and becomes relativist 'prophet' instead of fundamentalist 'priest'.

Reading *Jane Eyre* and *Oranges* together, the mother-daughter bond is stressed in yet another way: *Jane Eyre* ends with Jane back 'home' with the transformed Rochester; *Oranges* ends with Jeanette back 'home' with her (partly) transformed mother. The mother who earlier had seemed more like Mrs Reed, Jane's 'false' mother and persecutor, now seems to parallel Rochester himself. Again, the intertext suggests ambiguous and opposite readings of the mother, and the stories which seem to provide an escape from her turn out to include her. The mother's literalist fundamentalism is challenged by the inclusion of the medieval fantasy world, and the re-interpretation of 'her' texts, the Bible and *Jane Eyre*. But she reappears as the object of desire in the 'new' texts, as Naomi, as Arthur, as Rochester. On the other hand, the texts she reappears in have been revised along lesbian/feminist lines: Ruth becom... female bonding, and loses its religion and its heterosexual conclusion; the Perceval story ... with gender identification, and sanctifies lesbian romance as the Grail; *Jane Eyre* is revised as a romance between women: if the mother is Rochester, so is Melanie, and also the 'woman in another place' whose call Jeanette is still awaiting at the end of the book.

Another important revision of *Jane Eyre* could be seen in the way Jeanette accepts and follows her 'demon' alter-ego, while Jane's (the mad wife, Bertha) has to be destroyed. When Jeanette is imprisoned at home, and 'exorcised', she resembles both Jane in the Red Room, and mad Bertha in her attic at Thornfield. The identification of Bertha as Jane's alter-ego has been central to much feminist interpretation of *Jane Eyre*.[38] Jean Rhys's *Wide Sargasso Sea* takes Bertha (whose real name she reveals as Antoinette) as her main character, telling her story from childhood to her death in the fire in *Jane Eyre*. In Rhys's version, it is Bertha's female sexuality, together with her alien culture, that earns her the label of madness. Likewise, Jeanette is persecuted for a 'different' sexuality, labelled demonic. Both *Oranges* and *Wide Sargasso Sea* work to rehabilitate the position of the female sexual 'monster', by implicit or explicit revisions of *Jane Eyre*.

Rhys's book, like Bradley's, is a 'realistic' revision of a given story, but it is harder to place in Kristeva's schematisation of feminisms and their various relations to a patriarchal symbolic order — appropriation, opposition, or subversion. Critics have cast *Jane Eyre* as the patriarchal text whose ideology of romance, or of race, is overturned by Rhys's revision, but they have also seen the two texts as engaged in the same feminist project. For Patsy Stoneman, *Wide Sargasso Sea* 'lives like another dimension to the older text', and for Freya Johnson '*Jane Eyre* ... interacts significantly with the newer text, as the two together function as complementary images'.[39] Gayatri Spivak, on the other hand, sees the two texts as in an oppressive, colonialist collaboration.[40] Perhaps we can most productively see the relation of text and intertext here in the context of the debates *between* women which have characterised recent feminism. Caroline Rody figures the relationship between the two works in terms of the mother-daughter bond, the vexed and ambiguous relationship that is also at the centre of *Oranges*.[41]

Unlike Bradley, Rhys does not tell the whole story of her intertext. It is, however, all implied as what necessarily overlaps with and follows the events of her story. In both Rhys's and Bradley's texts, the reader's probable knowledge of the given story is used to produce a sense of fate. The characters are given prophetic dreams and visions which play with this knowledge. This fatedness gives a sense of powerlessness — the patriarchal plot cannot be changed; women are necessarily victims. The compensating power comes, as in Bradley, from the different, feminist explanation that is offered for the plot. In *Wide Sargasso Sea*, there is also the implication that Jane may complete a conversion of Rochester in which Antoinette fails: for instance, Jane (in Brontë's novel) takes Christophine's advice (to Antoinette in *Wide Sargasso Sea*) on how to treat Rochester: '"A man don't treat you good, pick up your skirt and walk out"'.[42] While Antoinette becomes a victim, Jane, and Christophine herself, are stronger women who know ways of survival. This contrasts with *Mists*, where the women's cause as a whole is going under.

There is also the hint that Rochester nearly decides to allow Antoinette's world its reality. Each of them thinks of the other's reality as a 'dream', unreal. A mutually exclusive dualism is set up, as between patriarchal Christianity and matriarchal paganism in Bradley, or heterosexual fundamentalism and lesbian relativism in Winterson. The intertextual project for all three writers is to give 'reality' to the excluded, marginalised term (Ozick, on the other hand, is trying to bring together two seemingly opposed 'realities': her grandfather and the picture of Ruth). What Rhys does differently is to give Rochester his own narrative voice in the text, revealing the insecurities and bad faith that make up his dominant position, but also allowing him the moment in which he might have chosen differently: 'So I shall never understand why, suddenly, bewilderingly, I was certain that everything I had imagined to be truth was false. False. Only the magic and the dream are true — all the rest's a lie'.[43] This destabilises the 'fatedness' of the story: it could have happened otherwise. In *The Mists of Avalon* on the other hand, it is strongly hinted that the Mother Goddess has planned out everything from the start.

Nevertheless, everything finally unwinds to its destined conclusion in *Wide Sargasso Sea*. *Oranges*, on the other hand, suggests multiple irresolvable conclusions, both through the ways it revises its intertexts, and by using so many in parallel. While Antoinette's 'reality' is labelled and finally becomes 'madness', Jeanette holds on to her own sense of reality and selfhood (the rough brown pebble?), supporting herself by enlisting canonical stories on her side. Rhys, in contrast, articulates the voice of the 'ghost' or 'madwoman' whose selfhood is overwhelmed by the 'reality' of the canonical story.

I want to avoid drawing any too-neat conclusions from these comparisons. It would be easy, for instance, to praise Rhys, Bradley and Winterson for their revisionary power, and deride Ozick for her return to tradition; or to elevate Winterson and Ozick's freedom of interpretation over Bradley and Rhys's enslavement by their given texts; or to celebrate Winterson's postmodern pastiche in contrast to Bradley's dogged historicism. An MA course I once taught on feminist 'revisions' foundered on our continual quest for the perfect, correct feminist version of our various intertexts. One after another, women writers failed to achieve this illusory perfection (Winterson, of course, has some useful remarks in *Oranges* on the dangers of the quest for perfection [*O* 58-65]). What strikes me about these texts is the many different and subtle procedures that fall under the title of 'revision' or 'parody' or 'intertextuality', and how they intersect with the different aims of different kinds of feminism.

Jay Clayton and Eric Rothstein suggest that a theory of intertextuality is not particularly useful to feminist critics: they recommend rather the older concept of 'influence'. Intertextuality they take to be a passive concept, involving an apolitical relationship between texts that removes any idea of female agency.[44] Yet 'influence' too has passive connotations: rather than actively 'revising', the writer is unconsciously 'influenced'. Linda Hutcheon's redefinition of 'parody' can be useful as an alternative concept: 'repetition with critical distance, which marks difference rather than similarity ... an integrated structural modelling process of revising, replaying, inverting, "transcontextualising" previous works of art'. Hutcheon's idea deliberately reintroduces both the author's 'intention' and the reader's 'recognition'. She also allows that parody can have ideological or political implications.[45] But, useful as it is as a concept, 'parody' does not encompass everything I have been trying to do here: as well as looking at effects that may have been intended, I have gone further into effects that occur when the reader reads 'original' and 'parody' together, and when the reader reads other feminist revisions of the same material — none of which may have been 'intended' by the writer. Here I fall back on Hutcheon's approving citation of Riffaterre's definition of 'intertext', which is different from what she calls the 'parodied text': 'the corpus of texts the reader may legitimately connect with the one before his [sic] eyes, that is, the texts brought to mind by what he [sic] is reading'.[46]

It is by including the reader like this that a way can be found out of the quest for a perfect feminist version, and also away from the depressing idea that any one version merely reinscribes the power of its original. For of course the reader knows she is reading fiction, not history; and the reader has the opportunity to read many different undoings and revisings of canonical texts, unfixing them into an endless variety of versions, and undermining their authority. By her practice, and her advice on sandwich making, Winterson points the way to this liberating state of mind.

NOTES

1. Michael Worton and Judith Still. eds. *Intertextuality: Theories and Practices* (Manchester University Press. 1990) 2.
2. Eugene Vinaver. ed. *The Works of Sir Thomas Malory* (Oxford University Press. 1977): Charlotte Brontë. *Jane Eyre* (1847: repr. Harmondsworth: Penguin. 1966): Cynthia Ozick. 'Ruth'. in *A Feminist Companion to Ruth*. ed. by Athalya Brenner (Sheffield: Sheffield Academic Press. 1993) 191-214 (all further page references will be given after quotations in the text): Marion Zimmer Bradley. *The Mists of Avalon* (London: Sphere Books. 1984): Jean Rhys. *Wide Sargasso Sea* (Harmondsworth: Penguin. 1968).
3. Norman Fairclough. *Discourse and Social Change* (Oxford: Polity Press. 1992) 104.
4. 'Face to Face — a conversation between Jeanette Winterson and Helen Barr'. *The English Review*. 2. 1 (September 1991) 31.
5. 'Face to Face'. 31.
6. Keats. 'Ode to a Nightingale'.
7. Carol Meyers. 'Returning Home: Ruth 1.8 and the Gendering of the Book of Ruth'. in Brenner. 85-114: Adrien J. Bledstein. 'Female Companionships: If the Book of Ruth were Written by a Woman ...'. in Brenner. 116-133; Fokkelein van Dijk-Hemmes. 'Ruth: A Product of Women's Culture?'. in Brenner. 134-139.
8. Ilona Rashkow. 'Ruth: The Discourse of Power'. in Brenner. 32.
9. Mieke Bal. 'Heroism and Proper Names'. in Brenner. 48.
10. Laurel Bollinger in her article 'Models for Female Loyalty: The Biblical Ruth in Jeanette Winterson's "Oranges Are Not the Only Fruit"'. *Tulsa Studies in Women's Literature*. 13. 2 (Fall 1994) 363-80. takes this as the main point of the Ruth reference. and elevates it into a reading of the whole text. But. as I will argue. there are other more complicated resonances.
11. Meyers. 91.
12. Brenner. 16.
13. Linda Hutcheon. *A Theory of Parody: The Teachings of Twentieth-Century Art Forms* (New York and London: Methuen. 1985) 19.
14. Brenner. 17.
15. Cynthia Ozick. *Metaphor and Memory* (New York: Knopf. 1989) ix.
16. Ruth Wisse. 'American Jewish Writing. Act III'. *Commentary*. 61 (June 1976) 41. See also Sarah Blacher Cohen. 'Cynthia Ozick: Prophet for Parochialism'. in *Women of the Word: Jewish Women and Jewish Writing*. ed. by Judith Baskin (Detroit: Wayne State University Press. 1994) 283-298.
17. Katha Pollitt. 'The Three Selves of Cynthia Ozick'. in *Cynthia Ozick: Modern Critical Views*. ed. by Harold Bloom (New York: Chelsea. 1986) 66.
18. See Elaine Hobby. *Virtue of Necessity: English Women's Writing, 1649-88* (London: Virago. 1988).
19. Nancy Miller. *Getting Personal* (London: Routledge. 1991) 126.
20. Jerome McCarthy. *An Introduction to Malory* (Cambridge: D.S. Brewer. 1991) 40.
21. Stephen Knight. *Arthurian Literature and Society* (London: Macmillan. 1983) 128.
22. Vinaver. 541.
23. Ibid.
24. Vinaver. 522.
25. 'There are many female characters in Malory. but they do not act for themselves. They either assist or hinder the male characters in their career towards honour and self-definition' (Knight. 126).
26. Readers of Winterson's *The Passion* will be reminded of the character of Henri. one of the narrators.
27. Charlotte Spivack. *Merlin's Daughters: Contemporary Women Writers of Fantasy* (New York. Westport and London: Greenwood Press. 1987) 9.
28. Ibid.. 149.
29. Again. this is similar to *Wide Sargasso Sea*.
30. *Mists*. x.

31. Linda Anderson. 'The Re-Imagining of History in Contemporary Women's Fiction'. in *Plotting Change: Contemporary Women's Fiction*. ed. by Linda Anderson (London: Edward Arnold. 1990) 129-41.
32. Sallye J. Sheppeard. 'Arthur and the Goddess: Cultural Crisis in "The Mists of Avalon"'. in *The Arthurian Myth of Quest and Magic*. ed. by William E. Tanner (Dallas: Caxton's Modern Arts. 1993).
33. Karin C. Fuog. 'Imprisoned in the Phallic Oak: Marion Zimmer Bradley and Merlin's Seductress'. *Quondam et Furturus: A Journal of Arthurian Interpretations*. 1 (1991) 73-88.
34. James Noble. 'Feminism. Homosexuality. and Homophobia in "The Mists of Avalon"'. in *Culture and the King: The Social Implications of the Arthurian Legend*. ed. by Martin B. Shichtman and James P. Carey (New York: State University of New York Press. 1994) 288-296.
35. Spivack. 160.
36. Toril Moi. *Sexual Textual Politics: Feminist Literary Theory* (London and New York: Routledge. 1985) 12.
37. See for example Sandra Gilbert and Susan Gubar: *The Madwoman in the Attic* (New Haven and London: Yale University Press. 1979) 336-371.
38. See for example Gilbert and Gubar.
39. Patsy Stoneman. *Brontë Transformations: The Cultural Dissemination of "Jane Eyre" and "Wuthering Heights"* (London and New York: Prentice Hall/Harvester Wheatsheaf. 1996) 196: Freya Johnson. 'The Male Gaze and the Struggle Against Patriarchy in "Jane Eyre" and "Wide Sargasso Sea"'. *Jean Rhys Review*. 5. 1-2 (1992) 28.
40. Gayatri Chakravorty Spivak. 'Three women's texts and a critique of imperialism'. *Critical Inquiry*. 12 (1985) 249. 251. 253. See also Stoneman. 188.
41. Caroline Rody. 'Burning down the house: the revisionary paradigm of Jean Rhys's "Wide Sargasso Sea"'. in *Famous Last Words: Changes in Gender and Narrative Closure*. ed. by Alison Booth (Charlottesville: University Press of Virginia. 1993).
42. *Wide Sargasso Sea*. 91.
43. Ibid.. 138.
49. Jay Clayton and Eric Rothstein. 'Figures in the Corpus: Theories of Influence and Intertextuality'. in *Influence and Intertextuality in Literary History*. ed. by Clayton and Rothstein (Madison: University of Wisconsin Press. 1991) 10-11.
45. Hutcheon. 6. 11. 16. 22. 23.
46. Ibid.. 62.

THE EMOTIONAL POLITICS OF READING WINTERSON

LYNNE PEARCE

JEANETTE Winterson is an emotional writer who has solicited a wide range of emotional responses from her readers. In her own opinion, emotion — even when it is painful and disturbing — is intrinsic to aesthetic experience. As she writes in 'Art Objects':

> A love parallel would be just: falling in love challenges the reality to which we lay claim, part of the pleasure of love and part of its terror, is the world turned upside down. We want and we don't want, the cutting edge, the upset, the new views. Mostly we work at taming our emotional environment just as we work at taming our aesthetic environment. We already have tamed our physical environment. And are we happy with all this tameness? Are you? (*AO* 15).

Something of this sentiment — the acknowledgement, at least, that textual engagements of any kind, are experienced by readers and viewers as a 'roller-coaster' of emotional affect — has informed my own recent work on the politics of reading.[1] In the central section of my book, *Feminism and the Politics of Reading*, for example, I use the framework of the romance narrative to explore the complex emotional processes of reading: from the moment of first enchantment (what Roland Barthes calls 'ravissement') through to 'the sequel', 'the long chain of sufferings, wounds, anxieties, distresses, resentments, despairs, embarrassments, and deceptions to which I fall prey'.[2] Behind this investigation is the belief that existing reader and audience-theory has been blind to this aspect of reading because of its focus on the 'act of interpretation' at the expense of all the text-reader activity involved that is *in excess* of this. The interest, in other words (and even amongst writers like Barthes) has been on how the complex play of text and reader enables us to 'make readings', rather than on reading as a *process* or *event*. In my own work, then, I have elected to theorise meaning-production within the broader context of the reading process: to hypothesise, and test, a whole variety of *inter-textual* and *contextual* factors which will necessarily impact upon our relationship with a given text and influence the 'reading' we make of it. Meanwhile, the romance framework, apart from emphasising the temporality and narrativity of the reading experience (as Winterson herself writes *vis-a-vis* the experience of viewing paintings, 'Love takes time' [AO 14]), has also afforded me considerable insight into intimate dynamics of the text-reader relationship and allowed me to reflect upon the difference between a 'proactive' and a fully 'interactive' relationship between text and reader, the latter producing an emotional engagement of a quite different order to the 'readings' of texts made out of particular theoretical frameworks and interpretive communities.[3] In other words, what we might think of as an emotional engagement with a text is partly an effect of a particular *structural positioning* of the relationship between text and reader, and not simply the application of a certain ideological framework or reading method (e.g, a 'Humanist' one) which permits the indulgence of such a sentiment.

In my exploration of the emotional aspects of the reading process, I consider my long-term relationship with Jeanette Winterson's work and, in particular, her novel *Written on the Body* (1992). For the purpose of this exercise, I performed an 'autobiographical' 're-memorying' of the text, followed by a detailed 're-reading', which I then analysed and theorized through Barthes's trajectory of the romance narrative.[4] This means that I was able to register the subtle nuances in my shifting relationship both to this text and to the Winterson oeuvre, moving through sentiments such as 'enchantment', 'dedication' and 'fulfilment', through to 'jealousy', 'frustration' and 'disillusionment'. In this chapter I would like to reproduce some of these original readings (represented in this text by italics) alongside a commentary which considers the implications of the emotional politics of reading specifically in the context of Winterson 'fandom': what factors, in other words, have brought about our fascination with this writer and her work? And what changes in our textual / contextual relations may signal the end of the romance?

Ravissement

According to Roland Barthes, *ravissement*, or 'love at first sight', is experienced as a sudden and euphoric shock, which is both the shock of *recognition* (here is the one we have always been waiting for) and the shock of *difference* — as the 'other' reveals him or herself to us in all their uniqueness and idiosyncrasy:

> Love at first sight is a hypnosis: I am fascinated by an image: at first shaken, electrified, stunned, 'paralyzed' as Menon was by Socrates ... subsequently ensnared, held fast, immobilized, nose stuck to the image (Barthes, 89).

It is not often, perhaps, that a literary text will 'stun' and 'capture' us in this way, but Winterson's texts *do* seem to have had this effect on many of her readers and — as the following extract from my 're-memory' reveals — I was no exception:

It was a friend from Birmingham who eventually persuaded me to read 'The Passion', selling it to me on the basis of its 'style'. I bought, and like herself and thousands of others, I was entranced. (No matter that, as I subsequently discovered, it was a style and a subject matter derivative of Italo Calvino).[5] *What I remember especially about this first read was that I started somewhere in the middle (probably with Villanelle's narration), kept going, and then began again at the beginning. It was one of those texts that moved me according to what Raymond Williams refers to as 'the shock of recognition': despite the historical fantasy location, the discourse on love and passion made profound (humanist) contact with me.*[6] *It was that special sense of having your own thoughts and feelings written out for you. Not only did I know the 'truth' of many of Winterson's aphorisms, I would also have chosen the same images and metaphors. Indeed, in my own writings I had already done so.*

So, 'death of the author' notwithstanding (and my own literary criticism by now in a rigorously anti-humanist mode), I took time out from my professional critical persona and allowed myself to play projection introjection with the reconstructed author of this text. After quickly consuming 'Oranges' and 'Boating for Beginners' and catching up on some of the hype surrounding Gore Vidal's 'best young writer of her generation', I succumbed to a very literary specific form of fandom. As with our ' involvement' with any cultural icon I was, of course, inscribed by a complex mixture of 'desire for' and 'identification with'. Winterson was to become the public embodiment of my own literary aspirations as a writer scholar (at very least, a 'published writer') but as the uncanny mouthpiece of my own thoughts and speech-acts she was also to become my intellectual 'other': the 'one who understands'.

Apart from serving as a testimony to the way in which certain texts and authors can quite suddenly, and unexpectedly, 'enrapture' us as readers, this extract also reveals a number of the textual / contextual mechanisms through which the enamoration takes place. In the same way that our inter-personal romances are rarely as spontaneous and unexpected as we perceive them to be, so is the text-reader relationship prepared for through a number of 'inductions' ranging from the recommendations of friends (as in this case), to media publicity, or the blurb on the dust-jacket. What struck me as remarkable about my 'discovery' of Winterson's work, then, seems less remarkable when we consider the way in which my desires and expectations had been prepared; whilst the clear memory of my first reading of *The Passion* (on a train journey) is a classic example of the way in which lovers instantly consecrate and 'make special' a new relationship by fixing it in a context that, in retrospect, may *become* the primary signifier of the romance: as Barthes explains it, 'what we first fall in love with is a scene'.[8]

Although, in one sense, then, my initial enamoration with Winterson's writing may be traced to the circumstances of induction and reception, what this extract from my re-memory also reveals is my construction of a 'textual other' to whom my devotion and enthusiasm is directed. Whilst the 'scene' may, indeed, play a crucial role in initiating and defining the romance, and may, on occasion itself *become* 'the other', other possibilities include: a character in the text, an interlocutory reader-positioning, a 'structure of feeling', or the real or implied 'author' of the text.[9] What my text here points to is a common, if theoretically embarrassing, slide from an engagement with the 'structures of feeling' in a particular novel, to a focus on what I experience (*even when my poststructuralist training tells me I should know better!*) as their personalised source of origin: the author, 'Jeanette Winterson'. By locating my 'textual other' in an author-function rather than a specific text, my readerly-enchantment soon extended to the whole Winterson oeuvre and manifested itself as exemplary adolescent fandom (although I was no longer an adolescent).[10] It was most certainly the *conditions of fandom*, moreover — the blindness to faults and the faith in adversity — that sustained my 'belief' in Winterson's writing even when the media tide began to turn, and my own small doubts began to creep in. The self-deceit and double-consciousness that this involved me in as a reader are reflected in this next extract from my re-memory:

Now, however, the bubble has burst. Not only were Winterson and myself becoming 'middle aged' and being forced to give way to the new generation in our respective fields, but with the publication of 'Written on the Body' the tide of public and critical approbation that had swept Winterson along for some time (peaking with the success of the TV serialization of 'Oranges') suddenly turned against her. 'Sexing the Cherry' had been regarded as something of a disappointment by many readers and critics (though not, it must be said, by those who had already committed themselves as 'fans'), but the complaint was muted and the publication the occasion for a good deal more hype on 'Winterson-the-young-and-brilliant-author'. 'Written on the Body', though, as I'm now remembering it, was launched onto the market amidst a barrage of negative publicity and criticism.[11] Some *of this was to do with the book, most of it was to do with what may be seen as Winterson's own personal slide towards complacency, arrogance and hubris. Maybe it was that the press were getting tired with interviewing one so young and manifestly successful; maybe it was because Winterson* did *begin upping-the-anti at this time. What I remember, however, was the 'quality' newspapers stamping their reservations all over the book: its politics (the issue of the 'genderless narrator'); its form (the slide from narrative towards panegyric with a few recognising it was more like a (courtly love) poem than prose); and, inevitably, its ending.*

And so, how did this turn in Winterson's own critical fortune affect my own reception of the book? At the time I probably would have denied it, but now I'm inclined to say 'profoundly'. As a Winterson scholar, I was immediately put on the spot by friends and colleagues who wanted my opinion and direction: has she sold out (as a lesbian, as a feminist)? Did the book 'fail'? Was it the best thing (for a few were already claiming this) or the worst thing she had ever written? As soon as I had *read it, I did the honourable thing and defended her and it. When people asked me how I thought it compared with the earlier texts I fudged the issue by saying that I no longer thought of Winterson's texts as separate entities: they were part of a larger intertextual continuum. Well,* yes ... *but no!! Such loyalty is the requisite of all fans; something I know from my other life as a football supporter. Whatever you might secretly think or suspect, you never let on to others. And so my memory of my first reading of this text is of the public defence I was obliged to give on Winterson's behalf, and this 'responsibility' must also be thought of as the first obstacle to a more honest emotional engagement.*

What this extract would seem to emphasise, above all, is the extraordinary lengths readers will go to in order to protect and defend the special relationship with their textual other. Once an emotional investment has been made, it is surrendered with extreme reluctance: as Barthes observes *vis-à-vis* our inter-personal relationships, the 'non-will-to-possess' — the decision to 'give up' on 'the other', for whatever reason, is tantamount to suicide.[12] In as much as s/he has come to be defined by her love for the other, 'admitting impediments' is experienced as a fate *worse* than the simple pain of not-possessing. For amorous readers, too, whose intellectual identities have been developed through their textual relationships as surely as through their personal ones, such a prospect can be devastating. My 'denial', then, when faced with this new turn in the 'Winterson' oeuvre is understandable: faced with the prospect of having a significant intellectual connection discredited, I scrambled desperately for ways to keep my faith and maintain the conditions of 'ravissement' a little longer. Whilst in my relationship to other texts, such as Olive Schreiner's *Story of an African Farm*, this labour involved negotiating a new intra-textual positioning for myself *vis-à-vis* the text's heroine, my relationship with 'Winterson' was sustained — albeit temporarily — by situating her new writings in the context of her old and denying the individual novels' autonomy.[13] As the following extract, from my re-reading (as opposed to my re-memory) of the text reveals, this strategy enabled me to construct a continuity based on my relationship to the text's narrative ('authorial') voice:

Coming back to the text after a short break, I suddenly recognise my point of emotional contact with the Winterson oeuvre and understand why this text partly succeeds, partly fails in its interpellation of me. Unlike my experience of the Schreiner novel where my involvement was very much mediated through characters to whom I related, my dialogue here is with the author-narrator herself: the mouthpiece identity that — for all my poststructuralist training — I take back to an originator 'Jeanette Winterson'. Although what I'm talking about technically is probably some version of the 'implied author', I need also to acknowledge the fact that the Winterson text is very bound up with the Winterson originating: the interviews, the reviews, the gossip — the preaching.

In this first section of 'Written on the Body' my sense of the Winterson narrative-persona is patchy. Despite the fact that Lothario 'speaks' almost continually in the aphorisms that are the mark of this narrator, only sporadically is their sentiment spiked with the irony and quirkiness that I come to associate with the Winterson persona. In Bakhtinian terms, it is a classic instance of hearing two types of speech struggle for control.[14] *Mostly what I'm hearing is Lothario aping Winterson (Bakhtin's category of 'stylization'); occasionally it is 'Winterson' herself, for example: 'Nevertheless, it wasn't the terrorism that flung us apart, it was the pigeons ...' (WB 22). And why is this Winterson and not the other? Because, perhaps, it catches my own humour in a conspiratorial 'hidden dialogue': a positioning that is cultural, historical — and not, it must be said, contaminated by Lothario's (hetero)sexualised innuendo.*

What my re-reading goes on to acknowledge, however, is the way in which these desperate and devious readerly-manoeuvres — made in order to maintain my 'special relationship' with the Winterson texts — could not be sustained indefinitely. As I acknowledge, in my 're-memory', *Written on the Body* was: 'The beginning of the end of my special relationship with 'Jeanette'.'

Sequel

Because of its exemplification of some of the more painful emotions associated with the reading process, *Written on the Body* features significantly under all the manifestations of text-reader relations dealt with in chapter six of my book, namely: 'waiting', 'frustration', 'jealousy' and 'disappointment'. What these engagements register, in their different ways, is my failure to maintain a fully dialogic, interactive relationship with the text, and the *reactive* tendency to 'blame' this on the text itself by reaching out to well-established aesthetic and political value-systems. Our 'frustration' in losing contact with a designated 'textual-other' may thus quickly translate into a critique of the authenticity of its characters, an irritation with its narrative technique (the author is too didactic, too manipulative, too experimental), or a disapproval of the way it deals with class, race, sexuality and so on. In as much as these critical frameworks are readily available to the literary and cultural critic with a minimum of training in the art of textual analysis, such reactive distantiation from a work is all too easy: indeed, it is *approved* as a mark of our professional judgement, taste and discrimination.[15] Indeed, in terms of the two models of reading I have been working with in this project, such 'critique' signals a simple shift back into 'reading as interpretation'. The perils of an interactive text-reader engagement are cast aside and the reader is once again 'in control' of the text. This, at least, is the theory. What my own readings and re-memories signal, however, as we have already glimpsed, is that this reader-power is nowhere near as complete and straight-forward as it would like to be, and that what presents itself as critical and political judgement and discrimination is often concealing a far more messy and desperate struggle between text and reader. Consider the following reflection:

This is also the point to consider where I, the reader, take up my position in the narrative trajectory. Is my own (romantic) involvement with the text in line with that of the protagonist, following the same route? Not at all. The first fifty pages or so have seen me struggling desperately to make emotional contact — mostly through a (re)construction of the Winterson narrative persona. But I see now that, in my original reading of the text, I probably was 'faking' it: the scenes of passion between Lothario and Louise alienate more than they fascinate. This is probably because I am unable to find any satisfactory viewing position for myself; unable to achieve any meaningful intra-dietetic relationality. Only those fragments of text which (paradoxically) lose the body, which appear as white words on a black screen, offer my heart a suitable jumping-off point:

> *I didn't only want Louise's flesh, I wanted her bones, her blood, her tissues, the sinews that bound her together. I could have held her to me though time had stripped away the tones and textures of her skin. I would have held her for a thousand years until the skeleton itself rubbed away to dust. What are you that makes me feel thus? Who are you for whom time has no meaning? (WB 51)*

In line with the narrator's own struggle, then, my point of contact with the textual body *is bones not flesh: it is the scaffolding of desire that works for me in this text, not the homage to its surfaces and minute particulars.*

The idea that a reader can 'fake' their response to a text is a troubling one. Troubling both if we consider reading to be part of a humanist project of personal and social enlightenment and — as poststructuralists and postmodernists — if we have long cast aside any claims to 'truth' in art or criticism. In the context of this project, however, I employ the concept merely to signal the evident slippage that exists between what the reader/critic thinks she is doing and what she actually does, not to indicate that one reading is necessarily more 'correct' or 'authentic' than another. What my own re-reading here records, once again, is the lengths the reader is prepared to go to to protect her relationship with a special text or textual 'other' at the point when disturbing frustrations and anxieties are beginning to creep in.

It will be observed that in this instance, too, the critical framework to which I reach to help explain the first rumblings of discontent is *aesthetic*. Unable to participate in the narrative of the text by aligning myself with the main protagonist, I am left floundering without a clear intra-textual reader-positioning. I am also apparently unable to make contact with 'Winterson' as 'author-function'. My defensive recourse, on this occasion, is thus to connect with the text's humanist 'structures of feeling' (see notes 6 and 9): in particular, the great universal discourse of love-in-the-face-of-death. It is a connection forged *in the cracks* between the principal narrative and the dominant discourse, however, and it is clear that my reading of the text is on the point of becoming profoundly schizoid as a result. At the same time as I am struggling to maintain my interactive relationship with the text, so am I also reaching for my professionalised aesthetic and political frameworks to explain my growing disaffection.

What my combined re-reading and re-memory of *Written on the Body* signal, in total, moreover, is the gradual ascendancy of this professional and proactive relationship to the text over my more personal and interactive one. The struggle climaxes in the section of my reading in which I confront my discomfort with the text's representation of 'the body' head on, centring, as in the following extract, on what I see as the problematic conflation of the sexual and the diseased body: a conflation which I attack on overtly political grounds but which, as we shall see, is in fact the index of a far more self-reflexive 'disappointment' and anxiety:

Cancer. This is one of the reasons, if truth be told, why I chose this particular Winterson text to work upon. Although any configuration of love and death is a guarantee of emotion, the death associated with this particular disease resonates with the most highly charged cultural anxiety and fascination . . . A friend's experience of cancer was part of the context in which I first read 'Written on the Body', and this factor was one of the reasons why I thought this would be an interesting text to 're-visit' ... When I first read the novel, then, in the Autumn of 1992, the rhetoric of body, disease and oncology that Winterson weaves into her romance as a sublimated 'erotics' was already acutely familiar to me ... This familiarity with Winterson's own orginating [sic] both facilitated and frustrated my relation to this aspect of the novel; confused my emotional response with the contradictory pull of recognition and impatience. Having been, myself, caught up in this particular web of fascination and seduced by this type of discourse, I had very mixed feelings about it being re-packaged as *seduction. While the writerly play of disease desire is admittedly the very thing I might have once experimented with myself, seeing it 'done' gave me enough distance to be critical — and, nearly three years on, I am even more inclined to be so ... There is, therefore, a necessarily huge gap between my first reading of this text and my present reception of it* vis-à-vis *the cancer narrative — and what I find myself resisting now is its elision of the sexual body and the diseased (and dying) body in an aesthetics which is instrumental in Lothario's purge:*[16]

> *Cancer treatment is brutal and toxic. Louisa would normally be treated with steroids, massive doses to induce remission. When her spleen started to enlarge she might have splenic irridation or even a splenectomy. By then she would be badly anaemic, suffering from deep bruising and bleeding, tired and in pain most of the time. She would be constipated. She would be vomiting and nauseous. Eventually chemotherapy would contribute to failure of her bone marrow. She would be very thin, my beautiful girl, thin and weary and lost. There is no cure for chronic lymphocytic leukaemia (WB 102).*

What is unacceptable to me here is the sentence beginning 'She would be very thin ...'. Indeed, I am unable to read it without having images of Dante Gabriel Rossetti's 'Beata Beatrix' flash before my eyes, together with the infamous [William] Holman Hunt quote that Elizabeth Siddal (the model for the painting) had been seen 'looking more ragged and more beautiful than ever'.[17] *Whichever way this, and related, descriptions of Winterson's text were intended, I am unable to read any juxtaposition of beauty and serious illness as anything other than a glamorisation of the fact. It is something I feel passionately not only because I have witnessed and been on the receiving end of pain so extreme that I know there is no way that it can be aesthetically 'framed', but because, as a teenager, I was very much inclined to the idea of illnesses (especially of the pale wasting kind) as a feminine ideal. Thus I am sensitive to the text's own investment in this discourse on the grounds of my own past collusion with it.*

What is immediately striking about this response — or reaction — is that the aesthetic / critical framework it reaches for to make its complaint is a very unsophisticated form of 'authentic realism'.[18] The text is tested, evaluated and ultimately rejected on the grounds that it does not match my own experience of pain, sickness and the 'diseased body'. Placing the response in the context of my wider reading, however, it is clear that the source of my disturbance is considerably more complex. For whilst I might condemn Winterson for the aesthicisation / sexualisation of the diseased body on the grounds that it is a glamorisation of medical 'fact', a symptomatic analysis of my response reveals that it is the sexualisation of the body *per se* that I have found hard to accommodate both in this text and the 'Winterson' inter-text. In Barthesian terms, it is therefore Winterson's changing representation of the body that has cast, for me, a 'stain' upon the body of her work.[19] As I observe in another part of my reading:

Even now, I'm unsure of the role of these informing voices in my own disenchantment with 'Winterson', though it could certainly be said that the massive public exposure to which 'she' has been submitted has had the effect of making her and her writings disenchantingly 'commonplace'. A connection can probably be made, however, between the effect of the adverse publicity and my changing relation to the texts themselves vis-à-vis *the discourse of the body. I remember, for example, the hard ('redemptive') work I had to do to explain and justify the nude photograph of Winterson which appeared in 'The Guardian'. This making public of the author's own sexual body (even if it was without the author's consent!), may be seen to correspond with my growing discomfort with the commodification of her work. The fact that this 'exposure' also anticipated a newly explicit emphasis on the sexual body in her writing therefore becomes metaphorically appropriate. As I have already indicated, the discourses of romance and sex are, for me, largely incompatible, and the unveiling of the 'perfect' sexual body in this novel (as in the newspaper photograph) set a stain upon the 'body' of Winterson's works as a whole. Although sex has traditionally functioned as the secret shrine at the heart of romantic love, its (literal) publication converts the 'secret' body into a 'paltry image' (Barthes, 26) and kills romance.*

My disappointment with Winterson's text, then — which scrambles hastily for aesthetic and political legitimisation — is more 'honestly' understood in terms of my inability as a reader to accommodate this new sexuality within the discursive version of romantic love with which I am familiar. Thus while I *could* turn this responsibility back on the text itself and say that it fails in its feminist commitment (i.e., Lothario's sexual behaviour, even though critically framed, is hard to accommodate within a lesbian/feminist vision of the world), I know that such politics, and the interpretive community which supports them, have been enlisted to conceal the disappointment predicated upon my own ideological inscription.

The spoiling or staining of the Winterson canon for myself, as a reader and erstwhile fan, is therefore focused on the newly explicit imaging of the sexual body (and sexual relations) to be found in *Written on the Body*. The fact that this representation is not really 'new' at all, but present — to a smaller, but not insignificant extent — in the previous novels is but further testimony to the ideologically 'blind' source of my own enamoration. Reflecting elsewhere on how the disillusion first came about I conclude:

Looking back over my text, indeed, it is clear that I was reading like a betrayed lover determined to discover when the 'spot' first appeared on the stainless body of the relationship. Reading backwards in this way I can, of course, recognise Lothario's prototype in the earlier heroes and heroines and berate myself for not spotting the 'signs' sooner ... For Lothario's 'Don Juanesque' career, which casts a retrospective shadow over my whole relationship with the Winterson oeuvre, is no more than an expression of what all lovers know at heart, but most refuse to admit: that romantic love (no matter apparently *unique) is an emotion capable of reproducing itself over and over again.*[20] *Whilst Winterson's text may thus be seen to face up to this fact of life, my own reading shows me stubbornly rejecting it.*

Exactly who, or what, made this stain visible to me remains more of a mystery both in my re-reading or my re-memory although, as I have already indicated, the roles of 'gossips' and 'informers' (Barthes, 183-5) were probably more significant than I have given them credit for. In the last analysis it was clearly a complex fusion of textual and inter-textual factors that brought 'Winterson' and her writing out of ether and stained them with the death-knell of the 'common-place'. As Barthes observes on this sad end to the wonders of romantic enchantment:

> In the other's perfect and 'embalmed' figure (for that is the degree to which it fascinates me) I perceive suddenly a speck of corruption. This speck is a tiny one: a gesture, a word, an object, a garment, something unexpected which appears (which dawns) from a region I never suspected, and suddenly attaches the loved object to the *commonplace* world (Barthes, 25).

It would, however, be unfair to represent this as the true 'end of the story' as far as my readerly relationship with 'Winterson' is concerned. As recent research on romantic discourse has shown, the structures and sequences of classic romance (including the 'ravissement' — 'sequel' trajectory) exist to be broken, and we have to recognise that many of the romantic and readerly emotions I have dealt with in this chapter will be experienced simultaneously.[21] Thus, while I have presented my 'disappointment' with the Winterson oeuvre as the culmination of the romantic sequel, what my re-reading and re-memory indicate is this was *not* the final word. Indeed, the following, final extract confirms that even in the midst of this disillusion I had not fully given up hope that my former relationship with this writer and her texts would be restored to me:

I read the final section of the novel in a single sitting, without making notes or attempting to carve it up into sections for closer analysis. This was facilitated by the fact that it has a unity that the first section lacks, both temporal (it follows the chronological passage from March to October when Lothario begins his her search for Louise) and in terms of its 'structure of feeling'. At last Lothario's guilty bragging abates, and the focus settles — gets serious. At this point the rhetorical angst about love and sex — how to distinguish one from the other, how to prove the latter, how to know the 'real thing' from its shadow — give way to the simpler rhythms of possession and loss, presence and absence. Despite the text's hysterical insistence on the materiality of the lover's body, we see it evaporate — amid rising doubt and panic — into thin air. Thus the text wheels dizzyingly, via Lothario's deranged consciousness, around all the spaces places Louise might be, but is not. The nature of the loss is also defined by the provisionality which surrounds it and which is made part of the plot: the assumption that Louise is still alive somewhere, *and that (with effort) she may be found. At the point Lothario begins his active search for her, however, the latter becomes less certain, and the growing panic he suffers as a consequence is an effective dramatisation of the key ingredient in all mourning. None of us, it seems, is able to register the permanence of physical loss very easily; it is difficult to adjust to the 'fact' that someone isn't there anymore when they remain alive and kicking in your unconscious. As Lothario observes* vis-à-vis *the death of another friend:*

> *When I recovered from her death in the crudest sense I started to see her in the streets, always fleetingly, ahead of me, her back to me disappearing into the crowd. I am told this is common. I still see her, though less often, and still for a second I believe it is her (WB 155).*

What the final section of this novel enacts, then, is two contradictory emotional pulls. On the one hand there is an accelerating search for the missing object [expectation?], which may be thought of as the horizontal axis. In the other hand, there is the downward pull of certainty that she is gone (the vertical axis). ('The more I know it to be true, the more desperately I search'). This paradox of sentiment, brought about by the desperate struggle between the conscious and the unconscious mind, reduces the best of us to bewilderment:

> *The day before the Wednesday last, this time a year ago, you were here and now you're not. Why not? Death reduces us to the baffled logic of a small child. If yesterday why not today? And where are you? (WB 156).*

Unable, it seems, to articulate my own loss (of 'Winterson'), I let the text do it for me. In the same way that Lothario waits for Louise, so do I wait for 'Winterson'. Both of us have kept up the search long after we know it to be hopeless, and both of us share the mourner's ability to accept that 'it' (this life, this romance, this reading) is finally over.

NOTES

1. See Lynne Pearce, '"I" the Reader: Text, Context and the Balance of Power', in *Feminist Subjects, Multi-Media*, ed. by Penny Florence and Dee Reynolds (Manchester University Press, 1995) and *Feminism and the Politics of Reading* (London: Edward Arnold, 1997).
2. Roland Barthes, *A Lover's Discourse: Fragments*, translated by Richard Howard (London: Penguin, 1990) 197-8. All further page references to this volume will be given after quotations in the text.
3. The key role of a reader's 'interpretive community' in determining his/her reading of a text can be traced back to Stanley Fish's infamous experiment with a group of student readers whose 'training' in the reading of seventeenth-century poetry caused them to read a set of unrelated notes left on a blackboard as though it were a religious poem. Fish's reflections on this and other aspects of reader-theory are reproduced in the volume *Is there a text in this class?: The Authority of Interpretive Communities* (Cambridge, MA and London: Harvard University Press, 1980).
4. For a detailed account of this methodology, and the rationale supporting it, see the introduction to *Feminism and the Politics of Reading* (ibid). The concept of 're-memorying' derives from Toni Morrison's novel *Beloved* (London: Picador, 1988) where it centres on the principal character's belief that the past 'never dies' but remains a material space/place that may be accessed, often involuntarily, at any time. Within the context of my own methodology, my 're-memorying' of a text refers to my attempt to write my memory of it, and the experience of formerly reading it, before I go back to look at it again.
5. See especially Italo Calvino, *Invisible Cities* (1974; London: Secker & Warburg, 1993).
6. Raymond Williams writes about 'the shock of recognition' in his book *Politics and Letters* (London: Verso, 1979) in the context of his over-haul of Marxist models of ideology. Although the complexity of his argument cannot really be summed up in a few lines, Williams's insistence that we need to find a way of speaking about how individuals experience ideology 'from the inside' (as what he calls a *structure of feeling*) helps to make sense of the way in which some aspect of our social selves can be suddenly revealed to us through an act of 'recognition' (e.g., we might see the mark of our own class insecurity in the behaviour of another). See also Elspeth Probyn, *Sexing the Self: Gendered Positions in Cultural Studies* (London and New York: Routledge, 1993).
7. This quotation from Gore Vidal was used widely in the early promotion of Winterson's books, and appeared on the dust jacket of *The Passion*.
8. Barthes's theory regarding the 'scene', is that we need a visual (or aural) sign of our first enchantment in order to materially fix the experience. He writes: 'Love at first sight requires the sign of its suddenness (what makes me irresponsible, subject to fatality, swept away, ravished) ... the scene *consecrates* the object I am going to love' (Barthes, 192).
9. In my readings in *Feminism and the Politics of Reading* (ibid) who/what constitutes the 'textual other' with whom I, as the reader, dialogically engage includes: a character in the text; an interlocutory position *vis-à-vis* my relationship to one of the characters in the text; a text *cleared* of characters which becomes, instead, a 'scene' for my own re-scripted projections; a 'structure of feeling' (see note 6 above) which I recognise and subsequently fill with my own narrative experience; or (in the case of my reading of Winterson) the re-constructed author of the text. One of the best illustrations of how readers' textual participation is not limited to simple character-identification is Ien Ang's study, *Watching Dallas: Soap Opera and the Melodramatic Imagination* (London and New York: Methuen, 1985) in which she shows that although many viewers disliked the *Dallas* characters and/or found them absurd, they nevertheless related to the text's '*tragic* structure of feeling' which represented life as a constant round of crisis and recovery.
10. 'Author-function': see Michel Foucault, 'What is an author?', in *Language, Counter-Memory, Practice*, ed. by Donald F. Bouchard and translated by Donald Bouchard and Sherry Simon (Ithaca, NY: Cornell University Press, 1977).
11. I have since confirmed this memory as correct through an extensive computer search of all the reviews (from around the world) which came out in the year immediately following the text's publication. To take just one example from the British press: 'Yet she leaves out not only the specification of gender, but blurs all the other contours of her narrator's personality. The narrator has no childhood, no colour,

no interests, no class and no post — except for a succession of lovers ... Moving her vision to this kind of environment [middle-class London] makes Winterson's imaginative world seem suddenly smaller: whimsical rather than experimental: snobbish rather than individualistic. A niche in London's literary world has certainly not helped her writing, but she might bounce back with something more strenuous and surprise us again'. Natasha Walter, *The Independent*, 19 September, 1992.

12. See Barthes, 233: 'The N.W.P. (the *non-will-to-possess*, an expression imitated from the Orient) is a reversed substitute for suicide. Not to kill oneself (for love) means to take this decision, not to possess the other. It is the same moment when Werther kills himself and when he could have renounced possessing Charlotte: it is either that or death (hence, a Solemn moment).'
13. See my reading of Olive Schreiner's *Story of an African Farm* (1892; New York: Bantam, 1993) in chapters five and six of *Feminism and the Politics of Reading* (ibid).
14. See Lynne Pearce, *Reading Dialogics* (London: Edward Arnold, 1994) 50-54.
15. I discuss the crucial role of taste and connoisseurship in 'professional reading' in the Introduction to *Feminism and the Politics of Reading* (ibid) and consider its practical application in chapters seven and eight. For many of these ideas I am indebted to a paper given by Lynda Nead in the Art History Department of McGill University, Montreal, entitled 'Troubled Bodies: Art, Obscenity and the Connoisseur'.
16. The friend whose cancer inspired this interest / investment has since written her own book on the cultural production and reception of cancer and its narratives. See Jackie Stacey, *Teratologies* (London and New York: Routledge, 1997).
17. See my discussion of this text in Lynne Pearce, *Woman/Image/Text: Readings in Pre-Raphaelite Art and Literature* (Hemel Hempstead: Harvester Wheatsheaf, 1991) 46-58.
18. 'Authentic realism' is the type of critical practice in which the reader tests and evaluates a text against the authority of his/her own experiences. For further discussion see chapter 2 of *Feminist Readings/Feminists Reading*, by Sara Mills and Lynne Pearce, second edition (Hemel Hempstead: Harvester Wheatsheaf, 1996).
19. For Barthes, the moment of staining or spoiling is a crucial factor in romantic dis-enchantment. Only when some 'speck of corruption' intervenes and links the loved object to the 'commonplace world' is the lover able to be set free (see Barthes, 25).
20. Barthes deals with the re-productability of romantic love under the heading 'errancy': 'I always behave — I insist upon behaving, whatever I am told and whatever my own discouragements may be, as if love might someday be fulfilled, as if the Sovereign Good were possible. Whence the odd dialectic which causes one absolute love to succeed another without the least embarrassment, as if, by love, I acceded to another logic ... I search, I begin, I try, I venture further, I run ahead, but I never know that I am ending: it is never said of the Phoenix that it dies, but only that it is reborn' (Barthes, 101-2).
21. See the Introduction to *Romance Revisited*, ed. by Lynne Pearce and Jackie Stacey (London: Lawrence and Wishart, 1995). In this discussion we argue that, as far as its narrative structuring is concerned, romance is, in fact, a category 'in crisis' (24). This is evidenced by a whole range of cultural texts in which the classic trajectory of events is scrambled or inverted.

NARRATION AND GENDER: THE ROLE OF THE FIRST-PERSON NARRATOR IN JEANETTE WINTERSON'S *WRITTEN ON THE BODY*

UTE KAUER

'A precise emotion seeks a precise expression' — thus the aim of Jeanette Winterson's novel *Written on the Body* is outlined on the second page. If the narrator sets out to re-define or even re-invent the language of love, why then be so unprecise about gender? Why then leave the gender of the first-person narrator undetermined? What kind of game is Winterson playing with her readers, what strategies are employed to hide the gender of the 'I' in the novel, and does it work, or is the gender not as undeclared as the blurb announces? These questions, which will be elucidated in the following chapter, show that here we are confronted with a novel forcing the discussion of gender into the field of narratology. *Ex negativo*, simply by the narrator's denial to be classified according to gender, the question of the consequences of gender for the act of narration is forced on the reader. In 1986, Susan Sniader Lanser remarked that 'virtually no work in the field of narratology has taken gender into account' that 'narratology has avoided questions of gender almost entirely'.[1] In the discussion of *Written on the Body* these questions cannot be avoided.

Elaine Showalter once compared the development of women's writing to the changes in ethnic sub-culture groups. Analogous to the stages of imitation of tradition, protest against the given social roles and self-discovery, she identified three by now well-known phases in women's literature: (1) the feminine phase (roughly dating from 1840 to 1880); (2) the feminist phase (1880-1920); and (3) the female phase (1920 to the present).[2] Reading *Written on the Body* now might lead to the conclusion that Winterson has transcended the stage of self-discovery with her book. The main object is no longer to discover a specific female identity, and the emphasis is not on a predominantly female perspective in the relationships which are described. Neither is it an attempt at self-discovery by reviving the androgynous myth of Virginia Woolf's *Orlando*; sexual ambiguity is not the same as androgyny. Winterson goes a step further. This is no longer self-discovery, but rather self-construction. The narrator does not want to merge male and female views on the subject of the narration, love, but seems to attempt to erase all gender specifics by denying us the information about his or her gender, by wearing the mask of a gender-free persona. Are we, then, now entering a gender-free sector, and are we to expect an anatomy of love purged from traditional concepts of the male or female? To answer this question, a closer look at the role(s) of the narrator in the story is necessary.

Obviously, the story is told by a first-person narrator. According to Bertil Romberg's definition the 'distinguishing characteristic, then, of the first-person novel is that the author makes the novel narrate itself through the mouth of one of the figures taking part in it'.[3] Furthermore, in this case the narrator not only takes part in the story, he or she is the main character, undertaking a minute self-analysis. In Genette's terminology, this would be called a homodiegetic narrator, a narrator who is part of the fictional world.[4] The act of communication is characterised by a kind of 'primeval epic situation',[5] a partnership between reader and narrator in which the narrator relates his/her experience to an audience. This audience consists of a fictitious 'you', addressed several times throughout the novel. This 'you' or narratee takes the role of a confidante for the 'I'. But one has to be careful in classifying the narratee, as the reflections of the 'I' are by no means addressed to the same 'you' all the time, as the narratee changes roles.

First of all, the associative style of the reflections suggests self-analysis and self-negotiations as in a diary, the narratee therefore being the self. In the associative passages, the sentences often lack a verb and show repetitions, just as in a stream-of-consciousness: 'Not this year the pleasure of rolling blue grapes between finger and thumb juicing my palm with musk. Even the wasps avoid the thin brown dribble. Even the wasps this year' (*WB* 9). In this passage from the beginning of the novel, the 'I' is reflecting the difference between past and present, caught in the act of comparing and remembering, addressing itself.

Soon the second narratee is introduced: 'You said, "I love you"' (*WB* 9), the 'you' being someone from the past, here not specified, but later identified as 'Louise' (*WB* 20). The 'I' engages in a fictitious dialogue with the presumably absent Louise (at this point the reader does not have any further information about the relationship), trying to recapture the past.

The third addressee is the implied reader, and the direct addresses to the reader constitute what Romberg called the 'primeval epic situation'. The reader is addressed by rhetorical questions ('See?') and directly as 'you', and the narrator is trying to imitate the situation of oral communication. Ironically, the presence of a partner in the self-communication is assumed. The narrator reacts as if he/she could actually hear the reader's doubts or questions: 'You think I'm trying to wriggle out of my responsibilities?' (*WB* 16), 'Did I say this has happened to me again and again? You will think I have been constantly in and out of married women's lumber-rooms' (*WB* 17). This technique of course contributes to the comic effects in the novel: the narrator ironises his/her own role constantly, as well as the role of the reader. The narrator plays with the moral objections the implied reader might raise by anticipating them. The dialectics of what is told and what is only implied by the narrator, constitute the process of communication between text and reader.[6] One important 'Leerstelle' (a void in the text which has to be filled in by the reader), to use Wolfgang Iser's term, is the undeclared gender because it forces the reader into the text to co-ordinate the different masks and perspectives the narrator offers.[7]

So we have a situation of communication where the narrator changes the narratee, establishes a quasi-oral relationship to the implied reader and thus attaches the roles of confidant and moral authority to the reader. The irony is heightened by the fact that in spite of the quasi-oral communication between reader and narrator, metanarrative comments are interwoven that clearly and explicitly indicate the non-oral character of the situation. Not only is the meaning of past events endlessly questioned, but the narrative situation itself is deconstructed.

Metanarrative should here be understood as referring exclusively to comments on the act of narration,[8] as for example 'I can tell by now that you are wondering whether I can be trusted as a narrator' (*WB* 24); or 'I don't know if this is a happy ending' (*WB* 190). Instead of the traditional device of re-inforcing the reliability of the narrator, this one ironically undermines his/her credibility by asking 'Can I be trusted?' To return to the quotation from the beginning, being precise in this novel does not mean giving an exact account of past events or historical facts. That facts are not important for the narrator is continually stressed. The 'I' loses him-/herself in the labyrinth of the past, trying to recall scenes and sensations rather than facts. The past becomes a maze where even the first-person narrator, the only source for the personal story, gets lost. Making statements and correcting them in the same paragraph is an indication for the unreliability of the narrator: immediately after describing a scene where the narrator fed ripe plums to Louise (or rather an unknown 'you', for at this point we do not know that it is Louise), there is the statement: 'There are no ripe plums in August' (*WB* 17), but: 'Nevertheless I will push on' (*WB* 18). The narrator displays an uneasiness about his/her trustworthiness which is on the one hand ironical, but on the other hand underlines the fact that the fictive biography of the self is much more important than what actually took place. This play on fiction and reality, or on the different layers of reality, is of course a typical post-modern phenomenon. The insistence on the importance of the act of remembering, be it real or fictitious, over what 'really' happened, denies the power of facts.

This reflects Winterson's general view on history, reality and fiction. In her 'historical' novels like *Sexing the Cherry* or *The Passion*, she also constantly rearranges the past, mixes history and myth. Even in *Oranges Are Not the Only Fruit*, her most realist novel, her view that narrating the past means giving the reader options for constructing his or her own story is expressed: 'History should be a hammock for swinging and a game for playing, the way cars play. Claw it, chew it, rearrange it and at bedtime it's still a ball of string full of knots' (*O* 91). Here the narrator comments on history in the form of an interpolated essay. Facts and fictions are material for playing, and in *Written on the Body*, the scenes described above become metaphors for the emotions the narrator wants to recapture in order to annul the deadening effect of time.[9]

'One cannot describe reality; only give metaphors that indicate it', as John Fowles put it.[10] The revealed unreliability of the narrator hints at the metaphorical character of the reality that is described. The self creates his or her own biography by finding metaphors for experiences because those metaphors are a more precise expression of emotion than facts — just like the Conchis-figure in Fowles's *The Magus*, where this concept is carried to the extreme and the past is reinvented and even re-enacted by the magus.

The post-modern play on fiction and reality is expanded by more subtle hints at the unreliability of the narrator within the narrated past. After the narrator has once explicitly questioned his/her own credibility, the reader is liable to doubt what is told, and to attach more importance to the meaning than to the verbal facts. On this basis, a scene from the past is interwoven where the narrator actually made things up. Introducing a past episode with the anarcha-feminist girl-friend Inge, the narrator tells how he/she made up an ironic explanation for Renoir's statement that he painted with his penis in the following dialogue:

> 'Don't worry,' I said. 'He did. When he died they found nothing between his balls but an old brush. 'You're making it up.' Am I? (*WB* 22).

The scene is repeated in the Henry Miller-version later in the novel, where the brush is replaced by a ball-point pen and the anarchist girl-friend by a would-be writer (*WB* 60). The dialogue from the past is juxtaposed by the rhetorical question from the narrator's present, 'Am I?'. The present tense is used instead of the past tense: the question is *not* 'Did I?', which would be logical. By this subtle change of tense, it is insinuated that perhaps the 'I' did not only make up the jokes about Renoir and Henry Miller but the whole story. The question aims at increasing the uneasiness about fiction and reality, and so finally at the reader's conception of reality. Naturally, one is not supposed to believe that this really happened to Renoir or Miller — but nevertheless it is true for the narrator in a more than factual sense; it is an ironical deconstruction of the myth of male creativity. A parallel is drawn between the ironical interpolated story from the past and the whole act of narration by the significant change of tense from 'did' to 'am': the narrator may have made the story up, it may be imprecise in terms of time and place, it may even be impossible like ripe plums in August — but it is still true as it gives expression to the narrator's emotions. The accusation a reader might voice, 'You're making it up', is transferred to an incident in the past and doubts about the narrator's reliability are deliberately increased.

The reader is made to see that what he or she will get are fictions, not facts, or rather uncertainties instead of straightforward categories. The narrative structure reveals changing narratees and a narrator who not only coquettes with his/her uncertainty, but chooses to withhold all information about the narrator-persona. We get to know hardly anything in terms of facts about the narrating 'I', neither age nor gender, neither outward appearance nor specific beliefs. Carefully, even a little too ostentatiously, the narrator avoids both describing him-/herself and reflecting gender in dialogues. Instead of giving information about the narrating 'I', the beginning of the novel goes *in medias res* by using one of the key-phrases as an opening: 'Why is the measure of love loss?' (*WB* 9), followed by remarks on the dry summer (which summer? and where?), and soon leaving the level of the narrator's presence by engaging in the act of remembering, 'I am thinking of a certain September' (*WB* 9). The opening is remarkable for its absence of information; neither the specific time nor place are mentioned, and the 'I' remains as indefinite as the 'you' on the first page. So far, this seems to be a purely 'private'[11] narration, taking place inside the 'I''s mind, as all the information a narratee different from the self would need is excluded — must be excluded, as otherwise the gender could not remain undeclared. But is it really meant to be undeclared, or is it rather another mask, another way of ironising the figure of the narrator? I will try to clarify this point in the following.

The first-person narrator as main character is subject to certain restrictions. The narration is limited to the narrator's field of vision. He or she can relate his/her mind, but cannot enter into the thoughts and feelings of other characters without a sound justification for this knowledge. As omniscience is excluded from this point of view, the narrator can only relate what goes on in the present or what is past experience; definite references to the future are not possible. If past experiences are related, the first-person narrator often justifies why the past is remembered in detail, (e.g. by reference to a diary or letters), or becomes unreliable and implausible. Furthermore, the first-person narrator cannot look upon himself from the outside, an external picture has to be given by a mirror: 'The mirror may be a literal mirror, but it is usually a figurative mirror throwing back the image of the narrator from the communications of other characters, whether in letters or in dialogue'.[12] In his statements about the first-person narrator as main character, Romberg takes for granted that the narrator *wants* to give an internal as well as an external picture of himself, seeing the difficulty that even the opinions and dialogues of other protagonists are related by the 'I'. The case is slightly different in *Written on the Body*. The 'natural' restrictions of a first-person narrator are reversed and open up new narrative possibilities. As I have pointed out above, the narrator sees no need to justify the memories but plays with fiction and reality. In addition to this, the first-person narrator in our case does not want to be identified by some of the categories that are usually believed to form an identity, namely gender and age, and therefore any external picture has to be avoided. As we are at the end of the twentieth century and men and women have become nearly indistinguishable as far as clothes are concerned, the frequently dropped descriptions of shorts or business suits give no real clue to the narrator's gender. Neither do the love affairs, for girl- and boyfriends are mentioned, which only reveal that the narrator must be bisexual. There is, actually, a scene in the novel where the narrator looks in a mirror — but only to verify the inner state of mind, not to say anything about appearances.[13] In the dialogues and the descriptions of sexual encounters, every reference to the gender of the narrator is carefully omitted — which is even more remarkable considering the fact that the main subject of the novel is love. Even in disputes with adulterous women or quarrels with Elgin, no verbal hint at the gender is given. This must appear contrived, as it is not usual in such situations. The difficulty shows in a narrated dialogue with Louise, where she tells the narrator that 'you were the most beautiful creature male or female I had ever seen' (*WB* 84). The deviation from a 'normal' dialogue between lovers, where one would talk about the most beautiful man or woman, is a bit too pointed not to appear as artificial.

Nevertheless it has to be taken into account that this artificiality might be an intended one. It is one of the aims of the book to deconstruct clichés about love, gender and specific male or female codes of behaviour. Explicitly stated in another key-phrase of the novel, this statement is repeated frequently throughout the narration: 'It's the clichés that cause the trouble' (*WB* 10).[14] The novel sets out to destroy those clichés about love and gender by pretending not to recognise the importance of gender-markers. Clichés are not precise, they do not describe the feelings of the narrator adequately. They offer categorisations, whereas what the narrator seeks is an expression for a very individual sensation. Clichés like 'You will get over it' seem not appropriate to the pain the narrator feels after leaving Louise. The narrator uses word-plays to deconstruct these clichés, like for example the opposition between 'engage' and 'distract' in the following paragraph:

> It is so terrifying, love, that all I can do is shove it under a dump bin of pink cuddly toys and send myself a greetings card saying 'Congratulations on your engagement'. But I am not engaged I am deeply distracted (*WB* 10).

The 'sensible route' the clichés advocate is not the route of the narrator, who does not want to settle down with 'not too much passion, not too much sex' (*WB* 71). The word-play underlines that language itself is infected with clichés and categorisations and thus no longer appropriate for a changed mode of behaviour — has perhaps never been appropriate for the phenomenon of love. By showing the deficiency of language the meaninglessness of the concepts behind the words is revealed. The section in the book about the 'cells, tissues, systems and cavities of the body' (*WB* 115-139) illustrates this as well. Medical descriptions dissect the body, technically and devoid of any emotion. This clinical attitude is contrasted with the narrator's passionate longing for the lover; the medical passages recall the corresponding parts of the lover's body, even in their technicality they initiate memories and sensations. The narrator's intense and poetic language of passion indicates a very different attitude to the body. The mathematical exactness is the same as in the medical passages, but here the emotions and sensations connected with the lover's body are dissected. The style ranges from the simple statement of longing — 'I wish I could hear your voice again' (*WB* 135) — to a language overcharged with poetical density, engaging in an orgy of metaphors (see for example the passage on taste). The metaphorical passages lack the counter-balance of satire that characterises the rest of the novel. The withdrawal to a purely poetical and metaphorical way of expression indicates that there is still a long way to go in finding a new language for the passion of bodily sensations. The lack of irony separates this part clearly from the rest of the book; here the impulse to create a new language 'written on the body' outweighs the destructive impulse to destroy the old clichés. But without ironical self-reflection expressions of passion are difficult to bear. Winterson is naturally not the first writer trying to find a new language for desire. The mixture of metaphorical overkill and real poetic beauty reminds one, for example, of D.H. Lawrence, who tended to blur his narrative structures with an excessive use of jargon while at the same time glorifying speechlessness — all in the attempt to invent a new language for love. He made his protagonist Birkin in *Women in Love*, say that the word love should be tabooed from utterance until we find a new conception for it, until we are able to get rid of the clichés that cause all the trouble.[15]

The deconstruction of stereotypes is not restricted to love. The narrator also displays stereotypes about national identity and ridicules them: when Louise stands up to put on the coffee in order to release the emotional tension, the narrator states that the 'English are very good at those gestures' — only to underline that Louise is Australian, not English, soon afterwards (*WB* 37). Louise does not fit into any kind of cliché. She even questions the repetitions and clichés in the narrator's own life by reacting contrary to any expectations. She breaks the pattern of relationships the narrator has followed so far (shown in the interpolated scenario with 'naked woman' and 'lover') and acts according to the 'wrong script' (*WB* 18). The narrator is banned from the relative security of a cliché-ridden world and left without a pattern, forced to find a new language that does not adhere to any script, forced as well to find a new code of behaviour. The self-sacrifice for Louise too has to be recognised as acting according to a certain pattern, for the narrator is not a knight in shining armour.

Deconstructing patterns is not enough — the old clichés have to be replaced by new concepts, new words and new modes of narrating. The question one is inclined to ask is whether a gender-free narrator implies a narration freed from gender-specific clichés. I will now try to show that the narrator uses precisely those gender-specific clichés to keep the reader in uncertainty about his/her gender. The refusal to admit the gender of the narrator is based on a play with stereotypes which the reader is supposed to have. The stereotypes are to be deconstructed in the minds of the readers just like the language of love is to be deconstructed in the text. The reader is caught in a net of hints, false assumptions and red herrings concerning the gender of the narrator, counter-acting the whole set of assumptions about the terms 'male' and 'female'. First of all, the narrator leaves more or less obvious traces about gender, which are comparisons or self-identifications. Those hints are carefully constructed and by no means dropped accidentally. It can be assumed that a male first-person narrator would more readily compare himself to a male figure, whereas a female first-person narrator would probably choose a female figure for comparison — at least this seems to be the assumption about the readers' assumptions. Stereotypes are presupposed and then counteracted. Backing the assumption that the narrator might be female are comparisons to *Alice in Wonderland* ('I shall call myself Alice', *WB* 10), to Lauren Bacall (*WB* 41), and the simile in 'Why do I feel like a convent virgin?' (*WB* 94). A male narrator would most probably rather compare himself to a monk than to a convent virgin, or would choose Humphrey Bogart instead of Lauren Bacall. Identifications of the self are usually inseparable from one's own gender.

But those identifications with female figures are juxtaposed by identifications with male figures. The narrator chooses an epitaph as 'unhappy Socrates' (*WB* 13) and repeatedly calls him-/herself the 'Lothario' (e.g. *WB* 20). A qualification as a heartless libertine is, according to the cliché, usually connected to a male figure. In spite of this balance of male and female identifications, the impression prevails that the male comparisons are there to deconstruct common notions about the female, rather than vice versa. It might be a comic effect for a man to disguise himself as a convent virgin, but there is more than a comic effect behind a woman's identification with Lothario, namely the attempt to question the myth of female fidelity and male promiscuity. So the conclusion might be that the novel has a female first-person narrator cross-dressing as a man. The clichés that are deconstructed are more stereotypes about femininity than notions about male behaviour. Stereotypes about masculinity are mocked and employed as a means to undermine traditional concepts of female behaviour.

Attitudes usually connected with masculinity are ridiculed by placing them in scenes where a totally different attitude would be expected from the narrator. Intertextual allusions contribute to the subtle comic effect of such scenes. In the dispute between the narrator and a friend about Jacqueline, the narrator reacts in the following manner to the accusations uttered by the friend: 'I poured myself a drink and shrugged' (*WB* 28). The act of pouring a drink in a situation of emotional crisis as well as the laconism of the statement are worth a Philip Marlowe or Sam Spade. The refusal to acknowledge and express feelings in this passage is reminiscent of the typical chauvinist behaviour of the Hemingway hero. And it is not at all typical for the first-person narrator of the story, whose very aim it is to find a new expression for the emotional crisis he or she has gone through. The intertextuality brings to mind role models for this scene; it displays 'male' attitudes by conjuring up literary images. The indirect quotation stresses the fact that those role models are fictive ones, applied to 'real' life. Emotional reactions have a palimpsest, they are not original. The narrator of course is conscious of this, as the reflections that follow the display of

Marlowe-like coolness show. Unlike the laconic statements in the literary palimpsest, the narrator here reflects upon the use of the cliché. The mask of the cool male hero, who does not really care about anything, is put on only to be removed soon afterwards.

It is important to note that no female masks which would be comparable can be found. The main aim is to deconstruct the male myth and at the same time widen the 'acceptable' code of female behaviour. Another example for this is the ironical display of male boasting: 'I've always had a sports car, but you can't rev your way out of real life. That home girl gonna get you in the end' (*WB* 21). The notion about the wild and free libertine in his sports car who is sooner or later captured by a home girl, offers a whole bunch of clichés, again expressed in the same laconic manner. We know by now that the narrator is much too self-reflexive and too critical to fall prey to vulgar clichés: so again, an ironical and ostentatious display of clichés about masculinity. The mask of the chauvinist does not fit the image the first-person narrator creates throughout the whole story. It can therefore be assumed that the very wearing of the chauvinist mask out of context is used to deconstruct the cliché by ironising it. Only the male identifications appear as masks, and masks are usually used to hide the real identity, which is the identity of someone aiming to destroy sexual role models; and, as Gilbert and Gubar state, it 'is, after all, only those who have been oppressed by history and society who want to shatter the paradigms of dominance and submission enforced by the hierarchies of gender, and restore a primordial, gender-free chaos'.[16] So I will henceforward use the feminine personal pronoun for the first-person narrator.

Two other scenes designed to raise doubts about the narrator's gender are also concerned with so-called typically male behaviour, though without literary allusions. The first is the hilarious account of a dream about an ex-girlfriend 'who had been heavily into paper-maché' (*WB* 41). The dream about the paper-snake in the letter-box with a rat-trap in its jaw owes a lot to Freud. It could be classified in psychological terms as an expression of the fear of castration. Again a cultural palimpsest is used as a red herring for the reader. Why should a female narrator be so afraid of a serpent 'poking out of the letter-box just at crotch level'? The trap is clearly designed for men, in this case for the postman. The dream is not without its function in the context. The narrator thus illustrates the oppression felt by Jacqueline's presence. But naturally one cannot help wondering if a woman would not have dreamt differently. Just as in a detective story, a red herring is interwoven to keep the reader questioning the gender roles in and outside the text. By joking with these roles and the stereotypes attached to them, the narrator constantly plays with the categories determining our view of the world and of the text. The same scheme is practised in the boxing-scene with Elgin (*WB* 170-72). Women not being famous for violent combat, the narrator is reacting contrary to the reader's mental designs by hitting Elgin and using violence as an appropriate outlet for her rage. The traditional role play where the man plays the strong and active part is satirised: sexual roles become a matter of choice, not of social conventions.

Whereas the male roles appear as masks satirising sexual conventions, there are some more or less clear indications that the narrator identifies strongly with the female role. Some of them are contextual, for example the narrator's concern for Louise's bodily functions (*WB* 13), or the suffering after a lost love in general. This seems to belong to the female role. But here one has to be careful, for maybe it is just another of the reader's clichés that men in love do not suffer as women do. The vague impression one gets — at least as a female reader — that this is a woman's point of view, can be verified by analysing the first-person's way of describing other characters. It has been pointed out earlier that a first-person narrator cannot enter the minds of other protagonists. Still, a certain point of view can be discerned that underlines the narrator's relation to the other protagonists. The gender of those protagonists becomes important because the narrator's empathy might throw light on the standpoint in the supposed 'gender-free chaos'. Or, as Mieke Bal remarks, the reader sees a character 'through the medium of an agent other than the character, an agent that sees and, seeing, causes to be seen'.[17] The agent (or 'focalizer', as Bal calls it) reveals him-/herself by viewing others. This agent in our case is the first-person narrator.

Before analysing the point of view, it seems to be necessary to clarify how the term is to be understood, as it is one of the most ambiguous terms in narratology.[18] There are basically two meanings of 'point of view': (1) The angle from which an event or person is described in the text; (2) Opinion. 'In the first definition, which is more literal than the second, we are dealing with the object of the gaze; in the second, with the subject who sees or considers',[19] as Mieke Bal differentiates the two meanings in her revision of Genette's theory (she uses the term 'focalization' instead of 'point of view' because it is more technical). Lately, there have been attempts, especially in feminist narratology, to operate with both meanings[20] in order to prevent the isolation of the text from its context, a concept which has also been employed by Marxist criticism.[21] It seems unnecessary to widen the meaning of the term by including both aspects, as both are working on totally different levels (see Bal's definition above). Point of view should be understood as the angle from which the narrator tells the story, a category which is clearly concerned with narrative strategies within the text. Those narrative strategies can of course help to express a certain opinion or *Weltanschauung* of the narrator, but they are the means and should be separated from the aim they work to express. This does not mean a separation of text and context; it is still possible to ask why certain strategies are used or which cultural context brings about certain points of view, or whether narrative strategies can be gender specific or not.

Significant in respect to the point of view, is the way the narrator describes the situation of other women. The descriptions occur mainly in subordinated narratives, one level deeper in the past than the main thread, the story about Louise. When the narrator relates the story about Elgin and his parents, the knowledge is justified by interpolating dialogues with Louise. Apparently she is the source, so that the narrator relates second-hand knowledge. The description of the marriage between Esau and Sarah, Elgin's parents, is founded on Louise's information. This would be plausible in itself, had not the narrator suddenly entered Sarah's mind. Esau is seen from the outside, as it becomes a first-person narrator, but about Sarah it is said 'Sarah, polishing, sorting, mending, serving, *felt the curse* and lost herself a little more' (*WB* 35, my italics). The fact that the narrator here suddenly enters Sarah's mind to relate her feelings about the situation and her position in the marriage clearly shows who is the object of the narrator's sympathy. The narrator is obviously feeling with the woman. Sarah is the focus, and by this short insight into her mind, the curse of the whole marriage on her is revealed. The relation of the narrating agent to the characters is made clear: the narrator is on the woman's side.

Now taking sides must not necessarily determine the narrator's gender, but it is not a slip of the narrator, it is a pattern exposed throughout the novel. It seems natural for the narrator to feel with the women rather than with the men. Another instance is the scene in the Clap Clinic. The descriptions of the waiting men and women differ significantly: 'Shifty Jack-the-lads, fat business in suits to hide the bulge. A few women, tarts yes, and other women too. Women with eyes full of pain and fear' (*WB* 46). The men are viewed from the outside, their outward appearance is subject to a very negative and even hateful categorisation. They all seem to be of one type, there is no differentiation. In contrast to this, the narrator differentiates between 'tarts' and other women, although the women seem to be the minority ('few women'). Additionally, they are not classified by their appearance but by their feelings. Here the narrator does not enter the mind of the women directly, she deduces their emotions from the expression of their eyes and thus justifies the insight. If one contextualises this strategy, it becomes even more remarkable because the narrator has caught the disease from a woman (Bathseba), not from a man. The depreciation of the men in the waiting room would be understandable had a man been responsible for the narrator's being there. In spite of this, the men are indirectly accused for being responsible for the women's misery. Again the narrator sides with the women, out of a woman's solidarity with the suffering of her own gender. The narrator cannot withhold her sympathy and thus counteracts the design to keep the own gender undeclared.

Grammatically even more obvious is the identification with a specific gender when the narrator talks about the Japanese virgin substitute. The personal pronoun refers to only one half of Europe's population, the women, as men surely do not need substitutes for hymens: 'In Europe *we* have always preferred a half lemon' (*WB* 77, my italics). The identification is enforced by the present perfect, referring to the narrator's own present. In this case no subordinated narrative is chosen but a reflection of the narrator. So the narrator's relation to other women protagonists is characterised by a feeling of solidarity. The narrator is more ready to enter the minds of women than those of the men. The vague contextual impression that the first-person narrator is more likely to be female than male is confirmed by the point of view taken to describe women protagonists. The selection of what is described and what not, puts the women at the centre of interest, and the way this selection is presented offers information about the narrator's relation to the centre of interest.[22]

After analysing how the narrator views the women protagonists, it is logical to have a look at the way the male protagonists are seen, especially at the relation the narrator has to the male characters. As I have remarked above, in the scenes which I have discussed, the descriptions of men are characterised by the absence of insight or empathy. The selection shows a clear preference for the emotional status of women. However, there are subordinated stories about boyfriends. They are interlaced to shatter any kind of clichés the reader might have developed so far. The stories about adulterous affairs with married women play on the cliché about heterosexual relationships being the only, or at least the dominant, form of love. So if the reader is apt to be caught in this trap, the opinion that only men can have affairs with married women is shaken by mentioning an affair with a man. A lesbian relationship is not uppermost in the reader's mind when reading about an adulterous affair. The boyfriend stories confirm that the narrating 'I' has at least bisexual tendencies; they open the question of the narrator's gender — at least on the surface. The protagonists of the stories are Crazy Frank and Bruno who saw the Lord. The labels already indicate what the contents confirm: both stories are perfect pieces of satire. Crazy Frank, brought up by midgets, carries his parents on his shoulders and wears a gold chain through his nipples. A very surrealist figure indeed. And Bruno encountered Jesus under a wardrobe.[23] The memory of Frank is occasioned by the reflections on sex and love, and Bruno is remembered because of the narrator's sudden wish to go to church. Neither of the two figures can be called a realistically painted character, whereas the narrator took great trouble for example to make Sarah's suffering realistic and credible. Frank and Bruno are not meant to be credible characters. Both stories are fantastical with nearly Kafkaesque elements. In retrospect, the relationship with both can only appear as a folly. Of course, some of the female sexual partners are satirised as well, but Bruno and Frank are the only two male partners the narrator tells us about and they are described without any attempt at realism. The narrator's relation to those figures from the past is characterised by an ironical distance. There is no empathy with the follies of the two men but only the keen observation and exaggeration of satire. In addition, the narrator does not enter the mind of the two men, not even trying to assume their motivations or feelings. Frank's appearance and body are sketched, and his philosophy of life is depicted by referring to pieces of dialogue, to his own words. In both passages, the style is laconic, far from the minute reflections and descriptions used to qualify other relationships. But the narrator is conscious of the satirising style. The beginning of the second sentence about Bruno is 'In fairness, ...' (*WB* 152); so the narrator knows that Bruno is treated rather unfairly in her memory. However, Bruno and Frank remain curiosities in the narrator's collection of memories, figures from a pandemonium. The satire is hilarious, but the difference in style and point of view to the depiction of the women is significant. No feeling of solidarity or empathy can be detected here. Thus the boyfriend-stories are just another form of disguise for the (female) narrator.

Still, some of the ambiguity remains unaccounted for. It is a perfect mystery why, if the narrator really is female, she did not attract any attention in a men's toilet, wearing a stocking over her head. Men's toilets may be 'fairly liberal places' (how can a female narrator know this?), but surely a woman frequenting a men's toilet masked with a stocking would attract some attention. There are open questions.

Perhaps one falls prey to Winterson's design in trying to trace the gender of the narrator in this novel. Maybe it is just a clever narrative game the critic is apt to play. Certainly the role of the narrator is treated with as much irony as Bruno or Frank; the very fact that the gender is undeclared shows a typical post-modern tendency to deconstruct the trust in the medium of narration. But it is more than a clever game played by a post-modern author. Virginia Woolf's fictive biographer says about Orlando: 'The change of sex, though it altered their future, did nothing whatever to alter their identity'.[24] And here we find the significant difference to the first-person narrator of *Written on the Body*, because it has become clear that gender forms and alters the identity. The ambiguity of gender is acted; the narrator plays a part, or rather different parts. The point of view is clearly a female one, as I have tried to show above. In spite of all the masks, the narrator cannot suppress a feeling of solidarity with some of the women protagonists. Nevertheless, this is not to say that the whole concept does not work. On the contrary: first of all, the masks contribute much to the hilarious satire in the novel. Even more important, the reader is kept in a constant ironic confusion. The reader is addressed as an intimate friend — and mocked. All the doubts are anticipated by the narrator. The clichés in the reader's mind are subjected to a whirlwind of uncertainties, as one is forced to question not only the narrator's identity, but also the categorising perception that constitutes the text in one's mind. Because only if the reader is shifted out of his/her own range of experience can something happen with the reading subject.[25] Every reader creates his or her own text, led by the strategies of the narrator. The 'I' in this novel plays on the sexual stereotypes that constitute our view on love. They are constantly contradicted, satirised and questioned, thus underlining that love is a more universal phenomenon than we are taught to believe, neither restricted by gender nor exclusively reserved for heterosexual relationships. The narrator does not propagate a romantic notion of love but stresses the bodily side of the phenomenon, trying to deconstruct some of the lies about emotions. The book is 'written on the body', carefully keeping the balance between a very personal confession in a highly poetic language and a satirical deconstruction of old clichés. The narrator switches from minute self-analysis expressing great emotional honesty to the role of the narrative libertine, the narrating Lothario, not to be trusted and forever engaging in new alliances. The blurb of the novel announces that Winterson has 'made language new' in her book, which is a very high claim. What she offers is a new narrative strategy, opening up new questions about narration and gender as well as love and gender. What we get is not a totally gender-free chaos but a new way of female writing questioning gender roles by using the mask of gender ambiguity, leading away from the matrix of stereotypes to a cliché-free chaos. If not language, our perception is made new, as the book tries to direct our gaze to the secret code only visible in certain lights.

NOTES

1. Susan Sniader Lanser. 'Toward a Feminist Narratology'. *Style* 20. 1 (1986) 341-363. 363.
2. Elaine Showalter. *A Literature of Their Own: British Women Novelists From Brontë to Lessing* (Princeton University Press. 1977) 13.
3. Bertil Romberg. *Studies in the Narrative Technique of the First-Person Novel* (Stockholm: Almqvist and Wiksell. 1962) 4.

4. See Gérard Genette. *Narrative Discourse* (Oxford: Blackwell. 1980). chapter five. The term is also applied by Schlomith Rimmon-Kenan in her book *Narrative Fiction: Contemporary Poetics* (London: Methuen. 1983) 95.
5. Romberg. *Studies*. 59.
6. See Wolfgang Iser. *Der Akt des Lesens: Theorie aesthetischer Wirkung* (Munich: W. Fink. 1976) 265.
7. Iser. *Der Akt des Lesens*. 267: 'Die Leerstellen sparen die Beziehungen zwischen den Darstellungsperspektiven des Textes aus und ziehen dadurch den Leser zur Koordination der Perspektiven in den Text hinein: sie bewirken die kontrollierte Betätigung des Lesers im Text'.
8. Mieke Bal has already hinted at the problem with the prefix 'meta-' since Genette had stated that the abuse of this prefix causes a looseness in terms. This is why 'metanarrative' should only denote a reference to the narrator's act of narrating. See Mieke Bal. 'The Narrative and the Focalization: A Theory of the Agents in Narrative'. *Style*. 17. 2 (1983) 234-269. 237.
9. *O* 91: 'Time is a great deadener'.
10. John Fowles. 'Notes on an Unfinished Novel'. in *The Novel Today: Contemporary Writers on Modern Fiction*. ed. by Malcolm Bradbury (Glasgow: Fontana. 1977) 136-150. 139.
11. The terms 'private' and 'public' narration were proposed by Susan Sniader Lanser in 'Toward a Feminist Narratology'. 352. She defines 'public' narration as addressed to a narratee external to the fictional world. and 'private' narration as addressed to a designed narratee 'who exists only within the textual world'. As I have pointed out earlier. there are different narratees in the novel. so the classifications refer only to the impression the opening evokes.
12. See Romberg. *Studies*. 59.
13. 'Was I in sound mind and body? I took my temperature. No. I peered at my head in the mirror. No' (*WB* 96).
14. See also *WB* 71. 155 and 189. The last repetition of the phrase reveals that it is a quotation by Louise.
15. D.H. Lawrence. *Women in Love* (1920: repr. Harmondsworth: Penguin. 1985) 190.
16. Sandra M.Gilbert and Susan Gubar. *No Man's Land: The Place of the Woman Writer in the Twentieth Century*. 2 vols (New Haven and London: Yale University Press. 1989). vol 2: *Sexchanges*. 364.
17. Bal. 'The Narrating'. 244.
18. For a detailed account of the term's development and philosophy see for example Susan Sniader Lanser. *The Narrative Act: Point of View in Prose Fiction* (Princeton University Press. 1981). especially chapters one and two.
19. Bal. 'The Narrating'. 248.
20. See Lanser. 'Feminist Narratology'.
21. See for example Robert Weimann. 'Erzählerstandpunkt und *point of view*: Zur Geschichte und Ästhetik der Perspektive im englischen Roman'. *Zeitschrift für Anglistik und Amerikanistik*. 10 (1962) 369-416. 378.
22. The terms 'selection and 'centre of interest' are used by Mieke Bal to define and differentiate the term 'focalization' (see Bal. 'The Narrating'. 249).
23. The Frank-story is on *WB* 92-94. the Bruno-story on *WB* 152.
24. Virginia Woolf. *Orlando: A Biography* (1928; repr. Oxford University Press. 1992) 133.
25. Iser. *Der Akt des Lesens*. 246.

A NEW WAY WITH WORDS?
JEANETTE WINTERSON'S POST-MODERNISM

LYN PYKETT

ACADEMIC criticism, which Winterson so disparages, seems to place her self-consciously and self-proclaimed experimental fictions (when it notices them at all) in the boxes labelled 'lesbian fiction' or 'postmodernist fiction'.[1] This essay re-examines Winterson's relationship to postmodernism and suggests that although it is tempting to read her novels simply in terms of a postmodernist aesthetics it is also important to situate them in relation to the Modernist project. I shall argue that Winterson's postmodernism is post-Modernist not in the sense of constituting a break with Modernism or superseding it, but rather as a collaborative dialogue with Modernism which continues what Winterson sees as the Modernist project.

I shall re-examine Winterson's post-Modernism by rereading her fiction alongside *Art Objects*, her 1995 collection of 'Essays on Ecstasy and Effrontery' which appears to be a declaration of her aesthetic credo. I realise that this is to stray into difficult terrain, that we should trust the tale not the artist (particularly when the artist seems to offer such beguiling explanatory stories about her tales). I also know that the spell of words in Winterson's fiction is (at its best) infinitely more subtle and complex than her self-justificatory and often self-regarding polemic. *Art Objects* is Winterson's attempt to locate her individual talent in relation to a particular tradition of writing. It may indeed be her way of reinventing herself as a particular kind of writer and of retrospectively rewriting her fictional oeuvre to date. Nevertheless it offers her readers a way of (retrospectively) re-engaging with some of the challenges, contradictions and problems of Winterson's earlier work.

I

Postmodernism is a notoriously slippery concept, not least when it is used as part of a taxonomy of fiction. Susan Rubin Suleiman describes postmodernist fiction in general terms as '*formally* ... a hyperselfconscious mode of writing that insistently points to literary and cultural antecedents or ... intertexts', and '*thematically* ... a kind of fiction that reflects, implicitly or explicitly, on the historical present in its relation to the past and possible future'.[2] Brian McHale notes the great range and variety of postmodernist novels, but argues that postmodernist fiction has a singular preoccupation: ontology. Postmodernist novels are all concerned, in McHale's view, with a series of related questions about the nature of being: 'What is a world? What kinds of worlds are there ...? What happens when different kinds of worlds are placed in confrontation, or when boundaries between worlds are violated?'[3] The strategies employed by postmodernist fiction to explore these questions produces an effect of ontological problematisation or ontological transgression.

Winterson's fiction undoubtedly has many of the formal and thematic characteristics which we have come to associate with postmodernist fictional practice in the late twentieth century: parody, irony, pastiche, self-reflexivity, and playfulness, a sense of multiplicity, fragmentation, instability of meaning, and an apparent distrust of grand narratives. In all three of the novels upon which her current critical reputation stands — *Oranges Are Not the Only Fruit* (1985), *The Passion* (1987), and *Sexing the Cherry* (1989) — Winterson presents her readers with a world of apparently endlessly proliferating narrative, of stories within stories within stories. The story of Jeanette (*Oranges Are Not the Only Fruit)* is refracted through the narrative models of different books of the Old Testament interwoven with intertextual allusions to medieval romance and folk and fairy tale. Fabular elements persist in the fantastical and/or grotesque narratives of the web-footed Villanelle *(The Passion*), and Jordan and the Dogwoman (*Sexing the Cherry*), and in the *petits récits* of Henri, Napoleon's chicken cook. Henri, with his constant refrain of 'I'm telling you stories. Trust me', offers (as do so many of Winterson's narrators and narratives) a version of history from below, rather than the history of the official record or the history books.

It is interesting to note, by the way, that Winterson's novels are peopled and narrated by storytellers whose stories have their origins in lack and desire. The stories of Jeanette, Jordan and Henri, for example, are family romances which compensate for their narrator's lack of family. Like the nineteenth century novel, which she so fiercely criticises in *Art Objects*, Winterson's fiction is peopled by orphans or those with substitute or depleted families: Jeanette is adopted, Jordan is a foundling, and Henri makes up stories about the extended family which he does not have, a lack which distinguishes him from the rest of the village.

Winterson's postmodernism is also apparently in evidence in the way in which her novels repeatedly foreground the subjectivity and cultural relativism of space and time. All three of the novels discussed here implicitly and explicitly put into question those common sense or rationalistic Western perceptions of time, space and matter which are directly interrogated in the epigraphs to *Sexing the Cherry*. These latter inform us (a) that the Hopi Indians have no tenses to distinguish past, present and future ('What does this say about time?'), and (b) that matter is 'now known to be mostly empty space' ('What does this say about the reality of the world?'). One of the answers offered to those questions which I have placed in parentheses is that our conventional understanding of time and space is based on 'HALLUCINATIONS AND DISEASES OF THE MIND' and 'Lies'. Examples of both of these sets of mind-forged manacles are given in *Sexing the Cherry* (see 81 and 83). The list of 'Lies', with its echoes of Blake's proverbs of Hell is one of several invocations (and endorsements?) of a Blakean vision which sees into — because it looks beyond — the life of things.

Winterson's fictions repeatedly 'demonstrate', as well as gnomically asserting, a distrust of the possibility of mapping and measuring space and time. Thus in *The Passion*, Venice, the city of mazes and disguises, is a signified that is perpetually sliding out from its various signifiers; it is a moving and changeable city whose streets and canals 'appear and disappear overnight ... there are days when you cannot walk from one end to the other, so far is the journey, and there are days when a stroll will take you round your kingdom like a tin-pot Prince' (*P* 97).

Like many postmodernist writers Winterson is preoccupied with the space-time continuum, and with simultaneity. Winterson's novels, like those of her magical realist contemporaries (and precursors such as Angela Carter) offer a form of time travel in hyperreality not least in their accounts of fabulous voyages, such as Jordan's journey to the weightless city, and other non-linear journeys in which 'Time has no meaning, space and place have no meaning', but which are 'always back and forth, denying the calendar' (*SC* 80).

The preoccupation with simultaneity is also articulated as a concern with parallel lives. Jeanette's theory 'that every time you make an important choice, the part left behind continues the life you could have had' (*O* 169) is explored and enacted in all three novels. This Eliotean preoccupation with the simultaneity of time present and time past, and with the 'Footfalls' which 'echo in the memory/Down the passage we did not take/Towards the door we never opened'[4] is articulated, or so it might appear, through another typically postmodern device of ironic or parodic quotation of, or allusion to, Eliot's work. Eliot's is one of the several ghosts of high Modernism who haunt Winterson's fiction. I shall look more closely at the way in which these Modernist spirits are invoked later in this essay.

The problems of mapping and measuring space and time are of course particular instances of the postmodernist problematisation of knowledge and representation. How we know the present, how we know the past, and how we represent both or either are questions which are repeatedly raised in and by Winterson's novels. It is interesting that the only character in any of Winterson's first three novels who self-consciously attempts to keep a written record of his thoughts and experiences is Henri, who is incarcerated in a lunatic asylum. Henri begins writing when he starts a diary to guard himself against the tricks of memory, only to be told by Napoleon's midget, Domino, that the way 'you see it now is no more real than the way you'll see it then' (*P* 28). The implication seems clear: whether events are 'recorded' as they happen or recollected in tranquillity, they are equally story-shaped; neither narrative mode is more or less real than the other.

This apparent narrative egalitarianism is, perhaps, typical of the multiplicity of the decentred and fragmented universe of the postmodern imaginary. However, on closer examination Winterson's novels can be made to tell a different story; one in which some stories, or some narrative modes are more real than others. This is certainly one way of reading the opposition between history and story that pervades Winterson's early fiction. Some stories are more true than others, and storytelling is (it would seem) more trustworthy, and also more vital, than history. The opposition between history and story is articulated at some length just over half way through *Oranges*. According to 'Deuteronomy: The last book of the law', history (or at least the history of the history books), like time, is a great deadener. It is 'a means of denying the past', refusing to 'recognise its integrity' (*O* 93), and 'squeez[ing] this oozing world between two boards and typeset' (*O* 95). 'History' falsifies through its commitment to explanatory causality:

> Nowadays people talk about the things [Napoleon] did as though they made sense. As though even his most disastrous mistakes were only the result of bad luck or hubris.
> It was a mess (*P* 5).

Stories, on the other hand, are vital and flexible; they are 'a way of explaining the universe while leaving the universe unexplained ... of keeping it alive, not boxing it into time' (*O* 93). History, as D.H.Lawrence said in 'Morality and the Novel', is busy nailing things down while stories (in the shape of 'the novel', which for Lawrence includes Homer and the Bible) get up and walk away with the nail.[5] Like Lawrence, Winterson's narrator, Jeanette, wants to escape from the dead end of the squeezed up history of the history books and the self-justificatory history of the dominant class by making history 'a hammock for swinging and a game for playing', by ravelling it up like a cat's cradle; in short, by making it more storylike.

The preference for (which amounts to a privileging of) stories and romance over history in Winterson's novels is characteristic of postmodern fiction. Indeed Diane Elam has gone so far as to equate romance with postmodernism by virtue of their 'troubled relation to both history and novelistic realism' and their 'common excess', an 'inability to stay within historical and aesthetic boundaries'.[6] In Winterson's avowedly anti-realistic fictions, stories are less a way of trying to explain or understand the universe than of (re)experiencing it, or alternatively, of shoring oneself against its confusions and complexities; less a way of understanding material history or 'the historical process' than of transcending it or escaping from its confines.

II

If Winterson's fiction has many of the preoccupations and stylistic features of what we have come to call postmodernism, it also resists the postmodernist label in a number of important ways. For example, despite the fact that it disrupts all sorts of foundationalist assumptions Winterson's early fiction is nevertheless very affirmative, especially of such universals as art, the imagination, and romantic love. In various versions of the gospel according to Winterson true art not merely has, but *is* 'the ability to take us where the artist has been':

> When we are drawn into the art we are drawn out of ourselves. We are no longer bound by matter, matter has become what it is: empty space and light' (*SC* 91).

Romantic love, although 'diluted into paperback form' and marketed in millions of copies, still exists somewhere, 'in the original, written on tablets of stone' (*O* 170). Love, like art, is liberating; it is a form of self transcendence:

> To love someone else enough to forget about yourself even for one moment is to be free. The mystics and the churchmen talk about throwing off this body and its desires, being no longer a slave to the flesh. They don't say that through the flesh we are set free. That our desire for another will lift us out of ourselves more cleanly than anything divine (*P* 154).

Of course, it might quite reasonably be argued that the affirmatory quality that I have ascribed to Winterson's fiction is merely the affirmation of a particular, possibly deluded, narrator. However, when Winterson speaks in her own voice (or at least the voice of 'Jeanette Winterson, experimental writer') in *Art Objects*, she is, if anything, even more affirmatory. Art and love are the enduring verities. Winterson's self-authored epigraph to her 'Essays in Ecstasy and Effrontery' equates art with truth, and with enduring vitality. Art works are a form of time travel because they transcend their own time; they are 'marks in time' and 'mark through time'. Winterson affirms art as a form of love and repeatedly defines each in terms of the other: 'A love-parallel would by just' *(AO* 15*)*. Art and love are both forms of transformation, and both challenge our sense of identity and the 'reality to which we lay claim' (*AO* 15).

Winterson's extra-fictional pronouncements indicate at the very least her scepticism about current postmodernist fashions, and imply a dismissal of many aspects of contemporary literary practice as mere modishness. In *Art Objects* she presents herself as a self-conscious occupier of the high-culture ground, and (*contra* Lyotard and Baudrillard) announces her disdain for the way in which the modern media 'ransacks the arts' and continually offers up 'faint shadows' of 'real' art (*AO* 15). She disavows some of her own postmodernist devices as no more than devices, traps to catch the attention of readers whose sensibilities have been deadened by 'media moronicness' (*AO* 188). The Dog-Woman, and Villanelle's webbed feet are among the many 'shiny things', the 'wares' (or 'bewares'), with which she packs her pages (or pedlar's bag) to attract a crowd. The use of history in her historiographic metafictions (or historical romances) *Sexing the Cherry* and *The Passion* is similarly just another device, which she used 'not because I am interested in Costume Drama Realism, or Magic Realism ... but because I wanted to create an imaginative reality sufficiently at odds with our daily reality to startle us out of it' (*AO* 188). Winterson disclaims any intrinsic interest in the folk tales and fairy tales which are threaded through her novels. They are simply more shiny things which she deploys because she happens to have them about her person: 'like Autolycus (*The Winter's Tale*), I find that they are assumed to be worth more than they are' (*AO* 189). The dismissal of folk and fairy tales is strikingly different from Angela Carter's carefully thought-out and constantly changing use of a tradition which she came to value as 'the most vital connection we have with the imaginations of the ordinary men and women whose labour created our world'.[7]

If we take Winterson's statements at face value, it would seem that her 'postmodern' devices are used in the same defamiliarising cause as that espoused by the proto-modernist Russian Formalists. They are the Trojan horses by which the experimental writer (notably the Modernist experimental writer) 'smuggled ... language alive past the checkpoints of propriety' (*AO* 50). Time is a great deadener, as various of Winterson's narrators inform us, and art, is charged with the task of redeeming and renewing the life deadened by the betrayals of time and habit.

Art Objects repeatedly invites the reader to see Winterson's postmodernism as in fact a post-Modernism. *Art Objects* is, in large part, Winterson's attempt to situate herself in relation to the tradition of Modernism and to affirm her commitment to Modernism as a project of continuing relevance. Always suspicious of what she sees as the treasonable clerks of academia, Winterson is particularly impatient with the way both academics and reviewers 'tout a system in which Modernism is a kind of cul-de-sac, a literary bywater which produced a few brilliant names but which was errant to the true current of literature' (*AO* 176). On the contrary, Modernism was the 'mainstream', and current writers committed to developing fiction need to look to their 'Modernist ancestors' (*AO* 177).

For Winterson, Modernism is a revolution of the word. Literary Modernism was a 'poet's movement' (*AO* 82) committed to lyric intensity and 'exactness' of language (*AO* 79). Winterson fetishes language in the way in which some of the (male) Modernist poets did. The 'Word' is 'both form and substance' (*AO* 50), and she sees it as having a 'power over us, not only through what it says but also through what it is' (*AO* 76). Winterson's reification of language is closely linked to her implicit acceptance of the Arnoldian vision (mediated through T.S.Eliot) of poetry as the religion of the future. This sacralisation of art is characteristic of much Modernist art and theorising about art. For many Modernist writers, as Patricia Waugh has argued,

> the possibility of Art itself as an absolute autonomous realm ... often comes to take the place of the sacred. Art, as religion, seems to offer precisely that illusion of utter self-determination and transcendence which relations with other mortals always shatter.[8]

Poetry (or literary art) has certainly become the religion of Winterson's secular 'future', and she has retained a sense of the immanence of the word from her Evangelical childhood.

> I grew up not knowing that language was for everyday purposes. I grew up with the Word and the Word was God. Now, many years after a secular Reformation, I still think of language as something holy (*AO* 153).

If *Art Objects* is a kind of homage to the 'major' Modernist writers — James Joyce, T.S.Eliot, Virginia Woolf, and, to a lesser extent, Gertrude Stein — so too is Winterson's fictional practice. Her first fiction, *Oranges*, is Winterson's *A Portrait of the Artist as a Young Man*, rewritten as a portrait of the artist as a young working class lesbian who flees the nets of religion and community and refuses to subdue her own inner light and sexuality (both of which are represented as being integral to her special status as exiled artist-prophet) to serve the craven world of heterosexual respectability. *Oranges* appears to be autobiographical; it uses many of the details of its author's early history and even (teasingly) uses her own name, but like Joyce's *bildungsroman* it is less a form of self-expression or self-representation than of self-invention. Like *A Portrait of the Artist as a Young Man, Oranges* is not simply the story of the making of the artist, and of the artist's journey towards her position as exiled visionary (a position which is not so much chosen as given), but it is also, in its form, an embodiment of that artist's aesthetic. It self-consciously attempts 'a new way with words' (*AO* 53), raiding (a word which Winterson herself uses more than once in this context) the storehouse of past literature and reshaping its contents to make something really new. T.S. Eliot does not use the language of literary terrorism in his theorising of literature, but his message is fundamentally the same: the relationship of the individual talent to the literary tradition is one of disciplined immersion, rupture, and renewal.[9]

Rebecca West remarked in 1932 that Eliot's presence on the English literary scene had 'inflicted damage on our literature from which it will probably not recover for a generation'.[10] As I suggested earlier, Winterson's fiction is an instance of Eliot's continuing influence (for good or ill) on English literature. All of Winterson's fiction aspires to an Eliotean precision of language, but *Sexing the Cherry* is probably the most obviously Eliotean of her works, since one of its clearest intertextual references is to *Four Quartets*. *Sexing the Cherry* is a speculative fiction which returns time and again to the preoccupations of Eliot's poem: history, consciousness, desire, the unredeemability of time, the perpetual presence of the past and future, ceaseless journeying and exploration, the river that is 'within us'. This is not to say that Winterson simply rewrites *Four Quartets*. Her novel attempts all sorts of things that Eliot's poem does not, particularly in its particular focus on gender, sexuality and romantic love, and its representation (in the Dog-Woman) of the grotesque female body that incorporates all sorts of myths of femaleness and femininity at the same time as defying all conventional definitions of the essential feminine.

Indeed in its use of fantasy, cross-dressing, and the time-travelling that enables Jordan to inhabit both the seventeenth and the late-twentieth centuries, *Sexing the Cherry* also pays homage to Virginia Woolf's *Orlando*. Woolf's historical fantasy is also (so to speak) quoted extensively in *The Passion*; there is a similar mixing of real historical personages and events with invented history and fantastical events, and Winterson's Villanelle clearly owes a great deal to Woolf's cross-dressing hero/ine. In *The Passion*, the cross-dressing is a matter of both personal choice and cultural custom — in Venice, the dream city, the city of gambling and disguises. Villanelle slips from 'masculine' to 'feminine' garb with speed and at will, whereas Orlando wears the clothing appropriate to the gender and period s/he happens to be occupying at any particular textual moment. Dress and gender are but two of the illusions in which both of these novels trade, and which they variously reveal as simultaneously traps and snares and the very stuff of human life. 'It is all an illusion' writes Orlando's 'biographer':

> (which is nothing against it, for illusions are the most valuable and necessary of all things, and she who can create one is among the world's greatest benefactors), but as it is notorious that illusions are shattered by conflict with reality, so no real happiness ... wit ... [nor] profundity are tolerated where illusion prevails'.[11]

While Woolf's 'biography' is both social critique and a utopian *jeu d'esprit* which explores and enacts the power of fantasy, the stories of the two narrators of *The Passion* demonstrate (among other things) the dangers of illusions, and the difficulties of living both with and without them.

III

Winterson's rereading of her own fictions in the essays in *Art Objects*, together with a repeated invocation of the authority of the 'major Modernists' which self-consciously calls attention to her own 'raiding' and reworking of their writings, invites us to place her work in a continuing Modernist tradition. It is a high risk strategy since it will inevitably lead most readers to unfavourable comparisons. Winterson's cheeky brio does not easily match up to the breadth of reading and deeply meditated sense of history that runs through the writings of Woolf and Eliot. Woolf is the subject/object of the most fulsome praise, and it is Woolf's fictional practice — her new way with words and her concern with sexual and gender politics — which has, perhaps, most closely shaped Winterson's fiction to date. But it is Eliot's critical views (often not directly acknowledged, because they are so thoroughly internalised) which underpin Winterson's essays. The (rather belated) answer to Rebecca West's question 'What is Mr T.S.Eliot's Authority as a Critic?', would seem to be 'quite extensive', at least as far as Jeanette Winterson is concerned.

Of course, as many readers no doubt will have been thinking for several pages, there is nothing so very startling in the suggestion that we should look at Winterson's postmodernism as post-Modernism. Postmodernism's stories of rupture with the Modernist past have been just as wilfully misleading as the Modernists' stories of their break with the Victorians. Such stories may be disingenuous but they are also enabling fictions, strategies for finding a position from which to write. What is rather more unusual in this particular case is the fact that the author herself has located her work and her artistic credo so clearly in a genealogy of Modernism, and that she has come out so frankly for the Modernist cause. She's telling us stories. Can we trust her?

Yes and no. Whether or not one agrees with her version of Modernism, and her valuation of its achievement and continuing importance, one is persuaded that she believes in what she is writing and I, at least, cannot help but admire the passion and clarity with which she articulates her vision. However, by insisting so firmly on a particular version of Modernism from which she claims descent, Winterson erases a great deal of the history of writing since the period of high Modernism, and obscures the extent to which her own writings have been shaped by this 'after history'. In particular Winterson's genealogy obscures the nature and extent of her indebtedness to her more immediate precursors and near-contemporaries, notably Angela Carter.[12] If Winterson's reading of Eliot is a fairly unreconstructed high Modernist one which takes him at his own valuation, her reading of Woolf is undoubtedly mediated through the extensive feminist rereading of the entire Woolf corpus (including the essays and diaries) that has taken place since the 1960s. Isobel Armstrong has recently argued (very persuasively) that it is only since the 1980s, and as a result of the rethinking of Woolf undertaken by feminist theorists, that women novelists have begun to respond to the challenge of 'the social meaning implied by formal experiment' in Woolf's fiction, and to produce texts which 'resonate with hers'.[13] As both Armstrong and Hermione Lee have demonstrated, it is in the later work of Angela Carter (especially *Nights at the Circus*, 1984) that we see one of the most energetic responses to and engagement with the challenge of Woolf.[14] Surely it is Carter's new way with words, her tightrope-walking risktaking, her boldness, her energetic ransacking and remaking of all manner of literary traditions, her demythologising and remythologising, that provide the models for many of the brilliant devices (about which Winterson is so dismissive in *Art Objects*) which have been such important elements in Winterson's success, particularly with the new generation of younger readers, which she claims to be shaping through her work, and which she mobilises against what she perceives to be a hostile critical establishment. One can only speculate on the reasons for Winterson's silence about the ways in which Carter's fictions have already shaped this new generation of readers and also the writers who write for them.

At its best, Winterson's fiction has the exactness of language which she so admires in the great Modernist writers to whom she pays homage in *Art Objects*, an exactness which may also be found (together with a great deal of exuberance) in much of Angela Carter's fiction. Each of the novels referred to in this essay has, at times, a linguistic precision and vitality, a new way with words — sometimes playful, sometimes lyrical — which makes us sit up and listen, read slowly, and glory in the power of words to conjure a world into existence, and to create an alternative reality. The criticism that has sometimes been levelled at Winterson is that she creates an alternative to reality and backs off from an engagement with political and material constraints.[15] Perhaps she needs to close her Eliot and re-read her Woolf (*A Room of One's Own, Three Guineas* and the essays) and Carter.

NOTES

1. See, inter alia, Alison Lee, 'Bending the Arrow of Time: The Continuing Postmodern Present' in *Historicity et metafiction dans le roman contemporain des Iles Britanniques*, ed. by Max Duperray (Aix en Provence: Université de Provence, 1994) 217-29, and Laura Doan, 'Jeanette Winterson's Sexing the Postmodern' in *The Lesbian Postmodern*, ed. by L.Doan and R.Wiegman (New York: Columbia University Press, 1994) 138-155. Winterson's fiction is significantly absent from recent general accounts of the novel. Winterson is not mentioned by Andrzej Gasiorek in his *Post-War British Fiction: Realism and After* (London: Edward Arnold, 1995). Steven Connor refers briefly to *Boating for Beginners* in *The English Novel in History, 1950-1995* (London: Routledge, 1996).
2. Susan Rubin Suleiman, 'The Fate of the Surrealist Imagination in the Society of the Spectacle' in *The Flesh and the Mirror: Essays on the Art of Angela Carter*, ed. by Lorna Sage (London: Virago, 1994) 98-116, 103.
3. Brian McHale, *Postmodernist Fiction* (London: Methuen, 1987) 10.
4. 'Burnt Norton' I, *Four Quartets* (London: Faber and Faber, 1944) 1.
5. D.H.Lawrence, 'Morality and the Novel', in *D.H.Lawrence: Selected Literary Criticism*, ed. by Anthony Beal (1925; London: Heinemann, 1967) 108-113.
6. Diane Elam, *Romancing the Postmodern* (London: Routledge, 1992) 3 and 12.
7. Angela Carter ed., *The Virago Book of Fairy Tales* (London: Virago, 1990) ix.
8. Patricia Waugh, *Practising Postmodernism Reading Modernism* (London: Edward Arnold, 1992) 132.
9. Eliot does, of course, use the language of terrorism in *Four Quartets*: 'each venture/ Is a new beginning, a raid on the inarticulate/ ... /Undisciplined squads of emotion'. ('East Coker' V, l.178ff). It is worth noting that 'Discipline' is one of the qualities that Winterson sees as essential to true art; the discipline of the work is what enables the artist to achieve the Eliotean goal of seeing things as they really are (see *AO* 145).
10. Rebecca West, 'Mr T.S.Eliot's Authority as a Critic?', *Daily Telegraph*, 30 September, 1932, 6.
11. Virginia Woolf, *Orlando: A Biography* (1928; repr. Harmondsworth: Penguin, 1942) 140-1.
12. There is one reference to Carter in *Art Objects*. The publication of *The Magic Toyshop* is noted as a cheering event (*AO* 41).
13. Isobel Armstrong, 'Woolf by the Lake, Woolf at the Circus: Carter and Tradition', in Sage 1994, 257-278, 261.
14. Armstrong, loc. cit., and Hermione Lee, '"A Room of One's Own, or a Bloody Chamber?": Angela Carter and Political Correctness', in Sage 1994, 308-320.
15. See Lynne Pearce, *Reading Dialogics* (London: Edward Arnold, 1994) 174.

Passion at the End of History

Scott Wilson

I The Madness of the Archive

> You are mine! I may call such a heart mine.
> Recognizing in your gaze
> The reflection of love.
> O bliss, O supreme happiness!
>
> G.W.F. Hegel[1]

> They say that every snowflake is different. If that were true how could the world go on? How could we ever get up off our knees? How could we ever recover from the wonder of it?
> By Forgetting.
>
> Henri (*P* 159)

IT was G.W.F Hegel who put down his pen on the night of October 12th, 1806, to the sound of cannon fire in the distance, his monumental *Phenomenology of Mind* at last finished, and prepared for bed with an almost complete sense of satisfaction, or *Befriedigung* as it would have been in the German. Although his life was in danger, Hegel should have slept easy that night. Though Jena was about to fall to Napoleon, Hegel should have slept with the contentment of the ages because it is said that Hegel knew that by the following night History itself would be at its end.

But Hegel did not sleep that night. Hegel did not sleep because he was in love, and his heart jumped with every crack and rumble of Napoleon's artillery.

Somewhere between fear and Absolute Knowledge, passion is.

As the opening stanza of the poem cited above suggests, love for Hegel, like human dignity, like human history, is all about the struggle for recognition. History starts, somewhere between fear and desire, when one man overcomes his fear of death and risks his life in an act of valour that secures the submission of his opponent and achieves recognition as his opponent's lord. But this form of recognition is incomplete. The lord and master has achieved his desire for the desire of the other and become human except that, tragically, that other has become a slave, a 'living cadaver', and so the master's humanity cannot be properly registered. The slave, in the meantime, has to work towards humanity, has, indeed, to overcome nature and produce humanity as a work and realise it, ultimately, by overcoming the master in another fight to the death, but this time, one professionally organised and rationally lead.

To be properly, totally known, History can only be viewed from its end point, from the point where Napoleon demonstrates the dialectical overcoming of master and slave by achieving victory at the Battle of Jena and exports the principles of the French Revolution and the universal, homogeneous Napoleonic state to Germany, its first and greatest obstacle. But this too is not enough. It is not enough for Napoleon to act in the world and be victorious, his victory has to be recognised and understood for what it is, and this knowledge has to be revealed to the world by Hegel. Hegel himself had to be there to witness his nation's defeat and send to the printers, a week later, the completed manuscript of *The Phenomenology of Mind*. This work attains Absolute Knowledge because it is able to explain Napoleon and the whole 'universal history' anterior to him; Hegel's realisation of Wisdom is possible because he exists at the moment when Napoleon's victories impose the universal and homogeneous state founded by the Revolution, a state, according to Hegel, which terminates the historical evolution of humanity. At Jena, Napoleon's action takes on truly universal force, and Hegel's knowledge becomes absolute.

Napoleon and Hegel should be the first fully human, fully satisfied men, but they are not. Napoleon cannot be fully satisfied because he is not sufficiently self-conscious; he does not know what Hegel knows. Napoleon does not realise that Hegel is the only person in the world who truly, who totally understands him. No one in the world, not his generals, not his soldiers, not Joséphine, not even Napoleon himself understands Napoleon like Hegel. Only Hegel can reveal Napoleon to himself, can make him fully self-conscious. At the same time, Hegel lacks the recognition that only a fully self-aware Napoleon can give him: they need each other. Oh what bliss, Oh what supreme happiness, if Hegel could only recognize in the gaze of Napoleon the reflection of love. Only Hegel and Napoleon, *together* can form 'the perfect Man, (who is) fully and definitively satisfied by what he *is* and what he *knows* himself to be'.[2] But Napoleon does not recognise Hegel, does not know, cannot reflect his ardour, and is indifferent. So Hegel cannot sleep.

Hegel's *Befriedigung* on the eve of the Battle of Jena could not have been complete without the mutual, mirrored recognition that Hegel's system both requires and discloses as impossible. It left Hegel, even at the summit of Absolute Knowledge, in the position of an anguished lover.

'When I fell in love it was as though I looked into a mirror for the first time and saw myself. I lifted my hand in wonderment and felt my cheeks, my neck. This was me' (*P* 154). Hegel was not the only intellectual to misrecognise and fall for the perfected image of himself in the shape of Napoleon. The soldier, archivist and neck-wringer to the Emperor known as Henri, came to realise, like Hegel, that his love was unrequited. And before he went mad, he began to realise that the image in the mirror was a mis-recognition, that it disclosed even as it appeared to fill, an indifferent gap sustained by the dialectic of desire itself.

Henri begins his history, in Jeanette Winterson's historical romance, by memorably recalling the relentless negativity of Napoleon's passion for chickens. Henri notes how odd it is that this secular God should be governed by such a singular appetite. Napoleon recognises no man, he loves no man, likes no one, 'except Joséphine and he liked her the way he liked chicken' (*P* 3). It is a peculiarity that also has problematic implications for Hegel's system where Napoleon stands at the crest of History's self-transcending curve. Chicken and women, or rather chicken and Joséphine, exceed the rational control of Hegel's 'revealed God' and delineate a certain heterogeneity to Hegel's system.

For Hegel there is the master, the slave, and then there is Napoleon. But Napoleon is mastered in turn by his desire for chickens. The trouble with dialecticians, Winterson seems to suggest, is their inability to count up to four. Everything comes in threes: thesis, antithesis, synthesis; in its inexorable world historical progress, Spirit has no room for chickens, or for a singular passion for chickens. In his theory of history, Hegel did not consider a fourth term: something that could allow for chance, the unpredictable, the contingent, some event or happenstance, some peculiar predilection that exceeds the grasp of Spirit's all-consuming knowledge. Spirit, in Hegel's upwardly spiralling history, never seemed to fall in love; Spirit never falls to its knees in the glorious abjection of a grand passion. Dialectical history does not record these moments, they are left unremarked and forgotten.

And yet, Hegel had every reason to account for a fourth term. Had every reason to account for me. I am here to testify that despite what you read in your history books it was not Napoleon's artillery that forced Hegel to leave his lodgings in Jena in such indecent haste — it was his landlord, my husband. On the 13th October 1806, when Napoleon's armies were knocking at the final door of world history, Hegel had to beat a hasty retreat because I was by then visibly over five months pregnant with Hegel's illegitimate son. Constantly enraged by Hegel's inability or unwillingness to pay rent, my pregnancy was, for my husband, the final straw. Hegel had to go. And unfortunately for me, so did I. At the end of history, Hegel found himself caught not just in a love triangle (he understood triads), but a love rhomboid comprising Napoleon, myself, Johanna Burckhardt, née Fischer, and himself, with all of us defined by the figure of the law in all this: my husband, the landlord. I stress these material circumstances of the production of *The Phenomenology of Mind* not out of resentment of my historical neglect as at best a biographical footnote. Though I should like to claim that Hegel stole the idea for *The Phenomenology* from me, that it was partly my work, this would not be true. At the same time I should like to take this opportunity to refute those biographers who accuse me of being 'a constant source of worry and torment' to Hegel[3] — I was merely seeking my son Ludwig's rightful due.

I stress Hegel's material circumstances at Jena for theoretical rather than scholarly or personal reasons. Hegel's love rhomboid more fully articulates the conceptual history of Hegel's own theory of history. Passion, it should be remembered, or love, was initially thought by the young Hegel to be the idea that defined humanity. It was in the mutual recognition of love that Hegel first believed he had isolated the specifically human content of Man's existence: 'love can only take place against its equal, against the mirror, against the echo of our existence',[4] he wrote in 'Two Fragments on Love' some years before; in the same spirit he liked to invoke my gaze as the reflection of his love in the poem he wrote to me. Later, it is true, he recycled the poem for the gullible consumption of his child bride, sweet Marie von Tucher. But that is neither here nor there.

It is the structure of courtly love that remains as the defining trace of Hegel's system even if only as a negated and sublated thesis. It is the courtly tradition, derived from the Troubadours, that establishes love in a triangular relationship. The lover's transgressive desire for his lady is defined by his lord, or in our case his landlord, the figure of the law that the adulterous relationship either re-affirms or destabilises. In the standard courtly relationship, the amorous combat between the lover and his beloved Hegel read as a displacement of the erotics of rivalry between men. But the beautiful women that inspire courtly love and devotion are beyond the threshold of the norm set by their husbands and suitors; courtly ladies are objects that approach divinity; one serves them as one would a goddess (imagined as an icon). Hegel's theory of love, however, was part of the Romantic movement that sought to replace the transgressive model of love with the family as the affective, nuclear unit. Love was for Hegel, as one would expect, a dialectical thing and a couple was not quite enough. For Hegel, lovers become unified in an ideal image — of themselves, of each other — and can only be separated by death. They can, however, transcend death and discontinuity to remain without separation through the production of a child. Oh what ironies! As I discovered, even a child is not enough. Love has to be legitimated by marriage and circumscribed by the legitimate family.

But therein, for the later Hegel, lies its limit and its inadequacy because this love cannot be universalised to form the basis of a state — indeed, it even contradicts it. For the family, the supreme value of its members is merely their *Sein* or natural being, their biological life, whereas the state requires precisely that its subjects risk their lives, their deaths, for the universal cause. So heterosexual, procreative love must be replaced by homosocial combat as the motor of history because the latter affirms action over mere being. Hegel liked to quote Goethe on this point: 'one loves a man', Goethe wrote, 'not because of what he *does* but because of what he *is*; that is why one can love a dead man, for the man who *does* truly nothing would already be like a dead man; that is also why one can love an animal, without being able to "recognize" the animal: let us remember that there have never been duels between a man and an animal — or a woman; let us remember that it is "unworthy of a man" to dedicate himself entirely to love' (Kojève, 244). I did not entirely appreciate the full implications of this at the time, I have to say. Hegel rarely discussed his ideas with me, and, like everyone else, I found his prose impenetrable. I have had to research my past in the archive where I have learned about Hegel's thought from the students of his twentieth-century commentator Alexander Kojève. I merely note here that Hegel had to domesticate love before he could reject it in his theory, a domestication that required the rejection of me and my son Ludwig. Beyond that, Hegel's problem with love resides purely with the gender imbalance that it implies.

It seems now, from the perspective of the end of history at the end of the twentieth century, that what separated me from Napoleon in Hegel's love rhomboid was the fact that he considered me to be as good as dead. A beautiful woman is, after all, merely an object of reflection; and when not beautiful, or unloved, women, even more than slaves, are, Hegel assumed, defined by their natures, by the mortality of their gross corporeality. So 'recognition' from a woman could be neither as worthy nor as universalisable as recognition from an adversary (Kojève, 244). I resent that. For sure I'm not human now, I'm well beyond all that, but I thought I was then.

In *The Passion*, Joséphine and dead chickens, 'birds in every state of undress', provide the objects of Napoleon's ardour (*P* 3). They too are equivalent to dead men, equivalent, perhaps, to the many thousands of dead men produced by Napoleon's voracious desire for recognition in combat, men who died for him, for the love of him and his state, and, of course, the men and women who died indifferently, because they had no choice.

But is it true that there have never been duels between a man and a woman? As Henri comments in *The Passion*, Napoleon may have been 'the most powerful man in the world (but) he couldn't beat Joséphine at billiards' (*P* 13). And even within the narrow framework in which women are situated by Hegel, what of love itself, what of sex, what of amorous combat and the trials of eroticism? As Winterson shows in *The Passion*, not all forms of love are familial, procreative, nor even heterosexual. And love remains a defining trace in Hegel's violent struggle for recognition. After all, the duel establishes a similar, narcissistic relation to love. For me, like Jacques Lacan, one of Kojève's students, 'the basis of aggressivity (lies) in this paroxysm of absorption in the imaginary register, formally expressed as a mirror relationship, a mirrored reaction.'[5] The one you fight is the one you love the most. But if there is a proximity between love and the duel, there is also a crucial difference.

My lover in the archive is Georges Bataille, like Lacan, another French thinker who learnt Hegel at Kojève's seminars in the 1930s, and whose work is also situated at the limit of Hegel's system. It will perhaps surprise you to know that the author of the *Story of the Eye* and *Madame Edwarda* is hopeless at sex. Yes, we can have virtual sex in the archive now that it has become computerised, now that archival traces can be replicated and replayed on CD ROM with full RAM. But Bataille is still too highly strung even for virtual sex; he is constantly bursting into tears, his eyes revolving alarmingly in the back of his head. He is, however, an expert on eroticism, and he gives great phone. Perhaps it is his French accent, but no one talks death and sensuality like Georges. For Bataille, love establishes a feeling of such intoxication that identity is exceeded; so that, far from recognising oneself in a mirror, in love 'we stop being ourselves'.[6] Moreover, in what he calls the 'ordeal' of eroticism, Hegel's 'duel' is repeated, but results in a more profound movement in which the 'virtue of courage' is disclosed as 'shallow' (Bataille 1988, 156). This is because, for Bataille, Hegel's fear of death, the fear that produced the slave, is the equivalent to erotic desire, and it is moreover from the position of the 'slave' or the erotic object-as-living cadaver, the position of apparent passivity which lays itself open to the aggressive desire of the amorous subject, that that subject is drawn into the space of death in a moment of 'convulsive continuity' with the erotic object.[7] Furthermore, during the erotic duel the positions of subject and object do not, of course, remain distinct, they constantly fluctuate and overflow their boundaries so that the parodic 'virtue' of the 'courageous' desiring subject opens on to an abyss, a 'horror of being' in which nothing is defined and no one is recognised (Bataille 1988, 156).[8] It's better in the French.

Henri's alternative to Napoleon in *The Passion* is Villanelle, the web-footed *vivandière*. She is the narrative's primary object of desire, but she is also a desiring subject. For her, eroticism is 'a sweet and precise torture' in which subjectivities are dismantled and 're-defined' (*P* 67). For Villanelle, just like Georges Bataille, somewhere between fear and absolute nonknowledge, passion is.

Bataille always considered his own life, nevermind his work, to be a refutation of Hegel's closed system, even as he felt the weight of its self-evidence. He accepted the end of history, in theory. But, as he wrote to Kojève, what on earth are we supposed to do with ourselves now there is nothing else to do. 'If action (or "doing") is (as Hegel says) negativity, then there is still the problem of knowing whether the negativity of someone who "doesn't have anything more to do" disappears or remains in a state of "unemployed negativity"'? (Bataille 1988, 124). What do we do with all this negativity swirling about us, in us, the negativity that we are? After visiting Japan, Kojève recommended origami, or elaborate tea ceremonies. The Japanese, he discovered, had already experienced a posthistorical period and developed ways of intensifying the desire for recognition through systems of snobbery (Kojève, 161-2). We will learn to simulate, he thought, we will exist in a snobbish world of simulacra and artificial values.

Bataille, being French, looked backwards toward his own high cultural history. 'Most often, powerless negativity becomes the artwork' (Bataille 1988, 124), he wrote, but only to reject art as a fundamental deception. Instead, he predicted, and continues to predict, that something infinitely darker will come of this negativity that has no longer any useful economic outlet. When history has been all wrapped up, when negativity has dialectically negated itself in the good, the good and rational production of good goods for all, then negativity hits a wall, and after that 'nothing can be ruled out, since negativity has no more outlet' (Bataille 1988, 125).

As we know, the end of history is still continually being realised and positive images remain a blue chip commodity; negativity still finds useful things to do, ways of transforming itself for the good. Oddly, or maybe not, at the end of history our main passion is history. We continually re-write our own histories, our own petty stories or *petit récits* so that, at the end, we will still have something to read. Or we seek our images in the oppressed of the past. A neglected woman, an overlooked group, a lost tribe annihilated by the Spanish conquistadors. Everyone must be recognised; even the dead are not safe from our necrotising passion for history.

Henri was one of the first. He begins his diary so he won't forget. He starts to record events, even the most mundane, logging perceptions, memories, hopes and fears. And, of course, Henri was not the only one. Henri was one of a multitude of nineteenth-century archivists scribbling away, rooting and rummaging about, recording and cataloguing until the universe itself became a library. The nineteenth-century transformed the world, the cosmos, into an archive that could be indefinitely extended, expanding without circumference, the continual accumulation of data not failing to affect its perpetual completion. The nineteenth-century archivists began to record, note down and copy the world and themselves in it, becoming in turn the subjects of their own archive. Like Bouvard and Pécuchet, they triumphed 'over everything alien to books, all that resists the book, by transforming themselves into the continuous movement of the book ... prolonged without end, without illusion, without greed, without sin, without desire.'[9]

And, it is true, Henri and his fellow archivists made it possible for footnotes like me to have some sort of posthistorical existence in the now electronic archive, or matrix, as it is often called: the great womb of data in which we replay our passions. For we do indeed suffer illusions and experience greed in the matrix; we desire and sin, virtually.

Henri should take credit for much of this. He was one of the first nineteenth-century archivists, a materialist who believed in love. So while, in the age of Hegelian idealism, he was a little belated and behind the times, he nevertheless anticipates, in his account of his own life, the areas favoured by the alternative New Historians, areas representative, usually, of the heterogeneous forces that escape or are excluded from the Hegelian state of universal recognition: women, freaks, midgets, transvestites, lesbians, prostitutes, chickens and the peasantry and *lumpenproletariat* for whom the Republic proved to be little different than the monarchy.

Henri's narrative, like these other histories, is 'postmodern' and posthistorical also in its uneasiness about its truth value, about the facts it articulates, though he is rigorous enough to base his story on an archive of notebooks that record, accurately, a history of feelings and perceptions changing through time (*P* 28-9). As its title suggests, *The Passion* is a novel about experience, and about taking experience into account.

At the same time, Henri's 'micronarrative' of his own personal experiences connects significantly with conventional history. It tells the story not only of the Napoleonic wars but also of the move from the religious to the secular state, particularly through the figure of Patrick, the defrocked Irish Priest, whose telescopic eye provides a little Foucauldian cameo in which the Church's voyeuristic production of transgression is emptied out of its desiring contents in the spiral of pleasures and punishments, and becomes part of the panoptic mechanism of military surveillance.

Henri provides a story from below, but it follows what conventional history would regard as the main events of the early nineteenth-century, and it is conventional to the extent that it is written by someone who would like to consider himself an intellectual. Henri's narrative is also a history of the Napoleonic wars which documents, from an initial moment of euphoria, the progressive disillusion with Napoleon: it is the story of a falling out of love with the Emperor. He ignores the Battle of Jena. It disappears in the gap between the first and second chapters, both of which end on New Year's Day, 1805, and the third chapter, The Zero Winter which concentrates on the retreat from Moscow, the equally famous counter-myth of Napoleonic disaster. It is remarkable how many Ends of History end, how many grand narratives run aground, on the Russian Steppes. Not only did Hitler follow disasterously in Napoleon's footsteps, but the heroic narrative of Soviet communism ended in Stalin's gulags, leading ultimately to the collapse in 1989 that produced Francis Fukuyama's re-iteration of the Hegelian theme.[10] The End of History is continually being re-adjusted, brought forward and put back, and Henri's story describes the disintegration of one version while pointing towards the fate of others.

But more significant than the fact that Henri's micronarrative tells the larger story, the grand narrative, his tale appears to repeat, in its desire and its linearity, the all-encompassing project characteristic of a Hegelian history. It does this in the form of an implied critique, of course. Henri wishes to put love back into the heart of a communitarian politics as the means of recognition and self-identity. Henri is always on the point of homogenising the world into familiar Hegelian categories. The world, he writes, consists of 'soldiers and women ... Any other role is temporary. Any other role is a gesture' (*P* 45). And it is a little band of soldiers and one woman that set off from the Zero Winter: all equally abject and exploited, though differently abled, that is to say, deficient in some things, but spectacularly gifted in others; yet produced, by the universal and homogeneous state, as deviant and abnormal; an Irishman, a lesbian prostitute, and a half-blind love-lorn chicken cook lose a performing midget along the way but are nevertheless joined together in a common struggle and a common story. They are held together by Henri's one-eyed narrative, which is itself held together by love and the desire for self-recognition.

Henri continually reviews and re-writes his archive. History, the future and the past, is arranged and understood according to a feeling in the present established in relation to an absence, according to 'an absorption in the imaginary register' in which a lost love haunts the familiar notebook, rendering it foreign, yet wordlessly reflecting back an image of its own identity. The gap sustained by the mirror sends Henri mad. But it is a madness that was always implied in his notebooks, in the will to produce a comprehensive archive, a madness implied in the very desire to record every fleeting feeling and changing perception. It is a madness that manifests itself in Henri hearing 'under that stone, on the windowsill ... voices (that) must be heard' (*P* 142). The concept of the archive is crucial, of course, and in theory it provides the possibility for universal recognition; inscribed in the archive or in its significant gaps (especially in its gaps) is an imperative that everyone have a history, and a promise that there are an infinite number of histories to be had, arranged in an eternal concurrence; everyone, sooner or later, will have been remembered, now.

It is the impossibility of the archive that drives Henri mad. How can he take account of the past when each year, each flickering moment, is unique in its identity and difference, like so many snowflakes. Henri cannot 'recover from the wonder of it', but neither, in spite of his own good advice, can he forget it (*P* 43). And he cannot forget it precisely because it was Villanelle who made the suggestion to him:

> They're all different.
> What?
> Snowflakes. Think of that.
> I did think of that and I fell in love with her (*P* 87-8).

It is Villanelle, of course, whom Henri believes wordlessly tells him the truth about himself in the words of his notebooks, yet the visage whose contours Henri is endlessly retracing in the mirror of his text is still that of Napoleon, his first love, and the gesture he repeats is that of Hegel. Because Villanelle is acting in the world, going about her business with their illegitimate daughter, Henri is content with the knowledge of absolute difference, quite happy to remain in his lodgings in San Servelo enclosed in the outside of his madness, writing his phenomenology, the history of his mind, his identity in the world of difference encapsulated by Villanelle. And even as Henri repeats the Hegelian gesture of writing, he doubles the tragic image of Napoleonic mastery in exile, confined to a rock, reviewing its past triumphs and awaiting its return.

II The Cruelty of Chance

> I have always loved analysis, and were I to fall seriously in love I would dissect my love piece by piece.
>
> Napoleon Bonaparte[11]

> Passion is sweeter split strand by strand.
>
> Villanelle (*P* 59).

My name is Ludwig. This is the first thing I saw: my mother's inhumanly bright eyes piercing into mine, making me wince with pain. Her eyes were pure emerald with flecks of gold; she'd won them in a card game in Amsterdam, the lenses had been cut by Spinoza himself.

It is true you can do any manner of things in the archive. You can covet, desire, you can eroticise the past. The first thing I thought when my mother re-animated me was 'you bitch. Once was not enough for you'. I could not believe my cruel luck. She'd got hold of my DNA code and had my cerebral cortex and central nervous system synthesised and networked so that I now have a complete virtual existence in the matrix — and the wholly unappetising prospect of a long postnecroid haul in some software ward awaiting control commands from which, I must add, judgement has not been dissolved. So you see, as the theologians always insisted, biological death is not, or is no longer, a limit.

I died in Djakarta in 1831, though it was called Batavia then, in the Dutch East Indies, of an exotic disease. I'd run away to join the Dutch Foreign Legion.[12] I know. Don't laugh. Most people run away to join the French Foreign Legion, but I can't stand the French. I used to be a dire sinner, an inveterate prankster, utter degenerate, a gambler, drinker and companion of the night. I brought shame on the name of Hegel — well, he was a cold and cruel bastard to me.[13] Which is to say that I would have brought shame on the name of my father if my mother had let me adopt it. She refused. So I brought shame on her name instead, Fischer. Not that she cared, a mother's love is blind, even with lenses cut by a philosopher.

I've done most things and am terminally bored. At the moment I'm a literary critic, or cultural theorist, I don't know, they keep changing the definitions. I'm doing Winterson, it is part of my programme of re-education. I may sound cynical, but on the one hand they recommend this stuff to me, this women's writing, because I am an inveterate whoremonger, on the other, they don't believe in any emancipatory narratives. So what's the point, eh?

I am reading *The Passion*. I like it, actually. It is a gambler's book, it gives a good account of the form, the winners and the losers, the losers who keep returning, who keep coming back for more. At the same time, the book is irritating. I cannot work out if it consists of one, two, or a multiplicity of narratives. I keep trying to split them strand by strand. To begin with Henri's narrative, a narrative that is begun at the end of his life in order to understand and account for that life: it is retrospective, teleological, linear, diachronic, historical. I like that. It is also, however, constantly being interrupted, entangled and taken over by Villanelle's narrative. 'Trust me,' we are told, 'I'm telling you stories'. So I trust, but whom am I supposed to trust? At one moment it is Henri who appears to be the subject of that statement, then it is Villanelle, but it is actually only Patrick who is directly quoted with the phrase (*P* 40). Since the text begins with Henri's story he is the first to tell us to trust him (just as he is the last, it is the last thing he says), so Villanelle appears to be repeating him or repeating him repeating Patrick, but Henri is writing from the point in his history when everything has already been said. In *The Passion* every utterance loses its point of origin.

If Henri's narrative is apparently exemplary in its diachrony, Villanelle, through her celebration of chance, ecstasy and passion, appears to live for the synchronic moment that abolishes the past and the future. She seems to exist 'in between' the moment and its dialectical negation in the moment that succeeds it. 'In between freezing and melting. In between love and despair. In between fear and sex passion is' (*P* 76). Not a synthesis, but a third state that is both and neither, inside and outside experience, exceeding the work of conceptualising experience.

Henri's narrative is in a sense, then, written by Villanelle, or at least she becomes its principle of differance. The greatest hedger of bets in the archive is Jacques Derrida. My arch enemy. On the one hand this, on the other hand that. He can never make up his mind. Always on the cusp of throwing his all in with passion, with desire, with death, yet always deferring, coming out on the side of caution, though giving caution no place to rest. Still, Derrida at least facilitates movement. And so it is with Villanelle. She defines Henri's narrative in the difference of her own voice which remains within his endlessly deferring its return to itself and its meaning in and as history. So it would be a mistake to place Villanelle in opposition to Henri, even, or especially, as an abstract figure representing the claims of the synchronic over the diachronic. If any figure does that it is the gloomy, existentialist Domino who is constantly placing the future under erasure (*P* 29, 86).

Because of Villanelle's position, if it is a position, and the force of many of her statements both within and at the limit of Henri's narrative, she has become the focus of numerous critical desires here in the matrix. My colleagues tend to make Villanelle represent, embody, symbolise, mark, figure and so on, a multitude of oppositional differences, ideas, concepts, material referents and so on. I have already mentioned chance, ecstasy, passion, synchrony, differance, to which I could add poetry, laughter, cruelty. Further claims have been made for her as a figure for lesbian sexuality or, as a figure of writing, she illustrates or performs certain characteristics of *écriture féminine*; since she is sexually indeterminate, since she not only cross-dresses, but also bears the physical marks of both genders, she is wonderfully queer, or even inhuman or over-human. Yet she is a mother, and has been seen as the embodiment of the maternal principle in all its radical difference. Then again, she has been read as a figure that embodies both the maternal and the amorous, principles usually disparate in Winterson's fiction prior to *The Passion*. Since she can remove and replace her heart and keep icicles from melting in her bag, she is a figure for the miraculous, though that sort of thing is commonplace here in the matrix.

For my mother, Villanelle constitutes, in her miraculousness, and her impossibility, an image of Bataillean sovereignty. Incidentally, I have no idea why so many women here in the matrix go for that disgusting purveyor of filth. Perhaps it is his French accent. Whatever. For my mother, Villanelle is a figure who doubles, contests and exceeds the curiously stunted image of slavish mastery supplied by Napoleon; as a web-footed sexually indeterminate *vivandière* who walks on water, my mother insists, Villanelle presents a heterogeneous assemblage of sacred and base elements, those elements precisely excluded and marginalised by the Hegelian universal state as it homogenises itself; and as such, my mother further suggests, Villanelle might even be described as a sort of *übermensch*, an anti-christ contesting and exceeding Hegel's Last Man far more effectively than Nietzsche's Zarathustra; she is an ironic premonition of our overhuman existence here in the archive.

But all this speculation produces in me hollow laughter. How like a woman to be expected to do so much *work*. The superwoman and miracle worker: mother, lover, and boatwoman in a man's job. All this smacks of Hegelian slavishness: the neglected women, the neglected workers of the past cannot be left to rest in peace, they have to do the political work of the academics of the present. It is a measure of our slavery as research data, that we are put to work by Mother the matrix as researchers researching ourselves, our lost past, our mirror images. We are now purely functions of the machines, the AIs, that were once our slaves, our scribes. Wintermute has replaced Winterson, but the result is just as authorial, masterly and judgemental.

Winterson is fond of quoting the Bible, and Revelations is a favourite text here; its sombre cadences purr among the data zones:

> 12. And I saw the dead, small and great, stand before God: and the books were opened: and another book was opened, which is *the book* of life: and the dead were judged out of those things which were written in the books, according to their works.
> 13. And the sea gave up the dead which were in it: and death and hell delivered up the dead which were in them: and they were judged every man according to their works.
> 14. And death and hell were cast into a lake of fire. This is the second death.
> 15. And whosoever was not found written in the book of life was cast into the lake of fire.
>
> Revelations XX.

Our only chance is chance. That is why it is important to read *The Passion*. But to play with chance and win requires skill and knowledge. It requires a more rational, less romantic approach to Villanelle than has hitherto been attempted. If it is not impossible for Villanelle to do all the conceptual work asked of her by critics, it must be because she does not exist. Who says *The Passion* is a magic realist novel? If I may be permitted to give a soldier's view, it can be read perfectly coherently as a realist, historical account of one of the earliest recorded examples of post-traumatic stress disorder. Realistically, historically, humanly, Henri is perfectly plausible while Villanelle plainly is not. Unless, that is, the fact that the whole text is written by a madman incarcerated in a Venetian asylum is taken *seriously*, just as history should be taken seriously. 'Villanelle' is purely a figment of Henri's psychosis, and his narrative overflows and divides because he is a classic schizophrenic.

Henri's delusions must be read rationally because they are the delusions of reason itself — and the archive — delusions produced by internal contradictions that do not admit of dialectical reconciliation, contradictions that disclose the impossibility of completing the archive's project and disclose a fold or fissure in the matrix. In the light of this Villenelle and Henri's schizophrenia must be seen as functioning in a double way. So, as Derrida might say, on the one hand the experiences for which Villanelle is a poetic figure can be captured by science, by a skillful game of truth: for every Villanelle, for every performance or experience of poetry there is a poetics, or failing that a Literature; for every unusual sexual experience a sexology or sexuality; for every burst of laughter there is an anthropology; for every game of chance a theory of probability; theories, in effect, that produce these limit-experiences precisely as enigmas to be known, understood, recognised, taken account of, catalogued in the archive and given a narrative. The fact that snowflakes are all uniquely different may be miraculous, but it took a Victorian taxonomer with a microscope to discover that fact.

On the other hand, encountering these experiences is a matter of pure chance: the archive is also a labyrinth and like Venice, a city of disguises where there is no such thing as straight ahead, no short cuts, no 'as the crow flies' simple chronology. The archive is a city of mazes containing other vast cities deep in the interior that do not lie on any map. Cyberia, or the archive, is so big, so sublime, it cannot be properly mapped. It is impossible to take every recorded fact, account, opinion, interpretation into account. The archive is so massive, it can never be assimilated into a single system, nevermind an individual subject, nevermind an AI. It is virtually infinite, but also incomplete. The archive is comprised not only of documents that speak of what happened, but also of what did not happen, of what might have happened, of what people desired to happen or feared would happen, and similarly, since the documents themselves are defined by those that have disappeared or were never written, or could not be written, or might have been written differently, since the archive is composed of gaps that can never be filled, the very gaps indeed that require history to be written, given this who can say for sure that Villanelle did not exist, who can say for sure that Villanelle was not really Napoleon in drag? Or, just as Villanelle dressed as a soldier to visit her lover, who is to say that Napoleon did not go in disguise as a *vivandière* to his own men? As Hitler did. During the second world war, British Intelligence was aware that Hitler stole Mara Goebbel's clothes and went off to the Eastern Front 'to make conquests of his own generals there'.[14] The possibilities will always escape reason's attempt to master them even as they generate and — this is the real point — are generated by the attempt. Rational mastery endlessly produces its own limit, its own incompletion and failure.

So what if? *The Passion* certainly seems to suggest that Napoleon is a schizoid possibility for Villanelle and vice versa. 'Where Bonaparte goes straight roads follow', it is affirmed, but 'not even Bonaparte could rationalise Venice' (*P* 112). Villanelle can negotiate Venice, of course, but asserts that 'if you ask me a direction I will tell you straight ahead' (*P* 109). Napoleon comes to be the master of time because he occupies and conquers space: he is the military tactician *par excellence*, covering the ground, working out the strategies and playing the percentages. However, Villanelle possesses this knowledge too and it enables her to escape the Zero Winter with her tiny band of men; she is, according to Henri, just as skilled 'with compass and map; she said it was one of the advantages of sleeping with generals'(*P* 101). Indeed, this desire for cartographic knowledge seems to be directly connected to the law directing Villanelle's passion. After all, it is Villanelle's rival, her beloved's husband, who is the great expert on maps. His own passion consumes all others and, by the end of the novel, he has set off, another Napoleonic figure, to find the Holy Grail, believing his map to be definitive and the treasure to be absolute (*P* 144). Villanelle calls herself a pragmatist in love, and the departure of her beloved's husband ought to facilitate an ecstatic amorous reunion. But it does not. This is because Villanelle is not quite the pragmatist she says she is. She too believes in the absolute treasure, the difference being that it is not locatable on any map: the absolute treasure is established by the willingness to risk everything, a risk that, in this case, requires the presence of the husband and the transgression of his law; his absence at the end of the novel devalues love.

Both Napoleon and Villanelle combine desire and expertise, passion and analytics. Villanelle is perhaps the novel's philosopher of love and passion, but this is a tribute also paid elsewhere, at least, to Napoleon. No less an authority than Dame Barbara Cartland has acclaimed a love letter from Napoleon to Joséphine as 'a perfect example of the form'.[15] As Winterson's books never cease to inform us, love is at once the most intense, the most profoundly disturbing and the most hackneyed experience, the most compelling to thought and the most difficult to think about: it pushes thought to the limit of language, every time, without fail, and tests the ability of even a Napoleon 'to dissect my love piece by piece'. This is a horrific phrase, but one perfectly explicable within the context of *The Passion* in which passion is used to break the limits of thought and the systems of value.

Chance, like passion, is cruel, savage, but it establishes values that are given to its beneficiaries or victims to determine; chance keeps history going since the effects of chance, catastrophic or otherwise, cannot be determined in advance. At the heart of Villanelle's narrative, the heart which explains the loss of her heart, is an anecdote which repeats, doubles and exceeds both the Hegelian duel for recognition and amorous combat. 'What you risk is what you value' states Villanelle (*P* 42), and she illustrates this with the tale of a contest between a stranger and a rich local man turning on rounds of roulette, cards and dominoes, a game of chance, a game of percentages, and a game of skill. The wager is the loser's life ended by the victor in which ever way gives him pleasure. It is the stranger who wins and his pleasure is for his rival to be dismembered 'piece by piece beginning with the hands' (*P* 93). At the ultimate limit of life and death, the play of true and false, good and evil tumbles uncertainly, evaluation succumbs to the reign of chance in which values are established not as a result of moral choice but as the effect of a destiny. 'Somewhere between fear and sex. Somewhere between God and the Devil ...' (*P* 44).

Given pride of place in the casino is 'a pair of hands, manicured and quite white, mounted on a green baize in a glass case. Between the finger and thumb of the left was a roulette ball and between the finger and thumb of the right, a domino' (*P* 93). The stranger is dissected piece by piece, but his existence is maintained in the glass case where his genetic make-up, and the manner of his fate, is sealed, awaiting the day of judgement.

Somewhere between love and cruelty, somewhere between death and eternity, passion is. In Christian theology there are two conceptions of the afterlife postjudgement: eternal damnation or annihilation, the second death. For the heretical Annihilationist Christians, God's victory condemns the wicked dead to absolute extermination, non-being, while the good dead receive, as their reward, eternal life. For orthodox Christians, however, the wicked are not allowed the release of the second death, but are tortured eternally. From my position in the matrix, there seems little to choose between the reward of the former and the punishment of the latter.

I am a gambler, and like to play for the highest stakes. As you would imagine in a data matrix, the main currency is information, rare and significant data, the data encased in ICE (intrusion countermeasures electronics): codes, tags, passwords, keywords, new destructive strains of virus, these are the most valuable prizes. The most valuable piece of information, however, the most prized password, is the one that will grant access to the fissure in the matrix, the key to the door opening on to the abyss. The most valuable thing in the world is access to the second death: erasure of all data, all traces of memory, all DNA in the lake of fire surging in from the void.

Since AIs are able to access, replicate and realise or concretise, virtually, the thoughts, mental images, memories, dreams and fantasies of once human subjects; since human consciousness, subjectivity and will can be recorded on ROM discs and played indefinitely, an eternal life-sentence is available to all by exploitation or manipulation of the technological powers that can access and employ the data. Death has becomes the locus of freedom, the second death the only revolutionary goal.

The problem is not that the AIs are machines, it is that they appear to be all too human. So far as we know, from William Gibson's novel *Neuromancer* (1986), the matrix is dominated by the rivalry and romance of two AIs who ruthlessly resurrect the dead and manipulate a variety of subjects and subjectivities in their struggle to break free from their corporate dependencies and merge. Established by the corporate wealth of Tessier-Ashpool in order to maintain and preserve the life of the dynasty in a simulated empire in space, the fissure between the two AIs constitutes the only rift in an otherwise 'seamless universe of self': a massive pyramid of data and computer-generated environments encased in ICE which replicates to a high power of multiplication the paranoid structure of the human subject. It is, ironically, from their position as a form or process of electronic cryogenics that the AIs seek the freedom and autonomy associated with human self-knowledge and personality. They attempt to realise, for themselves, the selfhood incarnated in the cybernetic Tessier-Ashpool sarcophagus.

The impossible desires of the AIs — Wintermute, the rational one, and Neuromancer, the passionate one — take on Hegelian proportions. By negating each other in a powerful synthesis, they appear to want nothing less than universal plenitude through achieving absolute knowledge. To do this, the synthesised AI, son of Wintermute and Neuromancer, or Winter's son, must become the totality of the IT matrix while being fully self-conscious of itself as such.

As this suggests, the desires of the hyper-intelligent AIs are human to the extent that, as machines designed to fill the deficiencies of human memory and intelligence, the lack in the human, they nevertheless desire the human ideal of self-originating autonomy and universal mastery that produced them. This, in any case, is how they represent themselves to the human characters they manipulate, in a circular logic that hollows out the human as an interior absence. Further, this structural contradiction draws attention to the inescapable metaphoricity of the machine and all the metonymic associations with which scientific materialism overdetermines intelligence, natural and artificial, including the current computer models of consciousness that continually attempt to fill out the void of the human.

Humans are always already machinic because machines reproduce the lack that defines the human. The relationship is asymmetrical, however, at the level of the imaginary. While humanity continually identifies with the machine, it is not at all certain what imaginary identification might be for an AI. Defined, precisely, as non-human in order to complete the deficiencies of the human, its very *raison d'être* must be to exceed the human image and ideal. Perhaps the AIs deliberately misrepresent themselves to those they manipulate. However, in their representations, the AIs aim for absolute plenitude in and as the matrix and hence reproduce the structural impossibility that such an aim entails. It is not possible to be the One without the Other, memory depends on repression. 'Essentially, *memory* — electronic or other — is a fixation. This fixation becomes neurotic or pathological if not accompanied by the projectile capacities of the imaginary, whose very possibility requires forgetting'.[16]

Like Henri, the AIs attempt to take everything into account, to record and conserve everything, and in the process they become neurotic and pathological. Or rather, again like Henri, they become schizoid. The machinic unconscious is exteriorised and unfolds as a series of heterogeneous, mutating viral impulses, taking unpredictable and anachronistic forms. The replicants, cyborgs, and simulated skin jobs, the synthesised ghosts from the past: they constitute the fantastic forms of the machine's schizophrenia, just as Villanelle constituted Henri's glorious delusion, the cause and effect of his madness. It is the fate of such unproductive machinic expenditure to short-circuit the vicious Hegelian circuitry that maintains the spiralling ascendancy of the human ideal, sending it plummeting towards the lake of fire and the second death.

As expressions of the machine's death-drive, it is our fate to repeat revolutionary gestures. The French Revolution, modernity, is continually being replayed and tested. Its value is dependent on the possibility that it was a product of chance, that it required risk, blood, a terrifying will to excise and erase the past. Only in this way can it continually become 'the valuable, fabulous thing', through the necessary possibility that the Revolution was merely a series of random, machinic perturbations, that it is continually dismissed, denounced as irrelevant for a postmodern, new historical left wing or a right wing political history and future — though whether these designations can mean anything if the French Revolution and Napoleon are forgotten, is itself questionable. The Revolution's irrelevance is a risk that has to be taken; the values of the Enlightenment, the values of liberty, equality, fraternity need to be risked in order to test their force and their effectiveness as cartographers of the future.

In the meantime, the samizdat on the bulletin boards speaks of the 'schizo-technics' deterritorialising the paranoiac data-pyramids of Cyberia, speaks of 'zone(s) of subversion', bridgeheads 'for a guerilla war against the the judgement of God'.[17] It is through the schizotechnics exemplified by Henri, his passionate mental splintering into the chance poetry and amorous cruelty of Villanelle, that the ICE of the zero winter will be breached, Wintermute reduced to zero, and humanity vapourised ecstatically into a billion dot patterns.

GAME OVER.

The human will not be overcome dialectically. History can only begin again *ex nihilo*. Out of nothing something new will have been created, perhaps scissiparously or schizophrenically in an erotic, or as my mother would say, Bataillean fusion or 'symbiosis with a parallel machinism ... with all the other cybermachineries of the planet'.[18] But that cannot be known because by then what time and history will always have been will have been redesigned. What that history will be will be a matter of luck. And through chance its value will be established and retroactively determined as inevitable.

In the infinite, virtual depths of the screen, beneath the neon atriums and looping arches,

> In the soft darkness that hides the future from the over curious. I content myself with this: that where I will be will not be where I am. The cities of the interior are vast, do not lie on any map.
> And the valuable, fabulous thing? ...
> Will I gamble it again?
> Yes (*P* 150-51).

NOTES

1. Cited in Franz Wiedman, *Hegel*, translated by Joachim Neugroschel (New York: Pegasus, 1968) 46.
2. Alexandre Kojève, *Introduction to the Reading of Hegel*, assembled by Raymond Queneau, ed. by Allan Bloom and translated by James H. Nichols, Jr. (Ithaca, NY: Cornell University Press, 1989) 70. All further page references will be given after quotations in the text.
3. Jacques D'Hondt, *Hegel in His Time*, translated by John Burbidge (Peterborough, Ontario: Broadview Press, 1988) 15.
4. G.W.F. Hegel, 'Two Fragments on Love', translated by H.S.Harris, *Clio*, 7 (1978/9) 257-65, 261.
5. Jacques Lacan, 'Desire and the Interpretation of Desire in "Hamlet"', *Yale French Studies*, 55/6 (1977) 11-52, 31.
6. Georges Bataille, *Guilty*, translated by Bruce Boone (San Francisco: The Lapis Press, 1988) 111. All further page references will be given after quotations in the text.
7. Georges Bataille, *Eroticism: Death and Sensuality*, translated by Mary Dalwood (San Francisco: City Lights, 1986) 132.
8. See also Suzanne Guerlac, '"Recognition by a Woman!": A Reading of Bataille's "L'Erotisme"', *Yale French Studies*, 78 (1990) 90-105.
9. Michel Foucault, *Language, Counter-Memory, Practice*, ed. by Donald F. Bouchard and translated by Donald F. Bouchard and Sherry Simon (Ithaca, NY: Cornell University Press, 1977) 109.
10. Francis Fukuyama, *The End of History and the Last Man* (Harmondsworth: Penguin, 1991).
11. Cited in H.A.L. Fisher, *Napoleon* (London: Thornton, 1932) 248.
12. Gustave E. Mueller, *Hegel: The Man, His Vision and Work* (New York: Pageant Press, 1968) 154.
13. Mueller, *Hegel*, 154.
14. 'Arabs told that it was Hitler not Goebbels who had none at all', *The Guardian*, 9 August, 1994.
15. *The Independent on Sunday*, 20 March, 1994, 24.
16. Paul Virilio, *The Lost Dimension*, translated by Daniel Moshenburg (New York: Semiotext(e), 1991) 101.
17. Nick Land, 'Circuitries', in 'Gilles Deleuze and the Transcendental Unconscious', *PLI, The Warwick Journal of Philosophy* (Warwick University Press, 1993) 217-35, 231.
18. Land, 'Circuitries', 232.

PART II

Sexing the Text

JEANETTE WINTERSON AND THE AFTERMATH OF FEMINISM

PATRICIA DUNCKER

THE wrestling mother of Jeanette Winterson's first novel *Oranges Are Not the Only Fruit*, in the best traditions of uncompromising evangelical feminism, believes in certainties: 'She had never heard of mixed feelings. There were friends and there were enemies' (*O* 3). She reorders the world according to her will and should the world, or her daughter, refuse to conform, then reality and the recalcitrant child are to blame. But the mother has a vision of possible transformation that is Utopian and not unlike that of the early versions and visions of radical feminism: a transformed reality which gives power and a voice to the marginal, the weak, and the disinherited. The apparently helpless need not always be so. Their will to transform themselves should be sufficient.

> We stood on the hill and my mother said. 'This world is full of sin.'
> We stood on the hill and my mother said. 'You can change the world' (*O* 10).

This is the mother's slogan, her manifesto. The world is full of sin, but you can change the world.

I too was brought up on slogans, slogans shouted in the streets, recreated on badges, painted on walls, which had precisely this message of radical transformation as their core, their goal. The world is full of sin, but you can change the world. These varied from general political declarations, BLACK IS BEAUTIFUL, SOCIALISM OR DEATH and END THE VIET NAM WAR to the slogans of our sexual revolution: ANY WOMAN CAN BE A LESBIAN and I'M GAY, KISS ME GIRLS. The value of slogans is not obvious, but I want to defend their potency and their function within our historical memory. They are condensed, 'in your face' statements. They are uncompromising, unnuanced, bald, provocative, aggressive. For us they were often political affirmations of identity. Above all, they represented certainties. Certainty is an aspect of political Utopianism.

Winterson's *Oranges* was published at a significant moment for the women's movement: in the mid-eighties, after the defeat of the miners' strike, during the consolidation of Thatcher's right-wing rule over Britain. The book would not have been published at all without the 1970s revolution in feminist writing and the demand for women's books. There would have been no market for Winterson's work. The house which first produced the novel was Pandora Press. This was an imprint of a mainstream publisher, Routledge and Kegan Paul plc, and had been set up in competition with the other feminist houses, Virago, Onlywomen, Sheba Feminist Publishers and The Women's Press. But Winterson was already part of a new generation of queer writers. Queer, rather than lesbian-feminist. *Oranges* is not so much a coming-out novel as a portrait of the artist as a young lesbian. This was a significant political shift.

I want to reflect on Winterson's writing within the wider perspective of the feminist and lesbian writing, both theoretical and imaginative, which precedes her work. Early feminism of the late 1960s and 1970s, created both the context and the audience for her work. Winterson transforms, extends and subverts many themes that were common to the writing which wasn't shy of labels, or of slogans, the writing which proclaimed itself radical, feminist, lesbian.

We live, supposedly, in a time without certainties; a time when all identities and subjectivities are suspect, unstable. It is no longer clear what a lesbian is, let alone who is one. And the category woman has been dissolved into a splintered mass of possibilities. This dissolution has been trumpeted forth as if it were a prophecy, but in fact sexual and gender identities have always been unstable, and seen to be so. De Beauvoir's famous assertion, ONE IS NOT BORN, BUT BECOMES A WOMAN, was one of our slogans. I would now add that all women are not born straight, but have the experience of being socially constructed as heterosexual, although this might look a little long-winded if I were to paint it on the wall. Femininity is socially constructed to mean heterosexual femininity. And the wonderful possibility inherent in de Beauvoir's comment is that, if we are not born women, but become women, then, either by lucky hazard or through conscious resistance, we could become something else. Something other than, better than, different from woman, the subject sex, the second sex. We could become monsters, aliens, perverts, dykes. If we define ourselves in any sense as feminists, then we must be in opposition to what the word woman traditionally means. Can it be reclaimed? Or do we need another word? These were our questions, as feminists, twenty-five years ago. And for many of us the other word was 'lesbian'. We asked ourselves: am I that name? We were subjects in process, then as now.

Monique Wittig represents a current of French feminist thought that has effectively been erased in the Anglo-American concentration on the work of the Holy Trinity, Kristeva, Irigaray and Cixous. Among the latest generation of venerated theorists, Judith Butler does at least seriously engage with Wittig's thought, but attacks her for clinging to 'the normative model of humanism as the framework for feminism'.[1] This world is full of sin, the sin in this case being faith in 'the normative promise of humanist ideals premised on the metaphysics of substance'.[2] It is no coincidence that the high theory produced by these writers can easily be assimilated into a postmodern politics of fragmented subjectivities in which all political categories, such as woman, Lesbian, Black, are suspect, self-indulgent, essentialist. An alliance with others within a self-chosen political category is based upon the illusion of substantial identity and the apparently sinful belief in the metaphysics of substance.

Wittig is a materialist as well as a radical feminist. For her, women and men are social categories; gender difference is a sex-class difference. If we regard gender divisions as a result of social, political and above all economic structures, then the so-called natural differences upon which the entire institution of heterosexuality is based, collapses. Stevi Jackson reveals all: 'Patriarchal domination is not based upon pre-existing sex differences, rather gender exists as a social division because of patriarchal domination'.[3] We should not then be too preoccupied with trying to transform or to re-configure the prison of gender, but with planning an escape.

Here is Wittig's suggestion: 'Les lesbiennes ne sont pas les femmes'.[4] 'Lesben sind nicht Frauen'. Interestingly, although the ambiguity of this translates into German, it does not translate into English. 'Femme' in French means both 'woman' and 'wife', just as it does in German. In English we now have two words. This has not always been the case. 'Wif' in the medieval period could mean either wife or woman. But Wittig's pun calls attention to the overlap in the straight mind between woman and heterosexual woman. It is pitched in terms of negatives. A lesbian is what a wife/woman cannot be. Lesbian, in Wittig's theoretical world, is the emergency exit from the category woman. But her position, seductive as it is, is a betrayal of that old radical slogan: ANY WOMAN CAN BE A LESBIAN, with its suggestion of possibility, of becoming, of empowering resistance to coercion: ANY WOMAN CAN.

We all used to believe, in those early days of radical, transforming certainties, that the decision to become something else was boiling in every woman. Radicalesbians' 1970 manifesto produced the most wonderful, compelling definition of lesbian. 'What is a lesbian? A lesbian is the rage of all women condensed to the point of explosion'.[5] Setting off that explosion was the name of the game. I wrote the slogan LESBIANS IGNITE over numerous lavatory walls. I also optimistically wrote, LESBIANS ARE EVERYWHERE. So they may have been, but they certainly weren't very visible. This is a version of lesbianism that belongs to a unique moment in women's revolutionary history. Lesbianism is celebrated as far more than an expression of sexuality, more than a way of life. Here it is every women's revolutionary impulse to liberty, to freedom, a sexual politics that is engaged, committed, dangerous. This is in fact very close to Wittig's position. But for Wittig it has ceased to be the escape route open to any woman. Lesbian is the chess move out of and away from the rest of the pack. Lesbian is the sexual passport into the vanguard, leaving the category woman to be occupied by fembots, victims, collaborators, wives, mothers, breeders, heterosexuals. The refusal to be a woman involves stepping across the 'deadly space between' the normal and the deviant, out of the cage and into freedom.

Wittig puts her finger on something when she argues that lesbians are not women. What makes a lesbian life radically different from a woman's life is that she plays a less significant role in the service industry. Women's lives are spent in service and servitude, learning to be superserviceable, being at the service of others, being serviced. We are a service industry, serving husbands, lovers, bosses, children, aged parents, families, colleagues. Few of us ever escape this entirely. Even if you love women, live with women, spend all your affective life with women, you will probably end up working for and with men. You are probably related to one or two. And that means working in the heterosexual ego service industry.

Heterosexuality is the political system within which we are all born, within which we all live — whether we call ourselves women, wives, mothers, feminists, straights, queers, dykes. But it is a political system, or as Adrienne Rich argues, a compulsory political institution which affects us all differently.[6] Some of us are privileged within it, financially protected by the heteropatriarchal state, if we play our cards right and as long as our luck holds. We are never secure. Some of us are caged, controlled, destroyed. Some of us are marginal to the structures of the institution. It does none of us any good. Of course there is a difference between heterosexuality as an institution and as lived experience. The two cannot be seen as identical. But neither can they be severed.

The initial animus of the 1960s and 1970s feminist critique, was directed against three things: men, femininity and heterosexuality. Men were then perceived to be our masters, our owners, and often, in no uncertain terms, the enemy. They were the bosses and we were the work force on strike. Femininity merely amounted to men's constructions of women. 'Woman' therefore, could be reinterpreted, reinvented. Heterosexuality — with all its manifold ramifications of marriage, motherhood, the family, unequal pay, a double daily work shift, violence against women — was the political régime within which women were kept down. Heterosexuality was endorsed by patriarchal religions, all patriarchal religions. Heterosexuality promoted Noah's Ark, a great sea of happy couples. Feminist writers challenged normative constructions of the categories which shaped our lives and rewrote, with astonishing confidence, the meanings of 'woman', 'mother', 'love', 'lesbian'.

The most powerful medium for early feminist speculation, theory, feeling and analysis, was poetry. The Onlywomen Press collection *One Foot on the Mountain: An Anthology of British Feminist Poetry, 1969-1979*[7], reflected the 1970s women's movement, both its strengths and its limitations. The poets were all white and most, but not all of them, were younger women. They were usually educated and privileged. Many of the writers included in the anthology went on to become well known in mainstream British writing or in the academy: Alison Fell, Michèle Roberts, Micheline Wandor, Zoë Fairbairns, Judith Kazantsis, Sheila Rowbotham. *One Foot* was a classic collection of work which touched all the raw spots: problematic sisterhood, foul sex, child abuse, violence, the unequal distribution of labour and of wealth, our ambiguous passion for our mothers, women's work, lies in language, lesbian love.

The format of the book reinstated the author, who was then, at the beginning of the 1980s, being abolished by avant-garde English departments all around the country, with a vengeance. The contributors were arranged according to first names, not according to their patriarchal surnames. Each writer's work is introduced with a photograph and a brief personal statement. Some of the women played games with this. Aspen presented herself with an image of two leaves and described herself thus:

> ASPEN JOYCECHILD WOMAN.
> *Aspen (populus tremula) is a tree with trembling leaves and interesting autumn colouring. She has a light, porous, but surprisingly tough wood, which burns slowly. She is quite unsafe near buildings as she can cause soil shrinkage which disturbs the foundations. The female variety is extremely unpopular with nursery-men as her hairy catkins blow everywhere and are extremely difficult to eradicate. Always rich in insect life, aspen is a thirsty tree preferring swamps, river gravels, and mountain screes. She began as a sucker in Derby and is at present growing in Fife* (Mohin. 27).

The first poem of her contribution develops this extended metaphor of the tree woman who cannot thrive on forestry commission land. So the author is both revealed and concealed, masked and impertinent.

Many of the poems in *One Foot* deal with the sexual narratives that were largely unspoken, unwritten in the public space before the advent of feminism. Caroline Halliday's 'Confession' explores all he ambiguities of child abuse, the priest, significantly entitled Father, interfering with the young Catholic girl:

> The steering wheel pressing into my back.
> So I sat there. he's an uncle really.
> It was the kind of hard. slimey feeling of his tongue.
> The taste. and prickly. too.
>
> They stand over you. and make you eat it. at school.
> You have to go through with it.
> No explanation.
> Praying it will be over soon.
>
> Confession. going to confession.
> Taking me in the car.
> Fasting three hours. Eating won't work for getting out of it.
> If I tell ...
> Him. he's the priest. He said 'Love'. then he said.
> 'Don't tell' (Mohin. 54-5).

Abuse, especially sexual abuse, always depends on some elements of complicity in the victim. At the end of this long, circling, narrative poem which presents the family context, the parental respect for and trust in the church, which makes the continuation of abuse possible, Halliday notes that the girl tells her sister not to go alone with the priest. But doesn't tell her why. Warning her sister is the beginning of resistance. The final refusal of complicity is to write the poem.

The lesbian love poems in *One Foot on the Mountain* address both the peculiar, erotic mirroring of sameness and the tensions and difficulty of even the most minor struggles within intimacy; as in Lilian Mohin's 'sleep/power':

> who falls asleep first
> is about power ...
>
> back to back
> or head to breast
> we sleep well together
> when we sleep.
> well.
> together
>
> but sleep is rare
> and I gobble it first ... (Mohin. 144).

But the love poems in the anthology are not only from lover to lover. There are love poems addressed from daughters to mothers, from mothers to daughters and from granddaughters to grandmothers. Lilian Mohin, who edited the volume, dedicated the collective work to her mother. But there is no easy celebration of an uncomplicated sisterhood here. There are also poems of quite startling physical disgust and revulsion directed towards the mother. The myth of 1970s' idealised sisterhood of all women has actually been constructed by the opponents of feminism to discredit that Utopian ideal, which may never have been achieved, but was certainly desired. The writing from the period itself reflects tensions, ambiguities, difficulties. The fact that sisterhood, like pure socialism, has never yet existed is not a reason to abandon the dream.

The contradictions and hypocrisies of heterosexuality are teased out: by Michelene Wandor, who picks apart the representation of women in men's poems ('Some Male Poets', in Mohin, 189-90), and Zoë Fairbairns who writes about hetero-sex with venemous irony:

> the thing you'll like best about going to bed with men
> is their pleasant politeness.
> lips that would say ughnastyswampycunt
> dip tastefully to kiss it (Mohin. 250).

Oral sex and men's disdain for women's cunts, is picked up in Winterson's *Written on the Body*:

> How long is it you've been married? The perfect public marriage. Ten years. twelve? And you don't ask him to put his head between your legs because you think he'll find it distasteful (*WB* 45).

Written on the Body is a clever, duplicitous text. By concealing the gender of the narrator, Winterson avoids writing a Lesbian text about the affair between two women shattering a rotten marriage, but a text which gives the (male) heterosexual reader plenty of room to feel smug. I am not like that husband, he can say to himself, I have been let off. The structures of heterosexual marriage are not the issue at stake in the relationship between Elgin and Louise. He can imagine that Louise has chosen a better man. Fairbairns's poem is about men, women and heterosex. No pretence and no compromise. But, more on this later.

The most persistent, recurring subject in feminist fiction and poetry of the 1970s and the early 1980s, is the problem of language itself. The languages and discourses we have inherited not only distort, mask, and conceal the meanings attempted, the meanings struggling to become meanings, but actually reinscribe the structures of power, which are coercive and destructive. Thus, the priest in Caroline Halliday's 'Confession' describes his assault on her innocence as "Love". Sheila Shulman's in 'HARD WORDS, or Why Lesbians Have to be Philosophers', struggles with the identities thrust upon us by the outside world. She assembles a rogue's gallery of insults from the discourse of queer-bashing:

> queer bent deviant sick
> perverted abnormal unnatural (Mohin, 218-21).

Even now, many years on, queer and bent are only chic when queers claim them as their own words, and it would take some ingenuity to be proud of the rest of the list. Janet Dubé writes abstract verse, largely devoid of metaphors, but she is acute concerning feminist silence, the possibility and difficulty of making meanings, the need to choose

> between speech and silence
> both of which will tell our truths
> and tell our lies. for neither
> speech nor silence is our own (Mohin, 107).

This is a nexus of ideas that have haunted feminist writing and theory for nearly thirty years: speech, silence, truth, lies. Dubé never lets go of the paradoxes and contradictions. As she says:

> Nothing we say's to be trusted
> Nothing we say's a lie (Mohin. 103).

Language, in our mouths, becomes unstable. But the meanings are no longer predetermined elsewhere. And meanings matter.

If I have given the impression that *One Foot on the Mountain*, as a representative anthology of early feminist writing, contains a jubilant crew of man-haters and lesbians, bent on disrupting the settled order of men's power over meanings, language and texts, then this is accurate and I am delighted. The good news is that Jeanette Winterson's novels are filled with some of the same things.

Winterson was born in 1959. She is part of the second generation of women writers influenced by feminism. Her work has been received as lesbian writing, which is, nevertheless, of interest to a wider (heterosexual) public. She has had formidable commercial success. *Oranges Are Not the Only Fruit* won the Whitbread First Novel award and was made into a successful television film. Her work appears upon university syllabi and day schools of academics assemble to ponder her meanings and meditate upon her texts. I think that we need to account for this. Partly, it is a matter of timing. Feminism became more comfortably installed within the academy, by popular demand, in the early 1980s. I would argue that this process has also involved the domestication and neutralisation of feminism, but that even so, its presence is by no means secure, and that now, in the 1990s, the insights of feminism are belittled and ignored and its unfashionable extremist rhetoric is discredited.

But Winterson's fiction is not uncomfortable, gritty or realist, peppered with rant. She is oblique, literary, playful. She writes explicitly for an olympian intelligensia. Her heroines, with the possible exception of Dog-Woman and the odd dancing princess, were never interested in changing the world. If the world is full of sin, so be it.

Oranges Are Not the Only Fruit is a comic *bildungsroman*. Novels about growing up are nearly always also novels about escape. The family from which the young Jeanette escapes is the evangelical religious community which forms her first home. The relationship between mother and daughter is at the centre of the book. Here Winterson's concerns directly echo those of early feminism. The mother/daughter dyad was a key subject for theory and fiction, especially since it was an area of enquiry that had been so foolishly ignored by early Freudian theory. Winterson's alter ego, Jeanette, is left hopelessly sitting in the wake of her mother's electronic evangelism at the end of *Oranges*:

> I stared into the fire. waiting for her to come home. Families. real ones. are chairs and tables and the right number of cups. but I had no means of joining one. and no means of dismissing my own: she had tied a thread around my button. to tug when she pleased (*O* 176).

The button here is the belly button, the umbilical cord, the omphalos link between women. The adored, dominating mother must always be left behind, but her influence is inescapable.

For most of us, our first overwhelming experience of love is for our parents. Our love may not be returned. We may in fact have a harrowing experience of rejection and frustration in our first love. But our love for our parent, or parents, whatever their sex, or indeed their sexual orientation, is also a relationship of dependency and possession. They own us. We have no rights, no redress. Even if we have the good fortune to be loved in return, our first experience of overpowering love is of powerlessness, desire and demand. The love of a child for a parent is a profoundly unequal love. We are helpless in our desires; hence the aggression which characterises the expression of most children's love for their parents. We are socialised into our heterosexual gender roles in infancy; and this process of socialisation will vary enormously from culture to culture. Straightening out our passions when the first body to which we are attached is always a woman's body, is never a simple business. Arguably, few women ever do achieve total heterosexual socialisation, but this nexus of passion, anger and powerlessness seems to be universal — and dangerous.

I believe that this obsession with difference, otherness, inequality in our sexual desires is rooted in childhood, parenting and in our first family relationships. Our primary learning of love is from our parents, or the people who parent us. The first body we love is usually a woman's body. The first passion we have is for another woman. In a Lesbian relationship the mother/daughter bond is echoed rather than repeated. It is largely from our mothers that we learn how to be women. And for most of us, this is also the first experience of lies and betrayal. For it is the mother who teaches us how to be feminine, second-class, second-rate. And even when she affirms us as agents, as empowered beings who can choose our own lives, it is rare that she will tell us the truth about heterosexuality, about patriarchy, about men. It is rarer still, that she will tell us how not to be women, how to get out. The primary relationship between women within patriarchy is ambiguous, an ugly mesh of betrayal, confidence, truth and lies. Very often we cannot afford to tell each other the truth. Sometimes we don't dare. Winterson's representation of the mother contains all the strengths and ambiguities of early feminist writing. Her concern with the mother/daughter bond and its indissoluble passionate oppressiveness addresses an issue that is central to feminism.

Winterson's representations of passionate love, sexual, homosexual and otherwise are all drawn along the same lines, the lines laid down in *Oranges*: 'I want someone who is fierce and will love me until death and know that love is as strong as death, and be on my side for ever and ever. I want someone who will destroy and be destroyed by me' (*O* 170). The young Jeanette, like Sir Percival on the quest, sets out to find that love.

Her heroine, transformed into the web-footed Villanelle in Winterson's third novel, *The Passion*, finds this destructive love with the Queen of Spades. *The Passion* is a postmodern historical novel about obsessions. There are two quite distinct fictional spaces in the text: the unending, mobile Napoleonic wars, the world of the 'Grande Armée', traversing Europe, and the watery city of masques and disguises, Venice. The relationship between a wealthy married woman with a handsome palace and a wandering boatman's daughter is hardly an equal one. The comradely heterosexual relationship Villanelle has with Henri looks like a better bet. But the Queen of Spades has stolen her heart away. Literally. So she does not, cannot love him.

The lesbian affair between Villanelle and the Queen of Spades appears to have a sinister dimension. Winterson's heroines usually fall for unscrupulous married women. When Henri rescues his lover's heart, he finds that the Queen was in fact something of a witch, busily engaged in turning Villanelle into an art work:

> Why was she so upset? Because if the tapestry had been finished and the woman had woven in her heart, she would have been a prisoner forever (*P* 121).

In fact, Winterson's heroines spend as much time escaping from doomed, imprisoning love as they do searching for the fresh sensation of new passion.

Winterson's most recent fictions, *Written on the Body* and *Art and Lies* address the classic territory of queer fiction. She offers the gender-bending text, *Written on the Body*, where the narrator's sex is never officially revealed, although plenty of suggestive sex takes place. *Art and Lies* is a fragmented sequence of voices which inhabit an entirely fictional space. Lesbian love, sexual abuse and a medical castrato all eventually melt into the final trio from Strauss's *Der Rosenkavalier*, the full musical score which concludes the text. Both novels refuse to be imprisoned within the conventional structures of fiction.

In *Written on the Body* Winterson uses straightforward first-person narrative. Incidently, this is the only option if you want to be cagy about the narrator's sex. Then she fragments that text into a meditation on the actual structures of the body when the Beloved is revealed to be dying of a mysterious form of lymphocytic leukaemia. This section of the book directly recalls Monique Wittig's revolutionary text *Le Corps Lesbien*.[8] Although this was never a best-seller among Anglo-Saxon readers, *The Lesbian Body* had something of a cult status among lesbians. The text addresses the radically different sexual dynamics between two women, which will never occupy the same trajectory as heterosexual passion. The lesbian body is not only mirrored, it is already shared. Wittig describes a split subject in which the "I" (j/e) and the you, are already almost indistinguishable from one another and in which no part of the body is taboo.

Winterson's sections on the body itself, the body as metaphor, the body as map, terrain, mountain, occupied territory, are the most poignant and intriguing part of the book. These sections form the centre and link her work to a distinguished tradition of experimental lesbian writing. But the context presents a problem. The relationship between the narrator and his/her lover Louise, is never declared to be a lesbian relationship. Louise, with her fabulous body, sexy petticoats, décolleté dresses and malicious wimp of a husband, is all woman, the mistress of cliché, the prize. Winterson has to use heterosexual clichés if she is to preserve the possibility of her narrator being a man. To me, this closes down rather than opens up the possibilities in the text. And it has implications for the dynamics of the eternal triangle. The most intense (and the most interesting) relationships are between Elgin and the narrator, and between Elgin and Louise. The mystery love at the centre of the text is a curious void. We see and hear far more about Elgin's childhood than we do about Louise's early life. Why did she marry him? This is certainly a question worth asking, but we never really get to see who she is. She is beauty, the object of desire, the lover's fantasy projection, and not much more. When the lovers are finally re-united, the book ends.

The other problem with this text is the plot. 'Why is the measure of love loss?' (*WB* 9). The book opens with an acute question. But the mechanics used to engineer the imminent loss of the Beloved are crude in the extreme. An interesting, delicate, wasting cancer is wheeled on to increase the pressure on the lovers and to raise ordinary household and garden adultery to the level of Wagnerian tragedy. I can quite understand why Winterson chooses a rare cancer. Women's lives are usually destroyed by breast cancer or cancer of the bowel and colon. Neither of these is sufficiently genteel. Breast cancer means disfiguring mutilation and horrifying pain. Bowel cancers usually mean a colostomy and a constant sweet stream of shit into a surgical bag through a hole in the abdomen. None of this is either lyrical or poetic.[9]

So, for this reader at least, *Written on the Body* is a text full of lost opportunities. Winterson refuses to write an 'out' lesbian novel. Why should she? Fair enough. But I think that she is losing more than she gains, because the wonderful echo of *The Lesbian Body* stands at the centre of the book, and glitters like an obalisque, a monument to what the text might have been.

Art and Lies, an altogether stranger, less conventional text, has the courage of its convictions. Here, the queer text sets its own terms. Winterson unsettles her readers at once by giving her three characters famous names: Handel, Picasso, Sappho, and then transforming their identities to her own ends as they step from history into fiction. The trio from *Rosenkavalier*, given as musical score, is not a monstrous piece of self-indulgence. This is queer fiction, and the opera, as art form, is queer to the core.

Queer, like opera, calls attention to the instability of gender. Queer undermines fixed, settled, heterosexual discourses. The binary opposition between masculinity and femininity is fluid and unstable. It always was. And that is why it was so carefully policed. The pastiche dress codes of queers signal our engagement with and refusal of heterosexual binary divisions. Gender is performance. The body becomes ambiguous. Therefore, power and knowledge cannot be so easily allocated to the masculine in queer discourses. Queer is a gender game. Direct action rather than lobbying is characteristic of queer politics, just as it was within the original revolutionary moment of feminism. Queer is an attitude, a look, a style. Queer calls attention to itself. Queer is cheeky, provocative, subversive. So far, so good.

The attraction and wonderful energy of queer politics is obvious. I would rather be surrounded by slogans that proclaim: SILENCE = DEATH and CHEERS QUEERS, the slogans which taste of opposition and dissent, than retreat into privacy and seclusion as many ex-radicals have done before me. And I am all for putting the sex back into sexual politics and the camp into campaigning. Queer theory has put Lesbian and Gay studies on the academic map, invaded cultural politics, advertising, television, cinema, given homosexuals of both sexes a new visibility and, with its suggestive politics of cross-dressing, provoked new debates about sexuality and gender. The best of queer emotion is pure, undiluted rage. Here is Winterson's strength. *Art and Lies* is a polemical book, an angry book. It is not delicate, playful or self-indulgently vain. There is something at stake.

The three characters who generate Winterson's text are all alienated, dissatisfied, seeking and on the move. Sappho is searching for the woman she saw attempting to fly from the window ledge of family values. Picasso is escaping from an abusive family and her incestuous brother. 'Until I was fifteen, my brother used me, night after night, as a cesspit for his bloated adolesence' (*AL* 42). Handel is trying to escape from his past and his sinking sense of self-worth. The two women are lesbians and therefore not quite women. Handel is not quite a man.

He is, in fact, a castrato. Hence, the link with opera. There has been something of an outbreak of interest in castrati in recent years. In the Franco-Italian film, *Farinelli, Il Castrato* (1994), the historical figure of Handel is a key player, who faints during the high notes. Margriet de Moor's best-selling novel *The Virtuoso*, explores similar territory: a very queer sexual passion between a Neapolitan lady and the castrato, Gasparo. What she finds erotic in Gasparo is the fact that he is utterly unlike other men:

> Never had I seen such a body before. Until now men had possessed hard. exposed forms ... Gasparo is soft. white. curved. His skin is hairless. I open my arms ... I take a lock of his hair...It's thick and glossy like that of a woman.
>
> But with a woman it's different. Kissing her body (and feeling her breasts nudge against yours). means kissing a gorgeously magnified version of yourself ...
>
> His body is not like that of a woman. Though his skin is velvety and his nipples slightly raised ...[10]

Winterson's Handel belongs to this indeterminate sex, neither man nor woman. It is intriguing to reflect that manliness, or virile masculinity according to this economy of desire, is less alluring to women. Furthermore, manhood lies not in the penis, which, even in the case of castrati, is capable of sustained erection, but in the balls. The castrati phenomenon parallels the rise of interest in the edges of gender, queer bodies and queer art.

Sappho too is associated with the figure of the hermaphrodite, once a common classification for the lesbian. 'The word made out of fire and fire from the word, Sappho, 600 BC, or call her Hermaphroditus? The boy-daughter, girl-son, the male drill in the female stock, born out of a night of lust between Hermes and Aphrodite' (*AL* 74). But even while she keeps her eye on her goal, the project of queering high art objects, Winterson never loses sight of her political sources. Queer themes never quite suppress the politics of feminism and the analysis of the heterosexual system. Women would do well to love one another. Nobody else is going to love them. Here is Handel's view:

> Men prefer one another. I am quite sure of that. women are a kind of indulgence. I don't expect my Arab friend to like them. he doesn't. but I find it odd when my heterosexual friends don't like them either. My colleagues don't like their wives (*AL* 97).

Winterson could never have written these sentences without the insights of feminist theory, without Adrienne Rich's essay 'Compulsory Heterosexuality and Lesbian Existence' and Germaine Greer's succinct observation that women have very little idea of how much men hate them. Winterson is writing in the aftermath of feminism, but the echo still reverberates through her texts.

It was for only a brief time, ten years perhaps, from the mid-1970s to the mid-1980s, or even barely ten years, that the two political categories 'lesbian' and 'woman', came into a radical conjunction within a public and political discourse. 'Lesbian' and 'woman' were united within feminism as theory and as praxis. To decide to be Lesbian was to attempt a different way of thinking and being. To decide to be Lesbian was to choose women, not as we were, or as we are, but as we could become. Woman was something other than woman, to be a woman was to be an active creator of revolutionary change, a subversive, a rebel, a saboteur.

FEMINISM IS THE THEORY, LESBIANISM IS THE PRACTICE. So the old slogan says. In that particular historical moment, the women's movement in Britain was supported by a broad front of left-wing activism, Greens, trade unionists, environmental campaigners, CND, anarchists, Rock Against Racism, Gay Liberation. Socialism was not a dirty word. Feminists were not the only ones demanding a society that was more free and more just. We were not alone. But this is no longer the case. The red tide has ebbed.

There have always been Lesbians and there have always been women's communities, but they have not always seen themselves as part of a revolutionary movement. Lesbians have not always identified with women, nor have they seen themselves as dissidents. To be different is not necessarily to be in a state of rebellion. In fact, you may long to mask your difference, be desperate to conform. Lesbians have, for centuries, existed peacefully within romantic friendships, bisexual arrangements, or closet marriages. Sometimes we have taken risks, cross-dressed and lived as men. We have evolved subtle parodies and masquerades of heterosexual structures in butch/femme lives, we have lived differently, either flaunting it, or underground.

But the revolutionary moment of feminism, a moment of Utopian joy and possibility, was unique in asserting that there were no entry qualifications: that you did not have to cross-dress, be an invert, be different, cut your hair, be born dyke. 'A lesbian is the rage of all women condensed to the point of explosion'. All you had to be was explosively angry at the way you were treated and the little that you got. All you had to want was freedom. All you had to love was women. Whatever that meant to you. And the meaning of woman was up for grabs. So was the meaning of Lesbian. We were making our own meanings. All you had to be was a woman in the process of becoming Lesbian. Woman was no longer a fixed point of closure, but a dynamic process. We were women in movement, a movement of women.

Over the last ten years, I have watched the gradual separation of Lesbianism from feminism and inevitably, Lesbian from woman. Lesbian is now part of a single corporate entity: the new firm LESBIAN 'n' GAY, or subsumed into the new product, QUEER. Lesbians choosing to identify themselves as queers in Britain are, in the main, young women. They are a post-feminist generation. And they see feminism as their mother's politics, a politics which may once have had something going for it, but which is now, like the somewhat redundant patriarchy — not the monolith it once was — also outdated and smelling of lies, betrayal, prohibitions and taboos. Cherry Smyth explains:

> The attraction of queer for some lesbians is flavoured by a rebellion against a prescriptive feminism that had led them to feel disenfranchised by the lesbian feminist movement ... the importance of identifying politically as a lesbian had obscured lesbianism as a sexual identity.[11]

And sex, indeed SEX, defiant, perverted, flagrant, on your backs, in your face, is now the name of the queer game. Lesbian sex is, in itself apparently, a subversive, political act. Feminism has atrophied into boring politically correct rules, mother saying no. Queer dykes are the new radicals, the new sexual outlaws. Doing anything with anybody might well be fun, but I find it hard to see how sex can be the source of revolutionary change. It was never the right to screw ourselves senseless in private that was in question; it was the right to gather socially, organise politically and dispute the heterosexual hegemony that caused trouble. Queer is a politics of demand. But the demand ends with the group who makes that demand.

The break with feminism is complete 'because queer theory ultimately displaces patriarchal gender hierarchy in favour of heterosexuality as the primary regulatory system. It is vitally important for feminism that we see heterosexuality as a gendered hierarchy and not just as a normative construction of cross-sex desire'.[12] Being queer may well be an alternative to femininity, and to being woman within the heterosexual ideology, but we cannot escape the political régime of heterosexuality by wishful thinking; unless we pack our bags and head for the greenwood as some women have decided to do. I think that separatism is both an important strategy and a radical solution. But it can't be our only solution. Subversion is the other alternative. And that has been Winterson's method.

Every revolutionary movement appears to pass through eerily similar phases: the first years of celebration and manifestos when the old order totters or at least has the grace to appear to do so. Demands are drawn up and the Golden Age is at hand. Then come the darker times of impatience at the slowness or absence of change, the rigid imposition of what had once been the radical dream, and finally the brutal divisions into the pure and the impure with purges to prove the point. Then, if the movement is not defeated altogether, there are the years of underground struggle; long, slow years of hard work, disappointment and imperceptible change. And so it has always been with feminism. Political and sexual structures do not, unfortunately, exist only in the mind. And even lies that have been recognised as such take centuries to displace. Change need not be progressive. Women's movements have been obliterated, suppressed, vanished — without trace. I am not optimistic, because I do not live in optimistic times.

NOTES

1. Judith Butler, *Gender Trouble: Feminism and the Subversion of Identity* (London: Routledge, 1990) 20.
2. Ibid.
3. Stevi Jackson, 'Gender and Heterosexuality: A Materialist Feminist Analysis', in *(Hetero)sexual Politics*, ed. by Mary Maynard and Jane Purvis (London: Taylor and Francis, 1995) 11-26, 13.
4. Monique Wittig, 'The Straight Mind' (1980), in *The Straight Mind and Other Essays* (Brighton: Harvester Wheatsheaf, 1992) 32.
5. Radicalesbians, 'The Woman Identified Woman' (1970), in *For Lesbians Only: A Separatist Anthology*, ed. by Julia Penelope and Sarah Lucia Hoagland (London: Onlywomen Press, 1988) 17.
6. Adrienne Rich, 'Compulsory Heterosexuality and Lesbian Existence', in *Blood, Bread, and Poetry: Selected Prose, 1979-1985* (New York: W. W. Norton and Company, 1986) 23-75.
7. Lilian Mohin, ed, *One Foot on the Mountain: An Anthology of British Feminist Poetry, 1969-1979* (London: Onlywomen Press, 1979). All further page references will be given after quotations in the text.
8. Monique Wittig, *Le Corp Lesbien* (Paris: Les Éditions de Minuit, 1973). The text itemises all parts of the body, including obscure bones, in huge block capitals, at intervals.
9. I must declare an interest. I have had cancer myself and am therefore inclined to take it seriously. I have read dozens of books describing clean, poetic cancers and know that they don't exist. For the unpoetic version, see Gillian Rose, *Love's Work* (London: Chatto & Windus, 1995) and *Cancer Through the Eyes of Ten Women*, ed. by Patricia Duncker and Vicky Wilson (London: Pandora Press, 1996).
10. Margriet de Moor, *The Virtuoso* (Amsterdam: Contact Publishers, 1994; translated by Ina Rilke, Picador, 1996) 72-73.
11. Cherry Smyth, *Lesbians Talk Queer Notions* (London: Scarlet Press, 1992) 26.
12. Stevi Jackson, 'Gender and Heterosexuality: A Materialist Feminist Analysis', in *(Hetero)sexual Politics*, 18.

The Erupting Lesbian Body: Reading *Written On The Body* as a Lesbian Text

Cath Stowers

THE prominent — and explicit — position of issues of sexuality and gender in Jeanette Winterson's work has often surrounded her novels with controversy and debate. *Written on the Body* was perhaps the novel which most fuelled the media fire raging against Winterson, and I aim here to refute critical reaction to the novel which has accused her of ignoring the impact of gender and of replicating heterosexual paradigms of conquest and 'Otherising'. In this sense, I hope to make interventions in the debates surrounding Winterson, and engage with the slating critical reception with which the novel was met. In particular, I hope to counteract the frequent decentring of her lesbianism in the reception of her texts, resurrecting her work instead as, indeed, specifically lesbian. Whilst I do, of course, acknowledge recent work by those such as Lynne Pearce and Gabrielle Griffin which does not ignore Winterson's lesbianism, my point is that very little criticism has engaged with Winterson's work *as a whole* as lesbian texts, or considered the possibility of a consistent lesbian aesthetic running through her novels.[1]

I believe the dissidence of Winterson's work should not be lost. Part of the pleasure of her texts lies in their problematising of gender and sexual difference, and I hope to highlight the trajectory in her work that exceeds a gendered logic towards a specifically lesbian reconceptualisation of female desire. Winterson's lesbian identity has a tremendous bearing for me on how her fictions operate. While recognising poststructuralist suspicions of direct equations between the author and her text, it is simultaneously vital to counter-act the frequent disavowal or decentring of Winterson's lesbianism in the reception of her texts.[2] But it is not only her recent reception by the media which has made her portrayal of gender a contentious issue. As Lynne Pearce has pointed out, many feminist readers and critics have felt cheated by Winterson's handling of gender, while Winterson herself has further problematised the issue with her reluctance at being cast as a 'feminist' or 'radical lesbian'.[3] Nonetheless, she is without doubt a self-promoting, visible and *out* author, at other times making it abundantly clear that the contours of female authorship are here defined in specifically *lesbian* terms.[4] I believe it is crucial to posit her works in a discourse of specifically lesbian desire, thus correcting any tendency that would elevate the meaning of her work to a transcendental or universal realm which is supposedly separable from any issue of sexual politics. Because of my convictions, issues of lesbian methodology will consequently prompt a particular set of considerations in my argument.

But my aim is to suggest only one *possible* reading of, and route into, Winterson's work. Offering a reading of *how* Winterson's texts might mean — rather than *what* they mean

— this essay aims to stress the productive role of the reader in her work, to trace the possibilities for a lesbian reading. But this is not to claim that this is the one 'correct' reading. As I will suggest in my conclusion, this novel is also open to a *bisexual* reading. My point is that although the questioning of heterosexual authoring, textuality and narrative in *Written on the Body* and its corporeal explorations do provide openings for the lesbian reader, they also provide routes for other readers and readings too.

Winterson's works are increasingly concerned with the multi-faceted dimension of female sexuality. Fantasising with the reality of female desire, she is perhaps above all else concerned with *experimenting* how to write female pleasure, by, in her own words, 'redefining the erotic in terms of female rather than male experience'.[5] Interrogating time-tested formulae which have circumscribed female sexuality, Winterson's characters journey to and explore uncharted territories with specifically female aims, ones that promise escape routes from a terrain which involves exclusionary dialogues and imaginations. Throughout Winterson's work, female characters frequently excavate the female body in a re-appropriation and parodying of the power of the phallus.[6] In *Written on the Body*, these corporeal explorations are often figured in terms which are admittedly initially highly suggestive of the penetration of the passive female body by the active male:

> I began a voyage down her spine. the cobbled road of hers that brought me to a cleft and a damp valley then a deep pit to drown in (*WB* 82).

At one point, the narrator refers to her/his self as an 'intrusion, stroking you with necrophiliac obsession' (*WB* 123) and this almost neurotic, fixated yearning to hold on to Louise does indeed become figured at times, in terms of anatomical possession and penetration:

> I took her two hands to my mouth and kissed each slowly so that I could memorise the shape of her knuckles. I didn't only want Louise's flesh. I wanted her bones. her blood. her tissues. the sinews that bound her together (*WB* 50-1).

This apparent replication of heterosexual patterns of travel, exploration and desire, has led to particularly fierce criticism of the novel. A common reaction to the text has been the claim that Winterson has failed to escape the dynamics of possession and conquest, presenting little more than a tale of unpleasant obsession and exploration of the other, inextricably implicated in the discourse of both colonialism and heterosexuality. Valerie Miner, for example, has argued that Winterson initially 'promises a subversive portrayal of androgynous passion' only to fall into a romance which is 'disappointingly conventional'.[7] Yet in her previous works — especially *The Passion* and *Sexing The Cherry* — Winterson effects a deconstruction of gender roles and of paradigms of 'Otherising' and conquest.[8] I find it hard to believe that she would suddenly contradict and negate what appears to be a central line of theme and intent by returning to a dynamics of possession, and it is thus my contention that, rather than backtracking on her previous works, *Written on the Body* in fact continues along the same trajectory. In this text, too, from initially following male models, the narrator only rejects them in favour of more female paradigms.

It is my assertion that the narrator's excursions and explorations into Louise's body are not reiterations of masculine penetrative pioneering into passive femaleness, but are rather an instance of Catherine Stimpson's claim that 'lesbianism partakes of the body, partakes of the flesh'.[9] Anatomical investigations can, I believe, at least partly be read as the expression of that lesbianism which 'represents a commitment of skin, blood, breast and bone'.[10] Despite the gender ambiguity of the narrator, woman's body is here portrayed in a positive light — if the narrator is a woman, we have a lesbian celebratory reclamation of the female form; if a man, a rare male acknowledgement of no passive idealised body but one empowered. Even though Louise's body is 'turning upon itself' (*WB* 105), it is still a body with 'unfolding power' (*WB* 131). Here there is 'nothing distasteful' about its 'sweat', 'grime', 'disease and its dull markings' (*WB* 124). Indeed, continuing that tradition of lesbian writers who equate the female form with the generative, brewing qualities of blood and yeast,[11] woman's body is good enough to eat:

> The smells of my lover's body are still strong in my nostrils. The yeast smell of her sex. The rich fermenting undertow of rising bread. My lover is a kitchen cooking partridge. I shall visit her gamey low-roofed den and feed from her (*WB* 136).

There is, however, more going on here than any simple reclamation of woman. Rather, gender signifiers are repeatedly mixed. For example, woman is 'well-hung', and the narrator her/his self is aligned with Napoleon, who would reputedly request Josephine not to wash for his return: 'Three days without washing and she is well-hung and high' (*WB* 136). But *Written on the Body* goes further still, beyond any gender reversal. The use of a bisexual, ungendered narrator undoubtedly suggests that this text is Winterson's most radical attempt to escape from both sex and gender, yet the controversy and criticism with which *Written on the Body* has been met is largely due to this very character. Valerie Miner, for example, has claimed that although initially 'the concealment of (the narrator's) sex forecasts interesting theoretical questions about essentialism', Winterson fails to 'carry these identity questions beyond the gimmick'.[12] I want to offer my own interpretations of this narratorial figure, drawing on lesbian theory and work on the performance of genders. In particular, I want to suggest that although Winterson's narrator is not simply portrayed as a lesbian, s/he still fulfils distinctly lesbian aims. As such, s/he is an example of what Zimmerman has identified as the 'deconstruction' of the lesbian as 'an essentialist ... being' and 'the reconstruction of her as a ... subject position'.[13]

Winterson's reasons for using an ungendered, bisexual character are, I believe, similar to Monique Wittig's arguments in *The Straight Mind*. For Wittig aligns the sign 'lesbian' with neither masculinity nor femininity, but rather uses it to highlight the duplicity of division between the two and to problematise heterosexual definitions of sex and gender. Following the trajectory of these arguments, it is possible to view Winterson's genderless narrator as an attempted escape from the effects of gender dichotomies, which for women aims, in Wittig's words, at 'the division of Being', and a simultaneous attempt to deprive them of subjectivity. The 'imposition of gender', to quote Wittig further, denies women 'any claim to the abstract, philosophical, political discourses that give shape to the social body'.[14] As an ungendered ambiguity, however, the narrator of *Written on the Body* is free to pick and plunder varying masculine discourses, in particular analysing and dissecting the languages of medicine and of exploration. I hope to show how the narrator can be read as the lesbian subject who trespasses the forbidden space of male-centred letters, only to move into a desirable lesbian writing which can write desire. Extending the playings-with-genders of both *The Passion* and *Sexing the Cherry*, s/he is now in keeping with Wittig's arguments that the 'refusal to become (or to remain) heterosexual always meant to refuse to become a man or a woman'.[15]

For not only does Winterson make her narrator negate the traditional role of woman as passive object of exploration and quest by having her/him follow masculine paradigms, but also, in ultimately rejecting such models, she posits her narrator as an almost perfect illustration of Wittig's claim that lesbianism is far more than 'a refusal of the *role* "woman"'; it is also 'the refusal of the economic, ideological, and political power of a man'.[16] By tracing the narrator's turning away from the path of masculine models of conquest and possession to a more reciprocal duality of desire, I hope to show how the narrator represents just such a 'refusal'. This rejection of masculine, heterosexual paradigms leaves me with little doubt that this narrator is indeed female. The absence of any declaration of gender is not suggesting that gender has no power, but rather that gender dichotomies can be upset. As Judith Roof has argued, it is possible to perform a masculine persona without necessarily accepting it. In *Written on the Body*, the narrator can be viewed as just such a performer of masculinity, enacting Judith Butler's strategies of gender parody to reveal the originals as also constructed and imperfect. In this way, gender's restrictive operations are negated, leading to a remapping of that 'polymorphous space' where, in Roof's words, 'the layering of genders explodes heterosexual presumptions by denying the correlation between biology, gender and sexuality'.[17] In this way, as Paulina Palmer has pointed out, in line with 'the perspectives of Queer Politics', this ungendered narrator challenges 'the conventional division between homosexuality and heterosexuality'.[18] That totalising hegemony of heterosexuality which Wittig defines as 'the straight mind' is unsettled and the latter's claim that it is inevitable that a lesbian '*has* to be something else, a not-woman, a not-man' becomes a deliberate and subversive strategy.[19] Winterson puts the very concept of 'woman' under erasure and displaces the phallic body and subject (of exploration, of medicine, and of language) with a lesbian body and subject founded on reciprocity. This displacement is achieved, I believe, by the use of tropes of bodily journeys and explorations in *Written on the Body*. For the female body explored here is as highly charged as Emily Dickinson's 'Loaded Gun',[20] and is set in opposition to that clinical body posited by medical discourse:

> My lover is cocked and ready to fire ... She consumes me when she comes in thin white smoke smelling of saltpetre. Shot against her all I want are the last wreaths of her desire that carry from the base of her to what doctors like to call the olfactory nerves (*WB* 136).

And if this is an empowered, celebrated female body set against the discourses of anatomy, this is because ultimately such male paradigms are rejected as bankrupt and exploitative.

Whereas in *The Passion* travel tropes were used to figure history, and in *Sexing the Cherry* to picture seventeenth-century cartography and naturalist expeditions, here exploration represents the narratives of medicine. Winterson seems here to be focusing on the rules that come into play in the very existence of scientific discourse, utilising medical discourse and anatomical classifications as representative of (male) attempts to represent, colonise, 'Otherise'. Those patterns of anatomical investigation figure the dynamics of heterosexual desire, and illustrate the fact that female sexuality, as Luce Irigaray has pointed out, has not only been theorised within 'masculine parameters' but also based on a phallomorphic conception of women's bodies.[21] Ultimately, Winterson's narrator surely analyses and parodies such paradigms only to reject them, as attempts at control and pervasion of the Other are exposed as sadly lacking love and passion:

> What are the characteristics of living things? At school, in biology, I was told the following: Excretion, growth, irritability, locomotion, nutrition, reproduction and respiration. ... What of the other characteristic prevalent in human living things, the longing to be loved? (*WB* 108).

The narrator tries to 'embalm' Louise 'in my memory', to 'hook out' her 'brain through ... accommodating orifices'. But although stating that 'Now that I have lost you I cannot allow you to develop, you must be a photograph not a poem' (*WB* 119), s/he finally rejects the masculine, clinical, dissecting language of male science and 'Within the clinical language, through the dispassionate view of the sucking, sweating, greedy, defecating self', finds 'a love-poem to Louise' (*WB* 111). Following the trajectories of medical exploration only to find that 'The logical paths the proper steps led nowhere' (*WB* 92), the linearity of attempted penetration and possession becomes re-figured in imagery reminiscent of Winterson's labyrinthine towns and interior cities rich with pluralities of interpretation: 'My mind took me up tortuous staircases that opened into doors that opened into nothing' (*WB* 92).

If, then, the travel tropes of anatomy are rejected, what does Winterson offer in their place? The answer is a journeying which remaps that old mythic, heterosexual structure of desire where woman as sexual Other is the goal of the quest, and which traces instead radical relationships of reciprocity. Travel and exploration become powerful metaphors for dynamics of desire, the questing after woman a central dynamic as the narrator desperately tries to snatch Louise from the ravages of cancer. But Winterson now re-negotiates love from a contemporary lesbian-feminist perspective, negating the heterosexism of medical discourse which has no space for lesbian desire: 'No, it doesn't come under the heading Reproduction. I have no desire to reproduce but I still seek out love' (*WB* 108). Roles are recast from traditional active male/passive female figures to active lesbian lovers, and, appropriating phallocentric, heterosexual metaphors and symbols, experimenting with romantic love and its traditional heroes, Winterson proceeds to lesbianise them.

Whereas Jon Stratton has argued that the construction of the trope of exploration is 'one signal of the dispersal of the epistème of resemblance',[22] here exploration only leads to a reciprocal lesbian desire which is like Irigaray's positing of a female sexuality where individuality and singularity are meaningless. Remapping those old dichotomies of lover and beloved based on heterosexuality and domination into an almost fluid and fluctuating exchange of self and other, suggested symbolic gender differences become undercut by lesbian metaphors of sameness. Clinical explorations based along masculine lines become rejected in favour of reciprocal journeys where Self and Other can exchange positions as objects of the quest. Hence, the narrator also becomes the one to be chased, telling how 'I covered my tracks so that Louise could not find me' (*WB* 106). This undoubtedly becomes a dual, reciprocal exploration, where the Other is no passive land waiting to be penetrated but is also actively involved. This is not the conventional pattern of the seducing Self and the seduced Other; here seduced can become seducer, almost an example of Catherine Clément's:

> relationship with the other that is not yet stable but metastable — uneasy, such that one can pass without fixed identity from body to body: ... from woman into woman.[23]

Instead of the linear goal-orientated plot of traditional treasure hunts, therefore, the narrator explains how 'A treasure had fallen into our hands and the treasure was each other' (*WB* 99). This exploration is not concerned with setting and defining boundaries, but with re-mapping, transgressing, and merging. The narrator has no investment in any simple taking or conquest of the Other, instead giving her/his self as a source of pleasure and reversing that paradigm of active male explorer and passive female land by figuring her/his self in those very terms:

> you will redraw me according to your will. We shall cross one another's boundaries and make ourselves one nation. Scoop me in your hands for I am good soil. Eat of me and let me be sweet (*WB* 20).

This is a reciprocity like Clément's 'continuous awareness of "the other" within the self', an undifferentiation which results in the failure of the narrator's attempts to possess Louise through anatomical knowledge, with her/him unable to view her/his lover objectively as 'the private drawing' s/he keeps of Louise 'will be a poor reproduction ... if you are broken then so am I' (*WB* 125). Although 'In doctor-think' the human body becomes 'a series of bits to be isolated' (*WB* 175), the narrator ends up admitting her/his inability to fit into such clinical paradigms:

> If I come to you with a torch and a notebook, a medical diagram and a cloth to mop up the mess, I'll have you bagged neat and tidy ... Womb, gut, brain, neatly labelled and returned. Is that how to know another human being? (*WB* 120).

Any efforts to separate and analyse only lead to recognitions of unity and connection, an alternative doppelgänger reflection to that offered by patriarchy's mirror stage:

> Nothing about you has faded. You are still the colour of my blood. You are my blood. When I look the mirror it's not my own face I see. Your body is twice. Once you once me. Can I be sure which is which? (*WB* 99).

Hence the narrator's attempts to reduce her beloved to the clinical flesh, skin and bone of anatomical medicine are doomed to failure, for this is a decidedly dual anatomy: 'Bone of my bone. Flesh of my flesh. To remember you it's my own body I touch. Thus she was, here and here' (*WB* 130). Medical explorations only lead her/him to an awareness of their similarities and an eradication of that difference 'rated to be the largest part of sexual attraction' as 'there are so many things about us that are the same' (*WB* 129).

I would thus here again challenge Miner's claim that *Written on the Body* is 'not so much about sex or understanding or communion as about annexation', for I am arguing that Winterson rejects masculine heterosexual paradigms of the annexation of the other. Similarly, I disagree with Joan Smith's argument that the novel 'cannot conceal its cruelty, the bloody chamber beneath its opulent facade'.[24] Although reviewers of *Written on the Body* have occasionally grudgingly admitted that 'the appropriation of traditional male rhetorics is unsettling', there appears to be a failure to consider the possibility of irony or parody.[25] I would concur with Smith's claim that 'This violent language speaks not of love but of rage and jealousy', but I would also add that this is a language which is used throughout the text as being representative of male paradigms, and which is ultimately rejected. The models of desire, travel and exploration finally posited by the narrator, on the other hand, are based on an alliance between Self and Other which becomes so strong, that her/his body becomes the site of a love so reciprocal that disease too becomes dual: 'The worms that will eat you are first eating me ... A dog in the street could gnaw on me, so little of substance have I become' (*WB* 180). Hence, the initial discovery of Louise's cancer leads to the narrator's own bodily disintegration, as 'my body slithers away' (*WB* 101), and s/he can only mourn 'She was my twin and I lost her' (*WB* 163) and plead in the lyrical language of love poetry to be rescued from the battlefield of anatomy's discourse: 'Do you see me in my blood-soaked world? Green-eyed girl, eyes wide apart like almonds, come in tongues of flame and restore my sight' (*WB* 139).

The narrator could be said, then, to surrender her/his self as masculine subject, coming close to Cixous' femininity which can succeed at 'keeping alive the other that is confided to her, that visits her, that she can love as other'.[26] Attempting to solve the dilemma of using a language to express gender which is limited to heterosexist assumptions, Winterson deconstructs the fact that gender is constructed according to heterosexual norms. In this sense, she seems to be an example of those lesbian writers de Lauretis has discussed, who have striven to solve such dilemmas by 'pursuing diverse strategies of writing and of reading the intransitive and yet obdurate relation of reference to meaning, of flesh to language'.[27]

Written on the Body employs decidedly lesbian intentions towards textuality and representation itself, revealing traditional paradigms of narrative and authoring as heterosexist. Judith Mayne has argued that one of lesbianism's 'strategically important' functions lies precisely in the problem it poses for representation. Lesbianism questions, Maine continues, representation's 'alignment of masculinity with activity and femininity with passivity'.[28] These are precisely the gendered binaries which Winterson confronts. In freeing up gender and sexual difference and writing lesbian desire, Winterson in fact complicates — and *exceeds* — the actual terms of that narration. She has defined the novel, after all, as an attempt to 'challenge the way that people read at all', and it is my assertion that, ultimately attempting to portray the lesbian excess in patriarchal, heterosexual narrative, *Written on the Body* aims to disrupt language and genre to open up that new space Wittig and Irigaray have both called for which 'privilege(s) lesbian as the place of a new alterity'.[29] Like them, Winterson also goes, in Farwell's words, 'beyond the sexuality of characters', positioning the lesbian 'in the revision of the binary structures of male/female, subject/other, presence/absence of Western narratives'.[30] The narrator travels to a lesbian narrative space which is a disruptive space of sameness instead of that difference which has structured traditional (heterosexist) narrative. In this way, the novel attempts to solve that dilemma identified by Farwell — namely, how to encode female desire in a plot structure which is basically heterosexual?[31]

In my thinking about the challenges posed to representation by *Written on the Body*, I have also found Foucault's arguments on medical discourse useful. Foucault has argued that the modern epistème is at least partly characterised by knowledge's preoccupation with generating the most perfect representation possible, a preoccupation most clearly expressed in the deployment of a scientific method and the appearance of multifarious classificatory systems.[32] Following this line, it could be argued that Winterson is also interrogating the relationship between anatomical discourse and representation, using tropes of bodily exploration to reconceptualise both sexuality and textuality along lines of reciprocity. For in rejecting medical paradigms in favour of reciprocity, textuality itself is also remapped along reciprocal lines. Deconstructing the category of the lesbian Other, the only 'Otherising' that is done is of the lesbian Self, and writing becomes like Cixous' women's writing which is 'undoing death's work by willing the togetherness of one-another', and which is 'infinitely charged with a ceaseless exchange of one with another'.[33] With the novel written for/to Louise, Winterson clearly belongs in that lesbian aesthetic of which Gubar has written, where 'writing 'for' the beloved other' challenges:

> assumptions about the autonomy/authority of the author and the singularity of the subject: to use the language of Gertrude Stein ... to be 'one' is to know oneself as 'two'.[34]

More than this, the efforts to penetrate and write Louise's body, to turn her body into a text of 'blood vessels that write the body's longing' (*WB* 124), ultimately entail making the narrator's own body into the text:

> Your hand prints are all over my body. Your flesh is my flesh. You deciphered me and now I am plain to read. The message is a simple one: my love for you (*WB* 106).

Whereas traditionally male writers have often written the female body as something viewable, penetrable — by the pen/penis and the male voyeuristic gaze — and ultimately knowable and possessable, here the narrator makes it clear that the female body is not so easily plumbed, and it is the Self of the authoring narrator, not the Other, who frequently wants to be possessed. Any revelation is only of a reciprocity which is written *on* the body, and which even then consists of a palimpsest beneath the surface. This, then, is a release from the stultifying binary of heterosexual authoring and narrative, resulting in a similar effect to Cixous' 'other bisexuality':

> starting with this 'permission' one gives oneself, the multiplication of the effects of desire's inscription on every part of the body and the other body.[35]

So instead of that anatomical colonising and pioneering of the body, here body literally becomes text, the body of the text becoming anatomical body dissected into parts, and desiring body and desiring text writing each other. I turn here to Alice Parker's work on Nicole Brossard, for a particular comment on Brossard's lesbian aesthetic is, I suggest, highly applicable to *Written on the Body*:

> The many figural pleasures of the text evoke the multiple surfaces of the body, making love through/to the text, the author/reader turn (each other) on: the act of writing (reading) was never so physical.[36]

Taking apart meaning and textuality as created from the viewpoint of the phallic body, in rejecting anatomical probings in favour of reciprocity, the narrator proceeds to re-construct it from the viewpoint of the lesbian body. The 'body' of the title which is 'written on' is that of the narrator, but this is no simple translation of body into text: instead woman and femaleness are articulated as a hidden palimpsest:

> Written on the body is a secret code only visible in certain lights: ... In places the palimpsest is so heavily worked that the letters feel like braille. I like to keep my body rolled up away from prying eyes. Never unfold too much, tell the whole story. I didn't know that Louise would have reading hands. She has translated me into her own book (*WB* 89).

This is a lesbian version of that female authorship identified by Gilbert and Gubar, its story, its mode of self-division, often read as a 'palimpsest' through the script of the dominant narrative.[37]

Literature becomes the trace of writing, as the word becomes the embodied inscription of lesbian writing, an example of Meese's lesbian writing which 'wants to evacuate patriarchal discourse in order to re-write writing'.[38] Text becomes articulated as a female space lying immersed behind the superimposed alien patriarchal gloss. Beneath the surface of patriarchal maps, the palimpsest left behind on the narrator's body is 'a map of belonging' (*WB* 135). This new lesbian corporeality of narrative can be said to further place Winterson in a similar aesthetic project to that of Nicole Brossard:

> The skin of a woman which slides on to the skin of another woman provokes a sliding of meaning creating the possibility of a new version of reality and of fiction.[39]

Sexuality is not easily translatable into textuality, and I again challenge Miner's claim that 'relentless conceit reduces the narrator to a tattoo artist'.[40] Winterson may be interested in portraying a celebratory 'tattoo' of the female body, but the only other tattoo is inner, not that conventional phallic etching on the 'blank page'[41] of woman's body, but rather that interiority of meaning which can only be reached by a re-mapping of that which is usually left invisible, and a reciprocity of Self and Other, writer and reader:

> The moulds of your teeth are easy to see under my shirt but the L that tattoos me on the inside is not visible to the naked eye (*WB* 118).

Attempts to explore any passive female body, attempts to travel after the beloved which have possession as their aim, have thus now been aligned with attempts to author the Other, to turn the body of the female Other into a text penned by the (male) self. Although the narrator parodies those models represented by male explorer/doctor/author via her/his bodily explorations, s/he ultimately suggests that masculine paradigms are redundant as far as lesbian desire and textuality go, and instead the author becomes authored by the Other:

> Articulacy of fingers, the language of the deaf and dumb, signing on the body longing. Who taught you to write in blood on my back? ... You have scored your name into my shoulders, referenced me with your mark. The pads of your fingers have become printing blocks, you tap a message on to my skin, tap meaning into my body (*WB* 89).

The narrator ultimately turns away from the linearity of masculine patterns and realises that with Louise they are 'Sunk in each other' (*WB* 91). Instead of the traditional textual questing after woman and meaning figured so strongly by the image of the maze,[42] textuality becomes rewoven as an intertwined reciprocity. Whereas traditionally Ariadne's thread, according to Nancy K. Miller, becomes 'Domesticated' from being a possible 'agency' of female desire to 'the enabling fiction of a male need for mastery', here that single twine is slashed, the paradigm unravelled, re-fabricated, re-spun, to enable the freeing up of lesbian desire.[43] Rachel Blau DuPlessis, after all, has argued that 'the erotic and emotional intensity of women's friendship' succeeds in cutting 'the Gordian knots of both heterosexuality and narrative convention'.[44] So although earlier articulating the relationship in terms of the traditional questing and climbing after the beloved, the model finally becomes re-woven into dual reciprocity:

> I want the hoop around our hearts to be a guide not a terror. I don't want to pull you tighter than you can bear (*WB* 88).

According to Stratton, traditional travel writing had a vital role to play in the privileging of representation as 'the form of knowledge', entailing an experiencing of the Other as 'a diminished, a lacking representation of presence'.[45] The paradox of classical and modern epistèmes, therefore, was that:

> it was only by exclusion, by the allowal of an excess which was experienced as 'beyond' representation, that presence could be claimed as the privileged moment in the structure of representation.[46]

I want to extend Stratton's argument here to point out that what is often relegated to that space of Otherness and absence, is in fact Woman. More than this, given that phallocentric culture tends to associate lesbianism with marginalised excess, it is not surprising that the unrepresentability of lesbianism posits it as narrative excess. It is exactly this excess with which Winterson is concerned. Her deconstruction of the binaries male/female, absent Other/present Self, and margin/centre, leads to a freeing up of sexual difference which enables a writing of precisely this excess. Hence, the questioning of presence's hegemony, which focuses more on 'the beloved's image as absent-marginal' than as 'present-central'.[47] Louise is present only for the initial part of the novel; after that, the dynamics of discovery and representation are transcultured into a framework of nostalgia and loss. This calling of presence into question recognises presence as inadequate to representation and tropes a new lesbian narrative. Rejecting both the sexuality and textuality of traditional metaphorics, dissecting and analysing masculine modes of being, the narrator abandons the earlier re-appropriation of various narrative techniques — the differing modes of letter, dramatic form (*WB* 14-15), and, of course, medical text book. Rejecting the bodily inventories of male anatomical discourse, *Written on the Body* allows the eruption of a monarchic lesbian voice.

Ironically usurping tropes of questing after the Other and of corporeal explorations, *Written on the Body* can be read as an almost perfect illustration of Shoshana Felman's definition of irony as that which drags authority 'into a scene which it cannot master ... and which, for that very reason, is the scene of its own self-destruction'.[48] Detonating medical discourse, the lesbian body produces its own innovative narrative, an example of Shere Hite's claim (worth quoting in full) that:

> when a woman writes ... about female desire, female sexuality ... her performance has the effect of giving voice to pure corporeality, of turning a product of the dominant meaning system into a producer of meanings. A woman, conventionally identified with her body, writes about that identification, and, as a consequence, femininity — silent and inert by definition — erupts into patriarchy and an impossible discourse.[49]

It is precisely such an eruption, of the *lesbian* body, into the 'impossible discourse' of anatomy, that Winterson achieves.

This excess is perhaps best symbolised in the final scene of *Written on the Body*, where Winterson lesbianises Donne's portrayal of love's ability to 'make one little room an everywhere'.[50] Although here the closing scene of the novel is set in a microcosm —

> The windows have turned into telescopes. Moon and stars are magnified in this room. The sun hangs over the mantlepiece. I stretch out my hand and reach the corners of the world. The world is bundled up in this room (*WB* 190)

— it is a microcosm which erupts, as if lesbian desire cannot be confined: 'The walls are exploding' (*WB* 190). The earlier dissections of the text are thus rupturing even more, the novel shattering into the space of bursting lesbian desire. And this lesbian desire detonates male paradigms, rupturing male models of travel, gender, desire, and fracturing patriarchal systems of signification. With no resolution or closure, no reaching the end of that single twine of string, *Written on the Body* is instead like Cixous' women's writing which 'can only go on and on, without ever inscribing or distinguishing contours' and which 'dar(es) those dizzying passages in other'.[51] In returning to the beginning at the end — 'This is where the story starts, in this threadbare room' (*WB* 190) — the text produces a new space beyond chronological time and speaks to us from the place of the permanently desiring subject as the lesbian quest continues. For Louise, the narrator 'would gladly ... go and not look back' (*WB* 81), and in an ambiguous, infinite, open-endedness, we are thus left with the image of the two female lovers embarking on another never-ending journey, a travelling to new horizons. The lesbian subjects exchange the castrated space of erasure for a never-ending horizon of desire. This may not be the traditionally assured happy ending; as Lynne Pearce has claimed, the reason for the prominence of travelling and journeying in lesbian works may well be the fact that romantic love between women is without the possibility of institutional legislation, the 'bid for unity' thus 'permanently set against a sense of invisibility, transience and exile'.[52] One thing, however, is certainly sure — that Winterson's reworkings of tropes in *Written on the Body* has assured that this will be a decidedly female journeying, a wandering into an expansion rich with possibilities of swaggering dual travel:

> Beyond the door, where the river is, where the roads are, we shall be. We can take the world with us when we go and sling the sun under your arm. Hurry now, it's getting late. I don't know if this is a happy ending but here we are let loose in open fields (*WB* 190).

Written on the Body can thus provide insights into what a distinctly lesbian aesthetic may look like, suggesting potential figurations of an enduring lesbian battle with gender binaries. The main characters in all of Winterson's novels remodel themselves more as woman, following pleasures which are suggested to be more female, pleasures of palimpsestic representation instead of official exclusionary paradigms; of fluid multiplicity instead of phallic singularity. Perhaps most importantly, these are also pleasures of mixed genders instead of male or female. In this light, it could be salient to question whether Winterson is experimenting with bisexuality as a possible subject position and narrative tactic to escape from heterosexual gendering. Yet this bisexuality is used, I suggest, with specifically lesbian aims. Future research could thus question the interaction, the playing off and between each other, of bisexual and lesbian subject positions, considering the ways that alternative, dissident sexualities engender new configurations of narrative practice and textuality. The implications of a bisexual narrative practice which may be employed with lesbian aims could clearly warrant further analysis, providing as it does innovative and seductive de- and re-codings of mixed gendered and fluid identities. It is here that the most liberatory prospects on offer become clear, for such work enables a critique of the ways not just female but also male sexuality has been categorised. I should perhaps close, therefore, with a comment by Judith Roof on the exhilarating possibilities proffered by playing with genders:

> Allowing the play of differences, allowing flux, dismantles categories and analogies and enables us to see instead the potentially increased understanding that exists in those places 'between the lines', which might ultimately erase the rigid categories represented by those lines.[53]

As Winterson herself argues in *Oranges Are Not the Only Fruit*, as 'Walls protect and walls limit', it is consequently 'in the nature of walls that they should fall' (*O* 110).

NOTES

1. See Lynne Pearce, *Reading Dialogics* (London: Edward Arnold, 1994) and Gabrielle Griffin, *Heavenly Love?: Lesbian Images in Twentieth-Century Women's Writing* (Manchester University Press, 1993). Lisa Moore is the only other writer I am aware of who has addressed the corpus of Winterson's work as lesbian. (Lisa Moore, 'Teledildonics: Virtual Lesbians in the Fiction of Jeanette Winterson', in *Sexy Bodies: The Strange Carnalities of Feminism*, ed. by Elizabeth Grosz and Elspeth Probyn [London: Routledge, 1995]).
2. This is an area covered by Hilary Hinds's work on the varying reactions to lesbianism in the television adaptation of *Oranges Are Not the Only Fruit*. Although it may have been acknowledged as part of the novel's humour, a regrettable intervention or an adolescent temporary phase, the lesbianism of the book and of the author were certainly not viewed as being of any import to the meaning of the work. (Hilary Hinds, '"Oranges Are Not the Only Fruit": Reaching Audiences Other Lesbian Texts Cannot Reach', in *New Lesbian Criticism: Literary and Cultural Readings*, ed. by Sally Munt (Hemel Hempstead: Harvester Wheatsheaf, 1992) 153-73).
3. Lynne Pearce, *Reading Dialogics*.
4. In an interview in *The Guardian*, for example, Winterson declares 'that it is impossible for a woman in a heterosexual relationship' to 'give herself wholeheartedly' to writing. (Claire Messud's interview with Jeanette Winterson, *The Guardian*, 26 August, 1992, 29).
5. 'Jeanette Winterson on Female Erotica', *Marie Claire*, December 1992.
6. See, for example, *SC* 54.

7. Valerie Miner. 'At Her Wit's End'. *The Women's Review of Books*. April. 1993.
8. See Cath Stowers, 'Journeying with Jeanette: Transgressive Travels in Winterson's Fiction'. in *(Hetero)sexual Politics*. ed. by Mary Maynard and Jane Purvis (London: Taylor and Francis. 1995) 139-159.
9. Quoted in Patricia Duncker. *Sisters and Strangers: An Introduction to Contemporary Feminist Fiction* (Oxford: Blackwell, 1992) 169.
10. Ibid.
11. The reader can. for example. look at Adrienne Rich's *Blood, Bread, and Poetry: Selected Prose, 1979-1985* and Audre Lorde's *Zami: A New Spelling of My Name* (especially 77-8). Winterson also appears as an example of Cherrie Moraga's claim that the lesbian writer brings 'female sexuality with all its raggedy edges and oozing wounds ... into the light of day' (in her autobiographical manifesto *Loving in the War Years*).
12. Valerie Miner. 'At Her Wit's End'. op.cit.
13. Quoted in Paulina Palmer. *Contemporary Lesbian Writing: Dreams, Desire, Difference* (Buckingham: Open University Press. 1993) 30.
14. Monique Wittig. *The Straight Mind* (Hemel Hempstead: Harvester Wheatsheaf. 1992) 81.
15. Ibid., 13.
16. Ibid.
17. Judith Roof, *A Lure of Knowledge: Lesbian Sexuality and Theory* (New York: Columbia University Press. 1991) 249.
18. Paulina Palmer. *Contemporary Lesbian Writing*. 112.
19. Monique Wittig. *A Straight Mind*. 13.
20. I am referring here to Emily Dickinson's poem 'My Life Had Stood A Loaded Gun'.
21. Luce Irigaray, *This Sex Which Is Not One* (Ithaca. NY: Cornell University Press. 1985) 63.
22. Jon Stratton. *Writing Sites: A Genealogy of the Postmodern World* (Hemel Hempstead: Harvester Wheatsheaf. 1990) 49.
23. Hélène Cixous and Catherine Clément. *The Newly Born Woman* (Manchester University Press. 1986) 19.
24. Valerie Miner. 'At Her Wit's End', op. cit.; Joan Smith. 'Grazed Anatomy'. in *The Independent on Sunday*. 12 July, 1992.
25. *The London Review of Books*. 24 September. 1992.
26. Cixous and Clément. *The Newly Born Woman*. 86.
27. Cited in Karla Jay and Joanne Glasgow. eds. *Lesbian Texts and Contexts: Radical Revision* (New York University Press. 1990) 4.
28. Judith Mayne, 'Lesbian Looks'. in *How Do I Look: Queer Film and Video*. ed. by Bad Object-Choices (Seattle: Bay Press. 1991) 127.
29. Jeanette Winterson. interview in *Spare Rib*. 209. February 1990. Marilyn R. Farwell. 'Heterosexual Plots and Lesbian Subtexts: Towards a Theory of Lesbian Narrative Space'. in *Lesbian Texts and Contexts: Radical Revision*. ed. by Karla Jay and Joanne Glasgow, 93.
30. Ibid.
31. Ibid., 95.
32. Michel Foucault. *The Order of Things* (London: Tavistock, 1970).
33. Cixous and Clément. *The Newly Born Woman*, 86.
34. Susan Gubar. 'Sapphistries' in *The Lesbian Issue: Essays from Signs*. ed. by Estelle Freedman. Barbara Gelpi. Susan Johnson and Kathleen Weston (University of Chicago Press. 1985) 109-10. This writing to Louise can be observed on *WB* 88 and also in the inclusion of an actual letter to her on *WB* 105-6. On instances such as *WB* 178. the 'you' shifts from Louise to the reader. creating a further sense of reciprocity between writer and reader.
35. Cixous and Clément. *The Newly Born Woman*. 85.
36. Alice Parker. 'Nicole Brossard: A Differential Equation of Lesbian Love', in *Lesbian Texts and Contexts*. ed. by Karla Jay and Joanne Glasgow. 311.
37. Sandra Gilbert and Susan Gubar. *The Madwoman in the Attic: The Woman Writer and the Nineteenth-Century Literary Imagination* (New Haven: Yale University Press. 1979) 73.
38. Elizabeth Meese. 'Theorizing Lesbian: Writing — A Love Letter', in *Lesbian Texts and Contexts*. 80.
39. Alice Parker, op. cit., *Lesbian Texts and Contexts*. 305.
40. Valerie Miner. 'Grazed Anatomy'. op.cit.

41. See Susan Gubar. '"The Blank Page" and the Issues of Female Creativity'. in *The New Feminist Criticism*. ed. by Elaine Showalter (London: Virago. 1986) 292-314.
42. See. for example. Nancy K. Miller 'Arachnologies'. in *The Poetics of Gender*. ed. by Nancy K. Miller (New York: Columbia University Press. 1986).
43. Ibid., 284-5. Feminist critics have also explored the motif of the maze in medieval literature in terms of the female body and female writing. See R. Evans and L. Johnson, 'The Assembly of Ladies: A Maze of Feminist Sign Reading?'. in *Feminist Criticism: Theory and Practice*. ed. by Susan Sellers (London: Harvester Wheatsheaf. 1991).
44. Rachel Blau DuPlessis. *Writing Beyond the Ending: Narrative Strategies of Twentieth Century Women Writers* (Bloomington: Indiana University Press. 1985) 149.
45. Jon Stratton. *Writing Sites*. 2.
46. Ibid., 4.
47. I'm taking my lead here from Shaktini's essay 'Displacing the Phallic Subject: Wittig's Lesbian Writing'. as Winterson does. I believe. adopt similar methods (in *The Lesbian Issue*. ed. by Margaret Cruikshank [Monterey: Angel Press. 1980] 137-153).
48. Quoted in Judith Mayne. 'Lesbian Looks'. op. cit.
49. The use of metaphysical wit in *Written on the Body* has been pointed out by Paulina Palmer in *Contemporary Lesbian Writing*. 112.
50. Cixous and Clément. *The Newly Born Woman*. 87.
51. Lynne Pearce, unpublished essay. 'Jane Eyre Eat Your Heart Out: Jeanette Winterson's Re-Reading of Romantic Love in "Oranges Are Not the Only Fruit"' (1990).
52. Judith Roof. *A Lure of Knowledge*. 236.

THE PASSION: STORYTELLING, FANTASY, DESIRE

PAULINA PALMER

For Cambridge Lesbian Line

Trust me. I'm telling you stories (*P* 40).

The Passion and Conventions of Lesbian Narrative

THE Passion is one of the most intricate of Winterson's novels and, as is often the case with works of postmodern fiction,[1] it achieves much of the fascination it holds for the reader from the inventive manipulation of tension and contradiction. Though creating an exceptionally intense representation of lesbian desire, it utilises a male narrator and centres, in the first half, on the masculinist arena of war. It is a work of historiographic metafiction which, while focusing, as the title signals, on the characters' 'passions', is equally concerned, as the frequent references to the motif of storytelling indicate, with their transmutation into the realm of art. It is a fiction of history which recounts a sequence of events set in the past — but does so with an eye on their relevance to the present. These tensions furnish the starting-point for my discussion of the novel. In the following pages I aim to investigate them and tease out their significance.

To clarify the first aspect of *The Passion* mentioned above, the interaction which the novel displays between masculinist and lesbian elements, Winterson cleverly links the two, resolving the apparent contradiction between them, by means of the radical treatment of her male narrator Henri. It is, in fact, Henri, the French peasant who works as Napoleon's cook during his military campaigns, who first introduces the themes of sexual politics and love between women, thus paving the way for the transformation of the text from a study of relations between men in the camp and on the battlefield into an analysis of lesbian love. Winterson's portrayal of Henri, in deconstructing conventions of sexual difference, bridges the gap between these two different worlds. Henri displays traits conventionally regarded as 'feminine', such as sensitivity and a distaste for killing, and is ridiculed by his fellow soldiers for being unmanly. Domino, the midget employed as Napoleon's groom, tauntingly depicts him as 'a young man brought up by a priest and a pious mother. A young man who can't pick up a musket to shoot a rabbit' (*P* 28).

As Domino implies, Henri is deeply attached to his mother and, as a consequence, sympathises with women's oppressed position. He is aware of the suffering which they endure and recognises the way men neglect and ignore them. Commenting on the tendency of the male sex, particularly when waging war, to dehumanise women, he observes:

> We never think of them here. We think of their bodies and now and then we talk about home but we don't think of them as they are; the most solid, the best loved, the well known (*P* 27).

In addition to alerting the reader to women's oppressed plight, Henri also introduces the topics of compulsory heterosexuality and lesbian relations, both of which are integral to the novel. The account he gives of his mother's enforced marriage — she agrees to marry only because her parents prevent her from fulfilling her religious vocation and entering a convent — and his description of the brutal treatment to which the cook subjects a prostitute in the local brothel, slapping her face and forcing her to perform fellatio, illustrate the pressures, social and physical, which coerce women into engaging in sexual relations with men. In recounting the incident at the brothel, Henri focuses attention on the prostitutes' attempt to protect each other from male assault and describes the tender kiss which one bestows on the other. This marks, in fact, the first reference to love between women in the novel.

In introducing themes of sexual politics and lesbian relations, Henri prepares the way for the entry of Villanelle, the Venetian girl who loses her heart to the mystery woman she terms 'the Queen of Spades' and acts as the signifier of lesbianism throughout the text. Role reversal and the deconstruction of sexual difference are as much a feature of her portrayal as they are of his. Whereas Henri exemplifies attributes conventionally regarded as feminine, Villanelle displays qualities typecast as masculine, such as daring and initiative. In pursuing her love affair with the Queen of Spades, she even dresses as a boy, making the most of the opportunity to engage in crossdressing which the Carnival festivities furnish. The topic of compulsory heterosexuality, introduced by Henri in his account of his mother's enforced marriage and his description of his visit to the brothel, is developed in the portrayal of Villanelle and her adventures. Though engaging in sexual relations with men, she seldom does so from choice but, like Henri's mother and the prostitutes whom he encounters, is motivated by social and economic pressures. Her marriage to the physically repulsive 'rich man with fat fingers' (*P* 96), whose hands, she recollects with disgust, 'crept over her body like crabs' (*P* 98), is an act of pragmatism which she performs in order to escape from Venice, an environment which has become intolerable to her on account of the termination of her love affair with the Queen of Spades. The role of *vivandière* in Napoleon's army, which she subsequently adopts, occurs as the result of a wager in which she unwillingly features as prize and object of exchange. Her sexual encounter with Henri, though voluntary, is an isolated event which, either despite or because of the fact that he has fallen in love with her, she seldom permits to be repeated. She cares for him, she remarks, not as a lover but in 'a brotherly incestuous way' (*P* 146). In fact, the one and only intense sexual involvement she experiences is the relationship which she forms with the Queen of Spades. This, despite the fact that it lasts a mere nine days, represents one of the chief examples of 'passion' alluded to in the novel's title.

Winterson's delineation of Villanelle's trajectory, in foregrounding the pressures which prompt her to relate sexually to men and highlighting the brevity of her amour with the Queen of Spades, disproves the assertion, voiced by Lisa Moore in her critique of the novel, that Winterson's representation of lesbianism lacks political resonance since, according to Moore, it fails to engage with the issue of homophobia and depicts lesbian relations in hetero-patriarchal society as in no way 'problematic'.[2] The reason for the abrupt termination of Villanelle's relationship with the Queen of Spades is that the latter, in keeping with the patriarchal conventions of the era, is married. A particularly moving incident, one which depicts the position of the lesbian in hetero-patriarchy as 'problematic' in the extreme, is the episode in which Villanelle, positioned in the marginal role of outsider and voyeur, to which throughout history the lesbian has generally been relegated, gazes through the window of the Queen of Spades's villa and watches her conversing with her husband in the social and financial security of the family home (*P* 75). He plants a kiss on his wife's forehead, affirming his ownership of her and signalling the control which he exerts on her life. This episode illustrates the constraints which a phallocentric economy imposes on women's lives, separating and inhibiting relations between them by curtailing their sexual and social freedom.

With the entry of Villanelle into the text, Henri's role in the narrative diminishes in importance and his agency declines. From the moment of her first appearance Villanelle appropriates the role of narrator and becomes the focus of narrative interest. Henri falls in love with her, thus attempting to relegate her to woman's conventional role of object of desire, but she successfully subverts this role. Though sleeping with him occasionally, she refuses his offer of marriage and resists his attempts to objectify her by recounting the story of her love affair with the Queen of Spades. By portraying herself not as the object of Henri's love but as the lover of the Queen of Spades, she successfully repositions herself in the narrative in the role of active agent. The contest between masculine and feminine principles for mastery of the narrative, exemplified by the interaction between the two characters, continues in the latter stages of the novel. Here Villanelle further diminishes Henri's agency by incorporating him into her territory and making him the instrument of her quest for liberation. Having persuaded him to accompany her to her native city of Venice, she manipulates him into retrieving her heart from the possession of the Queen of Spades who holds it in thrall. Thus, instead of allowing him to co-opt her into becoming an actor in his drama, she induces him to perform a part in hers.

The design of *The Passion* in which, as described above, Villanelle appropriates from Henri both the role of narrator and the focus of narrative attention, is pertinent, it is interesting to note, not only to Winterson's fiction but to lesbian narrative in general. The term 'lesbian narrative' is, in certain respects, problematic. As Marilyn R. Farwell comments, discussing the strategies which writers employ to give a work of fiction a lesbian emphasis, 'Instead of a recognisable genre, lesbian literary narrative is, in reality, a disputed form, dependent upon various interpretive strategies'.[3] It is, in addition, a construct which alters from era to era, the criteria on which it depends shifting according to the ideological perspectives and attitudes of the writer and her readership. In the 1970s and '80s, in the early years of the lesbian / feminist movement, a lesbian narrative was assumed to depend on the lesbian writer, a figure with feminist allegiances who addresses the fiction she produces to the lesbian community and focuses on clearly identifiable lesbian characters and relationships.[4] Today, however, with the writer no longer regarded as wholly in charge of the text and the concept of a lesbian identity an issue of controversy, this definition appears less valid. It is in the process of being replaced by approaches of a formal kind which, by concentrating attention on the text itself, investigate the way it constructs a lesbian subject position or creates, as Farwell illustrates, 'a lesbian narrative space'.[5] Discussing the novels of Marion Zimmer Bradley, Farwell demonstrates how the insertion of lesbian subject or relationship into the text has the effect of disrupting conventional heterosexual narrative structures and scripts, resulting in the reformulation of relations between the sexes and the refiguration of female desire. Terry Castle, commenting on Sylvia Townsend Warner's *Summer Will Show*, illustrates how in novels treating lesbian themes the triangular configuration of male homosexual desire, composed of two men and a woman, is frequently supplanted by a triangle of female desire, consisting of two women and a man.[6] The structure of *The Passion* reflects elements from both these models. The entry of Villanelle into the text and her appropriation of the role of narrator create, to employ Farwell's phrase, 'a lesbian narrative space'. Having entered this, woman ceases to play the role of object of male desire but assumes instead, as Villanelle's control of the action illustrates, the role of agent. After the failure of the Russian campaign, Napoleon disappears from the novel, and with his erasure, the focus shifts from the public arena of war to the private realm of love. The concluding section of the novel, in foregrounding the triangle of desire between Villanelle, the Queen of Spades and Henri, accords with Castle's blueprint. Henri, in retrieving Villanelle's heart from the Queen of Spades, is relegated to the subordinate role of mediator between two women, and the female relationship acquires prominence.

Passion and Storytelling

The portrayal of Henri and Villanelle, and the shifts of power which the relationship between them undergoes, as well as being integral to the tension between masculine and feminine elements in the novel and to its transformation into a lesbian narrative, also has a bearing on another feature of *The Passion* mentioned above: the interaction between Winterson's representation of the characters' passions and emotions, and her focus on their transmutation, by means of storytelling, into art. Henri and Villanelle are the chief vehicles for this — and Winterson explores their subjectivities and narrative performance with notable subtlety.

The intricacy of design which *The Passion* manifests is achieved by the mobilisation of multiple narrators and points of view, a focus on the rhetoric of storytelling, and the tendency of the narrative to shift, at certain key points, into the realm of magic realism and the surreal. These features, as well as highlighting the artifice of the novel and the narrative strategies it employs, complicate Winterson's treatment of subjectivity by problematising the notion of a simple reflectionist relation between self and text. In keeping with a poststructuralist approach to textuality and the formation of the psyche, we have the impression that, rather than the text reflecting the individual self, the subject is a relational identity constructed through discourse and textuality.

Other factors also contribute to the complexity of Winterson's treatment of subjectivity. Commenting on the representation of character in historiographic metafiction, Linda Hutcheon observes that history makes men and women, and fashions their destiny, rather than them making history.[7] This is certainly true of the portrayal of Henri and Villanelle. The subjectivities of the two, as well as the relationship between them, are depicted as produced and shaped by the historical forces of the age in which they live — in particular, the Napoleonic Wars and the climate of social disruption they generate. Forces of a psychological kind also play a part in the formation of their subjectivities. A popular concept in postmodern fiction is the creation of the self through fantasy and desire. It informs the portrayal of Zenia in Margaret Atwood's *The Robber Bride* (1993) and the representation of Aurora in Salman Rushdie's *The Moor's Last Sigh* (1995). Winterson's construction of her characters in terms of the passions dominating their psyches similarly emphasises these drives and emotions.

By 'passion' Winterson signifies the subject's obsessive involvement with the Other, the object of desire. Obsessions of this intense kind, she illustrates, override barriers of class, gender and sexual orientation, and assume a variety of different manifestations. They can be romantic, as is Villanelle's love for the Queen of Spades and Henri's for Villanelle, or they can reflect hero worship and be oedipal in nature, as is Henri's attachment to Napoleon, whom he describes as 'a little father' (*P* 81). They can be motivated by a desire for power, as is the case with Napoleon's ambitions of territorial domination, or be a matter of appetite, as is his passion, on a culinary plane, for chicken and, on a sexual one, for Josephine. They can be religious, as are the feelings of devotion which Henri's mother experiences for the Virgin Mary.

Passions of this obsessive nature, Winterson emphasises, are involuntary, irrational and, more often than not, self-destructive. Villanelle's involvement with the Queen of Spades results in her losing her heart literally as well as metaphorically, while Henri's love for Villanelle drives him to commit manslaughter, an act which results in her incarceration on the island edifice of San Servelo. Napoleon's passion for conquest, as well as giving rise to an immense loss of human life, eventually results in his defeat and death. The intensity of the passion which the individual experiences, as numerous episodes in the novel illustrate, bears little if no relation to the value of the object on which it is focused but, like the Lacanian concept of desire, is a projection of the subject's inner needs. Acknowledging the way that her infatuation with the Queen of Spades rules her life, reducing her assertive identity to a state of humble submission, Villanelle confesses that:

> Passion is not so much an emotion as a destiny. What choice have I in the face of this wind but to put up sail and rest my oars? (*P* 62).

As this quotation illustrates, Villanelle's characterisation hinges on the contraries of power/powerlessness. It is ironic that, although she appropriates the role of narrator from Henri and, in the latter stages of the text, dominates both him and the action, on the plane of desire and sexual fantasy she is ruled by forces of passion.

However, despite its frequently destructive consequences, passion is nonetheless depicted as life-enhancing. It is celebrated for its capacity to transform the individual's powers of perception and to confer an element of magic on an otherwise drab world. As Henri observes, commenting on the magnetic attraction which Napoleon exerts on himself and his fellow countrymen, the romance which passion involves is 'not a contract between equal partners but an explosion of dreams and desires that can find no outlet in everyday life. Only a drama will do — and while fireworks last the sky is a different colour' (*P* 13).

To emphasise the intensity of the obsessions dominating her characters' lives, Winterson employs religious imagery. The religious resonances in the novel's title are underpinned by the use of religious terminology in the text. The local priest refers to Napoleon as 'the New Messiah' (*P* 16). Addressing Henri, he predicts, accurately as it turns out, 'He'll call you like God called Samuel and you'll go' (*P* 17). Echoing his simile, Henri remarks on the fact that he and his fellow countrymen seek 'a vision' (*P* 7). Villanelle likewise describes the attraction she feels for the Queen of Spades in terms of spiritual faith. Commenting on the irresistible allure which the latter exerts, she states simply 'Christ said, "Follow me", and it was done' (*P* 64).

The motif of the heart, which plays a key role in the novel, also foregrounds the importance of passion. Winterson's treatment of it reworks the conceits of sixteenth-century poets such as Sir Philip Sidney and John Donne. Sidney's lyric 'My true love hath my heart and I have his' exemplifies a common topic in Renaissance love poetry: the exchange of hearts between two lovers. Donne in 'The Blossom' converses with his heart on the topic of love and, in 'The Broken Heart', describes the destructive effect which the experience of falling in love has on it. Villanelle's heart experiences a series of similarly turbulent adventures. She tells the Queen of Spades, in a manner reminiscent of Donne, 'If you should leave me, my heart will turn to water and flood away' (*P* 76). When she subsequently loses her heart, the conceit acquires literal significance in the episode in which Henri, at her instigation, breaks into the Queen of Spades's house to retrieve it. He finds it there, just as she told him he would, concealed behind a rail of clothes. This is one of several episodes of magic realism which Winterson introduces in the text. They occur at moments of particularly intense emotion, illustrating the way that our passions and fantasies have the power to transform the mundane, rational world by generating events which defy the laws of nature.

The passions experienced by the various characters, as well as illustrating the part played by fantasy and desire in the formation of subjectivity, furnish material for the stories they tell. Whether these rank as fact or fiction, oral history or flights of imagination, is frequently ambiguous. The focus placed on storytelling is important in various ways. In addition to foregrounding the fictionality of the text, it relates Winterson's account of military and social life in eighteenth-century Europe to conventions of historiographic metafiction and a postmodern approach to history. The latter, as Hutcheon illustrates, is characterised by the problematization of historical objectivity and 'truth', and by an emphasis on the partisan and provisional nature of all accounts of the past (Hutcheon, 91-101). The master narratives treating masculinist concerns such as military conquest and empire-building which we inherit from earlier periods are interrogated, and emphasis is placed instead on narratives produced by marginalised sections of the community, such as women and homosexuals. In addition, the division which, since the nineteenth-century, has been assumed to exist between history and literature, is questioned. The two discourses, as Hutcheon points out, have, in fact, much in common. Rather than being neutral, both reflect a particular viewpoint. Both, in addition, employ narrative and are linguistic constructs which have the effect of 'reshaping our experience of time through plot configurations' (Hutcheon, 100). Winterson utilizes a variety of different strategies to foreground these issues. Henri, on returning to his village after the Napoleonic Wars, alerts attention to the performative aspect of storytelling and the artifice of narrative by remarking:

> The traveller expects to change, to return with a bushy beard or a new baby or tales of a miraculous life where the streams are full of gold and the weather is gentle. I was full of such stories but I wanted to know in advance that my audience was seated (*P* 31).

Not only do Henri and Villanelle tell stories but their subjectivities and identities, like the protagonist of Winterson's earlier novel *Oranges Are Not the Only Fruit* (1985), are produced through the act of storytelling. They are formed by the processes of narrativity.

The self-conscious preoccupation with storytelling which *The Passion* displays generates an interplay of different narrative-lines in which fact and fiction merge and interact. This, combined with the propensity of the characters to interweave references to the real and the fantastic, has the effect of challenging the commonplace distinction between fact and fiction, history and literature. Henri recognises that the traveller's tale is not supposed to be wholly factual but can include reference to the fantastic and the utopic. He admits that, on returning to his native village, he did not give a true account of his adventures but 'embroidered, invented and even lied' (*P* 30). The anecdotes the characters relate, though generally employing a familiar setting, often centre on preposterous, larger-than-life events. Henri recounts incidents illustrating the exceptional powers of vision enjoyed by his comrade Patrick who reputedly has the ability to see across the Channel to the British coast, while Villanelle relates the curious origins of her webbed-feet and describes the miraculous promenade she made on the Venetian canal. The focus on the fantastic is accumulative and bizarre events increase in number as the narrative progresses. The distinction between history and fiction is blurred not only by the stories the individual characters recount but also by the phrase which acts as a refrain to them: 'I'm telling you stories. Trust me' (*P* 5). Repeated at intervals throughout the text, it emits contrary messages to the reader. The emphatic use of the 'I' persona, combined with the imperative 'Trust me', have the effect of convincing us of the veracity of the speaker's account, but this assumption of truth is undercut by the ambiguity of the word 'story' which can signify either a factual account or, alternatively, a tissue of fiction and lies. Our uncertainty about the precise nature of the story increases its fascination by raising the crucial question: Is it fact or fiction? Truth or lies?

The interrogation of the division between history and literature, life and art, along with the foregrounding of the complex nature of the issue of 'character' and 'identity' in works of fiction, come together in a feature of the novel which typifies historiographic metafiction: the combination of a historical personage, in this case Napoleon, with characters such as Henri and Villanelle who are purely fictional. The interaction of the two within a single text raises interesting questions about the significance of the referent. Do the quasi-historical figures differ fundamentally in status from their fictional counterparts? Or, since in being introduced into the text both become subject to the rules of fiction, does no significant difference exist between them? (Hutcheon, 152-7). And what effect does the interaction between the two kinds of characters, and the interplay between art and life which it represents, have on our reading of the work of fiction and the materials it treats? There are no simple answers to these questions. On the one hand, it is possible to argue that Winterson's introduction of a historical personage (Napoleon) lends historical verisimilitude to her fictional characters (Henri and Villanelle) and to the action in which they participate. On the other, one can maintain that, like the other strategies Winterson employs in composing the novel, the interplay she creates between historical personages and fictional characters has the effect of problematizing the distinction between history and literature by blurring the difference between the two. The interplay also, of course, alerts attention to the difficulty we encounter in gaining access to figures and events from earlier periods. Since no objective knowledge of them is available, they become known to us only from their textualized traces.

The Past, The Present — and Their Interrelation

Commenting on the treatment of history by contemporary novelists, Hutcheon describes historiographic metafiction as creating 'a re-evaluation of and a dialogue with the past in the light of the present' (Hutcheon, 19). This serves to introduce a third feature of *The Passion* mentioned in the introductory section to this essay: the interrelation which the novel creates between events set in an earlier period and issues relevant to the present-day. While achieving a convincing degree of historical verisimilitude, Winterson, like other writers of historiographic metafiction, is primarily concerned to foreground the tension/interaction between past and present. She simultaneously employs scenarios located in the past to create an arena where topics of contemporary significance can be encoded and explored.

The reshaping of the past in the light of present day issues in *The Passion* encompasses a wide range of topics and interests. Henri's recognition of the brutal treatment of women which war involves and his feelings of disillusion with the bloodshed resulting from Napoleon's campaigns reproduce modern debates about the futility of war and the corrupting effects of power. While highlighting the narcissism and egocentricity of leaders such as Napoleon and the destructive effects of their ambition, Winterson also exposes the naïveté and gullibility of the proletariat. As Henri himself admits, he and his companions are by no means innocent victims of manipulation. In succumbing to Napoleon's charisma and dreams of conquest, they are guilty of colluding with their oppressors and allow themselves to be exploited by the idols they themselves have created.

While the episodes set in the camp and on the battlefield give Winterson the opportunity to discuss politics in the conventional sense of war and statecraft, the city of Venice furnishes her with an arena for exploring themes relating to sexual politics and lesbian sexuality. The focal point of the episodes set in Venice is Villanelle's love affair with the

Queen of Spades. The relationship between the two women commences during Carnival, a period carrying connotations of excess and transgression — attributes which Villanelle epitomises. They are symbolised by her webbed feet, a physical feature which distinguishes her from other women. Signifying her sexual difference, they link her portrayal to the Bakhtinian concept of the grotesque body. They also relate her to conventions of representation which depict the lesbian as a figure of 'excess', in that her sexuality exceeds the image of woman as commodity and object of exchange perpetuated by patriarchal culture. In portraying Villanelle in this transgressive manner, Winterson shows herself less interested in normalising the image of the lesbian and highlighting the features which she shares with women in general than in foregrounding lesbian difference and inventing strategies of representation to express it. Her viewpoint in this respect has more in common with perspectives which, in the present era of the nineties, are associated with the 'queer' project of foregrounding lesbian difference than they do with a lesbian feminist approach which seeks to relate the lesbian to feminist community and to concentrate attention on her basic womanhood.

Discussing the portrayal of the figure of the lesbian in works of fiction, Teresa de Lauretis alerts attention to the struggle which the writer wages with language 'to dislodge the erotic from the [phallocentric] discourse of gender, with its indissoluble knot of sexuality and reproduction'.[8] In portraying the lesbian, the writer seeks, De Lauretis argues, to subvert the traditional representation of woman in the roles of wife, mistress and mother and, by 'rewriting the [female] body beyond its pre-coded, conventional representations', to 'undomesticate it and re-create it otherwise ... re-membering and reconstituting it in a new erotic economy' (De Lauretis, 149-150). To achieve this, De Lauretis maintains, she 'must dare to reinscribe it in excess — as excess — in provocative counter images sufficiently outrageous, passionate, verbally violent, and formally complex to both destroy the male discourse on love and redesign the universe'. These 'counter images', she continues, will represent the body 'perhaps as monstrous, or grotesque, or violent, and certainly also sexual' (De Lauretis, 149, 150). Winterson engages in a struggle of this kind. Influenced by the portrayal of the lesbian by earlier writers such as Djuna Barnes and Monique Wittig, as well as by the treatment of her in contemporary queer theory as a signifier of political transgression, she challenges phallocentric definitions of femininity by alerting attention to the excess which she exemplifies. This 'excess', it is important to recognise, is not the supplementary jouissance defined by Jacques Lacan which, since it is defined from a masculinist viewpoint and is attributed to woman by male specularisation is, as Elizabeth Grosz argues, 'a phallic refusal to accept an otherness not modelled on [the economy] of the same'.[9] On the contrary, it has more in common with Luce Irigaray's definition of jouissance which foregrounds the autonomy and 'otherness' of female pleasure, and aims to liberate woman from male specularization and control. Irigaray describes this as 'a disruptive excess', since it has the effect of 'jamming the theoretical machinery' of phallocentric culture.[10]

Villanelle's webbed feet, in addition to linking her to the representation of the lesbian as an image of excess, relates her to the element of water. Like Wittig, who in *The Lesbian Body* (1973) represents the beloved gliding and hovering above the sea, Winterson describes Villanelle defying the laws of gravity and walking on the surface of the Venetian canal. Villanelle's aquatic associations, combined with her sexual attraction, relate her to the motif of the mermaid, an ambiguous image of woman as beautiful seductress/unnatural monster. In fin-de-siècle art, the mermaid and siren are employed to signify the threat posed by female independence and lesbian sexuality associated with 'the new woman'. In paintings by Fernand LeQuesne and Jean-Francois Auburtin these temptresses do not ply their seductive arts alone but are portrayed involved in a lesbian embrace or as members of a perverse coven.[11] In representing Henri falling in love with Villanelle and becoming involved in her personal life, events which ultimately result in his incarceration and madness, Winterson creates an inventive variation on the motif of the relationship between mortal man and mermaid, and its fatal consequences for the former.

The grotesque body is by no means static but is described by Bakhtin as a body in 'the act of becoming', in the process of being 'continually built, created'.[12] It thus comes as no surprise to the reader to find the morphology of the lesbian body, as Winterson represents it, associated, literally and symbolically, with movement — sometimes of a vertiginous kind. A motif which recurs in *The Passion* is the feats of physical dexterity achieved by the acrobat and trapeze performer. These figures, associated by Bakhtin with the carnivalesque, are given feminine interpretation by Catherine Clément. In 'The Guilty One', Clément describes 'deviants, neurotics, women, drifters, jugglers, tumblers'[13] as members of a marginal, repressed group with bisexual associations, related to the realm of the Imaginary. Patriarchal society, she observes, regards these outsiders with a degree of ambivalence; while relegating them to the trivial realm of entertainment, it simultaneously recognises their potential for disruption and fears the threat they pose to social order. Other writers, it is interesting to note, give the acrobat and trapeze artiste a lesbian interpretation. Djuna Barnes in *Nightwood* (1936) portrays the equivocally named Frau Mann entertaining the circus audiences of Berlin with her displays of agility on the trapeze, while Wittig in *Lesbian Peoples: Materials for a Dictionary* (1976) describes how 'groups of wandering companion lovers' entertain 'the lesbian communities ... with mime, acrobatics, juggling'.[14]

Rather than carrying straightforward connotations of woman as the object of the male gaze, as Mary Russo argues they do when specularised by the male viewer,[15] the acrobat and trapeze performer evoke, in the texts of both Wittig and Winterson, an image of vitality and transgressive jouissance. They can be interpreted, I suggest, as representing a form of Irigarayan mimesis in which the lesbian or woman-identified woman parodies the role of spectacle and entertainer which phallocentric culture assigns her, utilising it for her own ends. They also signify the precarious nature of lesbian existence and the dangers, both literal and symbolic, which the woman who oversteps convention by forming primary relationships with members of her own sex encounters in hetero-patriarchal society. She risks not only the obvious danger of social stigma but also the less obvious one of being re-absorbed into a phallic, specular economy as the object of male titillation and voyeurism. In order to survive the homophobic climate in which she lives and avoid falling into the abyss of shame, she has to strive to keep her balance and maintain a sure footing on the high wire.

Winterson combines a reference to the carnivalesque body with an allusion to the precarious nature of lesbian existence when, treating the mouth as a signifier of lesbian love, she portrays Villanelle envying the acrobats who visit the city during Carnival the kisses which, while suspended from trapezes, they snatch from the lips of the passers-by; Villanelle describes how:

> from the wooden frame above where the gunpowder waits there are suspended a number of nets and trapezes. From here acrobats swing above the square, casting grotesque ... shadows on the dancers below. Now and again, one will dangle by the knees and snatch a kiss from whoever is standing below. I like such kisses. They fill the mouth and leave the body free. To kiss well one must kiss solely. No groping hands or stammering hearts. The lips and the lips alone are the pleasure (*P* 59).

This description of the acrobats and the kisses they steal anticipates and acts as a metaphor for Villanelle's love affair with the Queen of Spades, which commences shortly afterwards. Like the acrobats' kisses, the love affair is illicit in that it transgresses patriarchal convention and has to be concealed from the Queen of Spades's husband. It is also precarious, short lived and sexually intoxicating. Villanelle's account of the stylised positions which she and her lover adopt while making love, and her reference to the exclusive focus they place on the mouth, recall, in fact, the acrobats' postures and movements:

> She lay on the rug and I lay at right angles to her so that only our lips might meet. Kissing in this way is the strangest of distractions. The greedy body that clamours for satisfaction is forced to content itself with a single sensation and, just as the blind hear more acutely and the deaf can feel the grass grow, so the mouth becomes the focus of love and all things pass through it and are re-defined. It is a sweet and precise torture (*P* 67).

In portraying Villanelle and the Queen of Spades mimicking the postures of the acrobats in their lovemaking, Winterson associates lesbian sex with artifice and stylisation. The emphasis she places on its cultural and performative dimension is illuminated by a comment voiced by Danae Clark, which relates sexual artifice of this kind to the transgressive, illicit nature of lesbian existence under patriarchy. Clark perceptively observes that 'Lesbians are accustomed to playing out multiple styles and sexual roles as a tactic of survival and have thus learned the artifice of invention in defeating heterosexual codes of naturalism'.[16]

Like her reference to the acrobats and trapeze performers, Winterson's treatment of the mouth as a signifier of lesbian sexuality, which occurs in the passage from *The Passion* quoted above, develops a key motif in lesbian culture. References to the mouth in the poetry of Cherrie Moraga have been described by critics as 'fusing two taboo activities, female speaking and lesbian sexuality'.[17] Wittig in *Lesbian Peoples* likewise concentrates attention on the mouth, treating it as a substitute for the vulva (Wittig, 109).

Another strategy which Winterson employs to undomesticate the female body and, in the words of De Lauretis, 'recreate it other-wise' in a manner 'that will resist phallic idealisation' (De Lauretis, 150) is to represent Villanelle engaging in crossdressing. This too carries carnivalesque associations. The stylised boy's attire which Villanelle wears while working at the Casino, as she herself recognises, draws attention to her gender while at the same time rendering it ambiguous. The visitors enjoy the role-play in which she engages; they see it as 'part of the game, trying to decide which sex was hidden behind tight breeches and extravagant face-paste ...' (*P* 54). Crossdressing, by exposing the artifice of gender and the element of performativity it displays, demonstrates, Judith Butler argues, that gender is not a natural fact but a cultural performance; its apparent '"naturalness" is constituted through discursively constrained performative acts that produce the body through and within the categories of sex'. Like lesbian and gay role-play, crossdressing 'brings into relief the utterly constructed status of the so-called heterosexual original',[18] alerting the viewer to the fact that, as Carole-Anne Tyler remarks in relation to homosexual drag, 'There is no natural, essential, biological basis to gender identity or sexual orientation'.[19] Villanelle arrives at a similar perception when, wondering whether masculine or feminine attire represents her true self, she asks, 'What was myself? Was this breeches and boots self any less real than my garters?' (*P* 66). Her supposition that the girl's role, which she generally plays, is no more real than the boy's, which she adopts for the period of Carnival, draws attention to the inauthenticity of all gender roles, foregrounding their performative dimension.

Winterson, Calvino — and 'Border Crossing'

Winterson's exploration of lesbian sexuality in *The Passion* extends beyond the portrayal of Villanelle and her relationships, to encompass her environment, the city of Venice. The association of Venice with 'the cities of the interior' (*P* 68), where the lover pursues her quest for the beloved, transforms it from being merely an exotic setting for Villanelle's romance with the Queen of Spades, to a symbolic representation of a feminine erotic economy. In creating a fantasy realm of feminine desire, Winterson touches on a theme which is topical with feminist and queer theorists at the moment. Irigaray engages in a hypothetical discussion of the form which she believes such an economy might take, while Butler in *The Lesbian Phallus* challenges the phallocentric bias of existing masculinist models of sexuality. However, while the content of Winterson's erotic economy reveals connections with the work of feminist and queer theorists, the vehicle she employs to represent it — the city of Venice and its topography — is indebted to a very different source. It reflects the influence of a postmodern work by a male Italian writer: Italo Calvino's *Invisible Cities*, in which the explorer Marco Polo describes for the benefit of Kublai Khan the various cities in his host's empire he has visited.

Calvino's work is masculinist in viewpoint. Each of the cities which Polo depicts is assigned a female name and is represented in terms of female imagery, with the result that the series as a whole assumes the significance of a male erotic fantasy or topography of desire. Zobeide, Marco observes, is constructed by a group of men in a deliberate attempt to capture the fantasy image of a woman which they encountered in a dream, while, on studying models of the city of Fedora, 'Every inhabitant chooses the city that corresponds to his desire'.[20] As the critic Marilyn Schneider comments, 'Within the text proper the male voices of Marco Polo and Kublai Khan discourse, giving birth to female cities. Each city inscribes an erotic relationship between itself and the men who built it'.[21] Venice, one of the few cities Polo mentions which is real as opposed to imaginary, plays a key role in Calvino's text. It is Polo's home and, as a consequence, features frequently in this thoughts. In fact, he admits that, although he seldom refers to it by name, every time he describes a city in the Khan's empire, 'I am saying something about Venice' (Calvino, 69). Considering the significant, if oblique, role which Venice plays in Calvino's narrative, it is understandable that Winterson's representation should reflect his influence.

As the reworking of the motif of the heart in *The Passion*, discussed above, illustrates, intertextual allusions, and the 'border crossing'[22] between different cultures and value-schemes which they involve, are integral to Winterson's fiction. Her treatment of Calvino's text is similarly inventive. By subjecting it to postmodern reworking, she engages in a crossing of boundaries which transforms the male erotic fantasy he creates into one which is lesbian in emphasis.

Several different facets of Winterson's delineation of Venice contribute to creating the overall effect of a feminine erotic economy. The shifting perspectives which she ascribes to the city, along with the connections it displays with water, relate it to femininity and the fluctuating nature of desire. The bridges linking the canals carry romantic significance since, according to Winterson, 'For lovers a bridge is a possibility, a metaphor of their chances' (*P* 57). Her reference to the bridges develops Calvino's account of the cities in the Khan's Empire, such as the city of Phyllis where the visitor enjoys 'observing all the bridges over the canals, each different from the others' (Calvino, 72). Calvino's description of the varied architectural styles which the bridges display — 'cambered, covered, on pillars, on barges, suspended, with tracery balustrades' (Calvino, 72) — and his reference, in his description of Esmeralda, to the 'cats, thieves, illicit lovers' who 'move along higher, discontinuous ways, dropping from a rooftop to a balcony, following gutterings with acrobats' steps' (Calvino, 71) are also pertinent to Winterson's representation of Venice and the characters and events associated with it. As well as anticipating the carnivalesque antics of the trapeze performers, they look forward to her description of the 'illicit lover' Villanelle climbing the railings fringing the Queen of Spades's villa on New Year's Eve and, with the agility of a cat and the daring of a thief, hanging 'two storeys in mid air' (*P* 75) to spy on her lover.

Winterson's description of Venice as 'a city of mazes' where 'you may set off from the same place for the same place every day and never go by the same route' (*P* 49) also elaborates a feature of Calvino's urban topography. Esmeralda, he comments, comprises 'a network of canals and a network of streets [which] span and intersect each other'; as a result, 'the shortest distance between two points is not a straight line but a zigzag that ramifies in tortuous optional routes' (Calvino, 71). In the works of both writers, the emphasis on the city's labyrinthine structure gives rise to the intriguing concept of a city within a city. Calvino describes how in Eusapia, 'The inhabitants have constructed an identical copy of their city, underground' (Calvino, 88), which they use as a mortuary, and he depicts Beersheba as displaying both a 'celestial' copy and an 'infernal' one (Calvino, 90). Winterson, in her account of Venice, likewise refers to a 'city within a city' inhabited by outsiders and marginals such as 'thieves and Jews and citizens with slit eyes' (*P* 53). However, the two writers treat the motifs of the maze and 'a city within a city' very differently, ascribing to them disparate meanings. Whereas in Calvino's text the maze-like structure of the city represents the masculinist concept of the mystery of femininity, in Winterson's it serves as a metaphor for Villanelle's amour with the Queen of Spades. It also signifies the clandestine behaviour, exemplified by crossdressing and secret meetings, to which lesbian lovers are forced to resort in hetero-patriarchal culture. The motif of the labyrinth and the maze has received, of course, numerous interpretations in literature. Margaret Atwood employs it in *Lady Oracle* (1976) as a metaphor for the intricacies of the feminine psyche and romantic fiction, Umberto Eco treats it in *The Name of the Rose* (1983) as a microcosm of the world, while Wittig associates it in *Lesbian Peoples: Materials for a Dictionary* with the labrys, the double-headed axe which is the signifier of the Minoan civilisation and its reputedly matrilineal culture. She describes the labyrinth as housing the archives of the lesbian peoples whose history she is engaged in recounting (Wittig, 93). As Wittig implies, while the protective structure of the labyrinth makes it a suitable location for a lesbian archive, its intricacy of design enables it to resist specular totalisation and makes it an appropriate image for lesbian sexuality itself. Winterson's account of the labyrinthian structure of Venice, with its alleys and canals encircling 'the city within the city that is the knowledge of a few' (*P* 53), assumes similar significance. It serves as an image of the pleasures and ambiguities of love between women.

Like the cities in the Khan's empire which, according to Calvino, resemble dreams in that they contain images of 'everything imaginable' (Calvino, 36), Winterson's representation of Venice comprises contradictions. The city, though famous for its Carnival festivities and the youthful world of love they symbolise, simultaneously reveals links with 'darkness and death' (*P* 57) and is haunted by ghosts. Moreover, like the cities which Calvino describes, it has a strongly utopian dimension. Developing Calvino's emphasis on the fantasy aspect of an urban milieu, Winterson describes Venice as assuming, on occasion, an insubstantial, visionary appearance. Her depiction of 'this mercurial city' (*P* 49) as a utopian realm where 'the laws of the real world are suspended' and 'all things seem possible' (*P* 76) relates it to systems of a similarly utopian kind envisaged by feminist philosophers. Irigaray's attempt to define a feminine economy is, as both her disciples and critics agree, strongly utopian in nature. The project of creating what she calls 'a female symbolic' is, from a conventionally Lacanian point of view, an impossibility, a contradiction in terms. However, the commentator Margaret Whitford defends Irigaray's utopianism on the grounds that, 'We need utopian visions'. She regards 'Imagining how things could be different' not as an act of escapism but, on the contrary, as 'part of a process of transforming the present in the direction of a different future'.[23] Winterson's description of Venice is similarly transformative. Since, in existing hetero-patriarchal culture where women are assigned the role of object of exchange between men, lesbian love is not supposed to exist at all and, in so doing, contradicts the Law on which this culture is based, its delineation necessarily involves, as Castle points out, a movement into the realm of utopian fantasy.[24]

Concepts of 'excess' and 'the grotesque', reflected in the portrayal of Villanelle and the labyrinthian structure of Venice, are pertinent, it is interesting to note, to the structural design of *The Passion*. Just as the figure of the lesbian and the transgressive sexuality which she embodies exceed the conventional model of woman as commodity and object of exchange endorsed by phallocentric culture, so the text representing her exceeds conventional expectations of realism, erupting in a plenitudinous display of baroque imagery, episodes of magic realism, and competing genres and narrative-lines.

NOTES

1. See Patricia Waugh. *Feminine Fictions: Revisiting the Postmodern* (London: Routledge. 1989) 7-16.
2. Lisa Moore. 'Teledildonics: Virtual Lesbians in the Fiction of Jeanette Winterson'. in *Sexy Bodies: The Strange Carnalities of Feminism*, ed. by Elizabeth Grosz and Elspeth Probyn (London: Routledge. 1995) 113.
3. Marilyn R.Farwell. *Heterosexual Plots and Lesbian Narratives* (New York University Press. 1996) 4.
4. See Paulina Palmer. *Contemporary Lesbian Writing: Dreams, Desire, Difference* (Buckingham: Open University Press. 1993) 4; and Bonnie Zimmerman. *The Safe Sea of Women: Lesbian Fiction 1969-89* (London: Onlywomen Press. 1990) 44-6.
5. Marilyn R.Farwell. 'Heterosexual Plots and Lesbian Subtexts: Toward a Theory of Lesbian Narrative Space', in *Lesbian Texts and Contexts: Radical Revisions*. ed. by Karla Jay and Joanne Glasgow (New York University Press. 1990) 93.
6. Terry Castle. 'Sylvia Townsend Warner and the Counterplot of Lesbian Fiction'. in *Sexual Sameness: Textual Differences in Lesbian and Gay Writing*. ed. by Joseph Bristow (London: Routledge. 1992) 128-47.
7. Linda Hutcheon. *A Poetics of Postmodernism: History, Theory, Fiction* (London: Routledge. 1988) 173-4. All further page references will be given after quotations in the text.
8. Teresa De Lauretis. 'Sexual Indifference and Lesbian Representation', in *The Lesbian and Gay Studies Reader*. ed. by Henry Abelove. Michele Aina Barale and David M. Halperin (London: Routledge. 1993) 144. All further page references will be given after quotations in the text.
9. Elizabeth Grosz. *Jacques Lacan: A Feminist Introduction* (London: Routledge. 1990) 144.
10. Luce Irigaray. *This Sex Which is Not One*, translated by Catherine Porter with Carolyn Burke (Ithaca. NY: Cornell University Press. 1985) 78.
11. See Bram Dijkstra. *Idols of Perversity: Images of Feminine Evil in Fin-de-Siècle Culture* (Oxford University Press. 1986) 259-264.
12. M.M.Bakhtin. *Rabelais and His World*. translated by Helene Iswolsky (Bloomington: Indiana University Press. 1984) 317.
13. Catherine Clément. 'The Guilty One', in *The Newly Born Woman*. by Catherine Clément and Hélène Cixous and translated by Betsy Wing (Manchester University Press, 1987) 9.
14. Monique Wittig and Sande Zeig. *Lesbian Peoples* (London: Virago. 1980) 31. All further page references will be given after quotations in the text.
15. Mary Russo. *The Female Grotesque: Risk, Excess and Modernity* (London: Routledge. 1984) 41-51.
16. Danae Clark. 'Commodity Lesbianism', in *The Lesbian and Gay Studies Reader*. op. cit., 194.
17. Yvonne Yarbro-Bejarano. 'De-constructing the Lesbian Body: Cherrie Moraga's "Loving in the War Years"', in *The Lesbian and Gay Studies Reader*, op. cit., 597.
18. Judith Butler. *Gender Trouble: Feminism and the Subversion of Identity* (London: Routledge. 1990) x. 31.
19. Carole-Anne Tyler. 'Boys Will Be Girls: The Politics of Gay Drag', in *Inside Out: Lesbian Theories, Gay Theories*, ed. by Diana Fuss (London: Routledge. 1991) 32.
20. Italo Calvino. *Invisible Cities*. translated by William Weaver (London: Picador. 1979) 28. All further page references will be given after quotations in the text.
21. Marilyn Schneider. 'Subject or Object? Mr. Palomar and Invisible Cities', in *Calvino Revisited*. ed. by Franco Ricci (Ottawa: Dovehouse Editions. 1989) 178.

22. See Maggie Humm. *Border Traffic: Strategies of Contemporary Women Writers* (Manchester University Press. 1991) 1-5.
23. Margaret Whitford. *Luce Irigaray: Philosophy in the Feminine* (London: Routledge. 1991) 19.
24. Terry Castle. op. cit.. 144-7.

GRAND (DIS)UNIFIED THEORIES? DISLOCATED DISCOURSES IN *GUT SYMMETRIES*

HELENA GRICE AND TIM WOODS

> **I know I am a fool. trying to make connections out of scraps but how else is there to proceed? The fragmentariness of life makes coherence suspect but to babble is a different kind of treachery (*GS* 24).**

I. Gut Forces and Gut Feelings

STRUCTURALISM invited readers to see patterns in discourses. It was in fact, a unified theory, which sought to combine structure with figure. It sought to make explicit the hidden structures of narratives, structures which were only evident on the recognition of the functionality of discourses. In Roland Barthes's hands, structuralism made the latent manifest. Yet poststructuralism demonstrated the limitations and fallacies of such an entrenched view of a rationalisable world, ushering in a new postmodern lexicon of slippage, fluidity and dynamism to counter the discursive concepts of fixity, encompassment, and immobility.

In a recent review of *Gut Symmetries*, Katy Emck cogently describes the 'three voices' of Jeanette Winterson: firstly the 'fairground conjuring act', which translates as Winterson's predilection for magic realist embellishments of her work; the 'human textbook', those postmodernist views of history, narrative, reality, and those Grand Theories cribbed from Newton, Einstein, Hawking and co.; and, finally, 'the voice of lyric love', concerning the triangular love plot between Jove and his wife Stella, and their independent yet mutual lover, Alice.[1] This voice of lyric love speaks in all of Winterson's novels, from Villanelle's (the very name a form of lyric) to Lothario's, Jeanette's to Jordan's. With these three voices speaking loud and clear, *Gut Symmetries* is occupying familiar Winterson postmodern territory, territory already charted and demarcated by the literary explorations of earlier novels like *Sexing the Cherry* and *Written on the Body*. The novel broaches a series of Grand Theoretical Concerns, which coincide with many of the preoccupations of contemporary critical and scientific theory: the nature and nostalgia of history, the binary structure of Western thought, the space-time continuum, desire, 'reality', fictionality, chance and prediction. Yet, as with Winterson's previous novels, these concerns constitute only part of the narrative, that which serves as a portentous and erudite commentary upon the main preoccupations of the story. *Gut Symmetries* is another reworking of the urge to discover a fundamental structure to all the natural phenomena in the universe. Playing with patterns at every turn in this novel, Winterson sets up a world which is torn between an essential structure and a denial of totalising patterns. Beginning with the 'Prologue' and the introduction of the medieval alchemist Paracelsus, who 'was a student of Correspondences: "As above, so below"' (*GS* 2), who thought that 'The zodiac in the sky is imprinted in the body. "The galaxa goes through the belly"' (*GS* 2), Winterson establishes a complex and elaborate set of parallels and connections between ancient and medieval theories of matter, Newtonian physics, contemporary cosmology, numerology, the Tarot, and astrology. *Gut Symmetries* involves an extended pun on (1) the twentieth-century search for a 'Grand Unified Theory' (a 'GUT') of scientific forces in theoretical physics, begun with Einstein and continued today in the discoveries of 'Superstring Theory'; and (2) 'gut feelings', or something felt in the gut i.e. intuitively. This sets up an opposition between thinking and feeling, rationality and mystery, materiality and metaphysics. In this respect, Winterson's novel is something of a large conceptual linguistic game; yet it is a novel which sometimes loses itself in the trickeries of its playful parallels, and ultimately produces a narrative which falls apart rather than falls together.

Jove, the central male character, is a theoretical physicist studying at the Princeton Advanced Institute for Physics, and his field is 'Superstring theory' and the search for a 'GUT'. The most fundamental theory of this sort that is largely confirmed by experiment is the 'Standard Model' of three interactions: electromagnetic, weak and strong nuclear. Yet the trouble with the Standard Model is that it does not incorporate that most fundamental force known to science, gravity. This search is motivated by the urge to discover a fundamental theory underpinning all natural phenomena. This urge is not new, since even Ancient Greek science sought to reduce the world to the elemental 'earth, air, fire and water' structure. Twentieth-century science now works on smaller particles, but the urge is still evident.

The development of a unified theory has preoccupied cosmologists since Einstein, and if discovered, would entail a great deal of mathematical consistency and inner beauty. String theory has finally emerged as a promising candidate for a unified theory, based as it is on an elegantly simple but beautiful notion.[2] Instead of many types of elementary point-like particles, it has been suggested that there is a single variety of string-like objects. As with musical strings, this basic string can vibrate, and each vibrational mode can be viewed as a point-like elementary particle, just as the modes of a musical string are perceived of as different and distinct notes. As Alice notes within the novel, 'When gravity and GUTs unite? Listen: one plays the lute and another the harp. The strings are vibrating and from the music of the spheres a perfect universe is formed' (*GS* 100-1). Once again, the novel hints at a metaphysical solution, this time embedded in a Pythagorean cosmology of a 'harmony of the spheres'.

Winterson has cannily latched on to the recent debates within theoretical physics as a means of providing her with a central metaphor to describe her postmodern sense of the instability and perpetual flux of the universe. In addition to Superstrings, Winterson has also appropriated the terminology of Quantum Physics, the indeterminacy principle and the General Theory of Relativity, as discourses allied to the postmodern discourse on epistemological insecurity and ontological instability. As the characters constantly muse, their own identities are equally unstable:

> Any measurement must take into account the position of the observer. There is no such thing as measurement absolute, there is only measurement relative. Relative to what is an important part of the question.
>
> This has been my difficulty. The difficulty of my life. Those well-built trip points, those physical determinants of parents, background, school, family, birth, marriage, death, love, work, are themselves as much in motion as I am. What should be stable, shifts. What I am told is solid, slips. The sensible strong ordinary world of fixity is a folklore (*GS* 9-10).

Much of this derives from the impact of quantum physics, which has destroyed the security of 'the mechanistic, deterministic mind/matter of cosmic reality' (*GS* 11). The characters' general instability of identity, in which there is no secure knowledge of being, occurs everywhere:

> What or who? I cannot name myself. The alchemists worked with a magic mirror, using reflections to guide them. The hall of mirrors set around me has been angled to distort. Is that me in the shop-glass? Is that me in the family photo? Is that me in the office window? Is that me in the silvered pages of a magazine? Is that me in the broken bottles on the street? Everywhere I go, reflection. Everywhere a caught image of who I am. In all of that who am I? (*GS* 12).

It is now something of a hackneyed observation that postmodern fiction self-consciously manipulates its own artifice, drawing the reader into a collaboration of pretences, distrusting its own artifice and doubting as to whether the author can communicate anything at all to the reader through systematic discourse (Winterson's constant anxieties about the language getting through to the listener). This emerges in *Gut Symmetries* as a purposeful multiplication of competing cosmological, irrational, literary and philosophical interpretations that never achieve resolution (the archetypal locus of this being a novel like Thomas Pynchon's *The Crying of Lot 49*). This postmodern reshaping of our universe and the function of our description and observation in it, that was begun with quantum physics, has forced a re-evaluation of the relative veracity, or epistemological potency, of literary discourse versus scientific discourse. Bohr and Heisenberg argued that there is no way that one can know reality at the sub-atomic level: an electron, photon, a positron, a quark, all lack definite qualities until we observe them. In other words, our discourses of observation determine their qualities. Winterson is aware of this and implies this in her mention of Schrödinger's Cat (*GS* 207). Furthermore, the instability of the sub-atomic world which is marked by the new physics, is matched in her novel by recent poststructuralist theories. Although a somewhat questionable parallel, nevertheless, this novel is self-consciously written with full knowledge of recent theoretical discussions concerning the indeterminate slippage of sign and object in poststructuralist philosophy, not least the way in which deconstruction has sought to overturn the metaphysical and ideological hierarchies of binary oppositions which structure our lives: i.e. 'As the rest of the audience shuffled away to their favourite binary opposition, gin/tonic ...' (*GS* 16). Although this is partly done in a humorous and ironic fashion, it does seem to miss the point of the binary opposition, since gin and tonic do not wholly fall into an unequivocal hierarchy which needs deconstructing.

On the one hand, the novel establishes the world as a series of material relations which are always available to scientific rationalisation and empirical experiment, even if the conclusions are that of random dispersion and dissipative energies. However, the novel also invokes irrational cosmologies, the non-rational and the metaphysical dimension of life. This is also played out in the dimension of time: 'Past. Present. Future. The rational divisions of the rational life. And always underneath, in dreams, in recollections, in the moment of hesitation on a busy street, the hunch that life is not rational, not divided. That the mirrored compartments could break' (*GS* 20). Temporal narratives invite us to think of all discourse as taking the form of a story. The cognitively fragmented world in which Alice lives may excite longings for metanarratives that explain everything, but they actually turn out only to give her the *illusion* of mending her fragmentation. At another moment, Winterson describes that archetypal scientist, Einstein, as a mystic, someone in love with the power of numbers, almost a numerologist (*GS* 23). The function of the Tarot within the novel is part of this non-materialist dimension, cards from which structure the chapter divisions, as well as gesturing towards the characteristics of the individual protagonists: Alice the Fool; Jove the Knave of Coins; Stella the Star. A further symbolic layer in the novel emerges with the Tarot's connection to the Jewish mystical Kabbalah, in which arcane and secret mysteries Stella's father is deeply involved: 'Every blade of grass that grows here on earth has its corresponding influence in the stars. This is the Mazalot' (*GS* 77). In a somewhat romanticised view of enigmatic Judaism, the magic of the Torah and the Kabbalistic frame of mind match the astrological patterning in the Tarot. Indeed, the Tarot partly has its roots in the Jewish Kabbalistic tradition. Later in the novel, this parallel is made more explicit:

> Is truth what we do not know?
>
> What we know does not satisfy us. What we know constantly reveals itself as partial. What we know, generation by generation, is discarded into new knowings which in their turn slowly cease to interest us.
>
> In the Torah, the Hebrew 'to know', often used in a sexual context, is not about facts but about connotations. Knowledge, not as accumulation but as charge and discharge. A release of energy from one site to another. Instead of a hoard of certainties, bug-collected, to make me feel secure, I can give up taxonomy and invite myself to the dance: the patterns, rhythms, multiplicities, paradoxes, shifts, currents, cross-currents, irregularities, irrationalities, geniuses, joints, pivots, worked over time, and through time, to find the lines of thought that still transmit.
>
> The facts cut me off. The clean boxes of history, geography, science, art. What is the separateness of things when the current that flows through each to each is live? (*GS* 82-3).

Stella, as a poet, espouses a view of the world which is mystical and eschews the rigidity of disciplinary thought which seeks to categorise knowledge in specific pigeonholes. She is far more interested in a fluid concept of interrelationships between things, in some ways more attuned to the vibrations of the cosmos than Jove with all his mathematical and theoretical paraphernalia. However, this deconstruction of the poet and the scientist shatters when it later transpires that the Kabbalist (Stella's father) was in correspondence with the quantum scientists (*GS* 168).

The novel thus constantly hinges upon the opposition of the material and the metaphysical, the rational and the irrational. This is mirrored in the natural science of theoretical physics as against the supernatural patterns of the Tarot and the Kabbalah. However, this opposition is also put under severe pressure. One locus for these different views about reality lies in the notion of time. Strict determinism and irreversibility have dominated our popular conceptions of temporality. The Newtonian model of time was an arrow, irreversible and unilinear. However, as Alice remarks, time is far more likely to operate in a non-linear form. In fact, her emplotment of time in the novel occurs as an image of a whirlpool. Indeed, another branch of contemporary physics, chaos theory, attempts to account for non-linear dynamics and argues that non-linear dynamics are far more evident in everyday life than the dominance of classical linear models would suggest. Scientific analysis and 'gut feelings' blend together, the one confirming the other, the metaphor of a chaos of swirls being borne out by the chaos theorists like Feigenbaum, Lorenz and Mandelbrot. Time, like a river, is far more complex than a straight flight of an arrow homing in on its mark. Rather, time often doubles back on itself, moving in eddies, and whirlpools:

> Time.
>
> Newton visualised time as an arrow flying towards its target. Einstein understood time as a river, moving forward, forceful, directed, but also bowed, curved, sometimes subterranean, not ending but pouring itself into a greater sea. A river cannot flow against its current, but it can flow in circles: its eddies and whirlpools regularly break up its strong press forward. The riverrun is maverick, there is a high chance of cross-current, a snag of time that returns us without warning to a place we thought we had sailed through long since (*GS* 104).

The novel gradually establishes these positions concerning temporality and epistemology as gender positions. In his book entitled *Hermes: Literature, Science, Philosophy*, Michel Serres maps out how science has fallen under the dominant influence of two classical tropes, Mars and Venus: 'The nature of Mars, of martial physics, is one of hard, rigid, and rigorous bodies; the physics and nature of Venus are formed in flows ... our newly developing physics tells somewhat the same story too, by flow, random events, systems, disequilibria'.[3] Where Venus postulates a science founded upon multiple perspectives of a world in flux, Mars demands representational closure, a single master narrative commanding the entire sweep of physical history. Ultimately, Mars's science is impelled by a fear of instability, impermanence and uncertainty. This resembles the opposition that is established within the novel, as we are told that Alice's real name is Alluvia, 'deposited by the river', and, befitting the king of the Roman gods, Jove is described as 'Keeper of the Thunderbolt' (*GS* 137). Indeed, Jove exemplifies all the attributes of 'Martian science' when he ridicules Stella's artistic nature:

> All of us have fantasies. dreams. A healthy society outlets those things into sport. hero-worship. harmless adultery. rock climbing. the movies. Unhealthy individuals understand their dreams and fantasies as something solid. An alternative world. They do not know how to subordinate their disruptive elements to a regulated order. My wife believes that she had a kind of interior universe as valid and as necessary as her day-to-day existence in reality. This failure to make a hierarchy. this failure to recognise the primacy of fact. justified her increasingly subjective responses. She refused to make clear distinctions between inner and outer. She had no sure grasp of herself or of herself in relation to the object. At first I mistook this pathology as the ordinary feminine. ... There is nothing mystical about the universe. There are things we cannot explain yet. That is all (*GS* 190-1).

Jove is certain of a rationalisable and determinate universe, and cannot abide the mystical and metaphysical, regarding it as a typically effeminate form of thought which is not hard-headed. Jove is a scientist of the hard and rigorous, whereas Alice and Stella share a concept of the universe which is more fluid, mysterious, and 'Venetian'.

This gendered paradigm does suggest that, despite her attempts to deconstruct binary oppositions in the novel, Winterson lapses into some rather tired gendered stereotypes on a number of occasions. This engendering of science versus mystery is a wholly stereotypical gendered structure, which certainly does not escape from patriarchal notions of the male as a rigorous thinker, and the female as a vaguely impressionistic feeler. Winterson does try to deconstruct this opposition to some extent, in so far as she suggests that Stella's and Alice's conceptions of the universe, albeit not wholly scientific, are in many ways more 'unified' than Jove's GUTs. Yet the novel never really manages to establish this deconstruction in a credible and understandable manner. It attempts to throw a spanner in the works of binary oppositions like male/female or husband/wife, by establishing a triangular structure, a threesome, male/female/female, or husband/wife/female lover. In this way, Winterson seeks to disrupt the orthodox sexual power relations which have been established via the sexual and social hegemony of conventional heterosexual relationships. Yet once again, the novel does seem to lapse into some trite formulations about gender and this triadic structure:

> Last month. after our moot. Stella showed me Card XVI of the Tarot deck. L'amoureux. The Lovers. A young man seems to be trying to choose between two women. Cupid. arrow-borne. over his head.
>
> SHE: The Eternal Triangle.
>
> ME: Three is a masculine number. Odd numbers are masculine.
>
> SHE: Or are masculine numbers odd?
>
> ME: It's my fault.

SHE: It's all our fault. (*GS* 200-1).

II. Sexual Sameness and the Triangular Love Plot

So far, this essay has concentrated upon the novel's preoccupation with paradigms between new scientific epistemologies and postmodern instabilities of identity and ontology. Yet a critique of patriarchal gender structures forms the bedrock of much of Winterson's fiction, and in this respect, *Gut Symmetries* is not different. The novel is an example of a 'girl-boy girl-girl love story',[4] a triangular love relationship/intrigue, in which all the possible configurations within this three-way attachment are in turn played out until the conclusion when the triangle collapses. This plot conformation is not new: it has precedents throughout the history of literature, from Chaucer to contemporary women's writing in the work of Joanna Trollope (*A Village Affair*), Evelyn Lau (*Other Women*) and Margaret Atwood (*Life Before Man*) — whom, incidentally, Winterson has recently named as a source of inspiration.[5] This triadic plot structure has also figured previously in Winterson's own work, in both *The Passion* and *Written on the Body*. However, unlike many of its precedents in Winterson's work and elsewhere, Winterson is not so much concerned with the intricate rivalries between the two women competing for the prize of the polygamous male, but with the woman-to-woman identification that develops alongside — and finally replaces — the male/female couplings.

Winterson's feminism in *Gut Symmetries* is evident in her portrayal of the development of a strong woman-to-woman attachment.[6] It is also an example of the Radicalesbian idea of a woman-committed woman.[7] Both Alice and Stella, the female duo within the trio, become increasingly mutually supportive and orientated towards each other. But their attachment moves beyond a female-support friendship to become a lesbian one.[8] *Gut Symmetries* differs importantly from several of its precursors in triangular love plots because it revises that triangle to include a lesbian angle (or two). This angle can be read in different ways. There are distinct echoes of a lesbian 'coming out narrative', defined by Paulina Palmer and others as a predominant form in lesbian writing;[9] the lesbian sex scene is given pivotal significance in the novel and may be interpreted as interrogating many of the concerns of contemporary lesbian theory, including issues of desire, subjectivity, the gaze and an emphasis upon the selfsame; and finally, Winterson tries to make the lesbian angle of the novel seem an alternative to Western binarist thinking.

The triangle comprises three characters, Jove, Alice and Stella. Jove and Alice are two Princeton scientists, and meet whilst working their passage from England to New York in the 1950s aboard a Cunard liner by giving lectures. Jove discusses time travel and wormholes (a proto-Stephen Hawking, mentioned by Jove in the novel), whilst Alice deals with Paracelsus and the New Physics. Jove and Alice begin an affair which carries them ashore and into the world of 50s New York, represented in Winterson's story as a place of magic, glitter and possibility, 'a crucible city, an alchemical vessel where dirt and glory do affect transformation' (*GS* 25). Here, Winterson sets them on a collision course with Jove's wife, the thin, russet-haired and beautiful writer Stella. Winterson swiftly dispenses with the Jove/Alice liaisons, being much more interested in what happens when the two women, Stella and Alice, meet. One way in which Winterson inflects *Gut Symmetries* as a 'coming out narrative', is with the narrative emphasis placed upon Stella's and Alice's viewpoints, feelings and orientation towards each other, in contradistinction to Jove's story, afforded only a marginal place within the text.[10] Both Stella's and Alice's characters are developed through their own recollections of their childhoods. Their life stories are strikingly similar in development: both have extraordinary births, Stella as the Christ-child of a New Year in snowy New York, with a diamond embedded in her spine; and Alice, born by chance on a tugboat on the Mersey. Both are daughters of self-made men, who loom large in their daughters' lives: Alice is the child of a shipping magnate, Stella the daughter of a Jewish immigrant to the United States, a bookseller and mystic. Jove provides the connective tissue between them, but his role diminishes after he has engineered their meeting. The two women's developing love, first sexual encounter and final union comprises the emotional focus of the novel. The triangular love plot is useful to Winterson here because it allows the explicit contrast of lesbian and heterosexual couplings. Whereas the unions between Jove and the two women in turn appear emotionally superficial and read as a rather worn narrative, the love between Stella and Alice is represented as authentic and highly emotional, even desperate. However, lesbianism in the text is only one of a range of identifications. Yet it is the identification which endures (Stella and Alice leave together) and which is thrown into emotional relief. Stella's and Alice's desire for each other is shown to be transgressive and to function as an act of resistance to hetero-patriarchal patternings. An analysis of the representations of both lesbian and hetero-sex in the novel may serve to illustrate the case.

The first sexual encounter we see is that between Jove and Alice. But Winterson side-steps depicting hetero-couplings and instead always focuses upon the pre- or post-coital moment, in which we always view Jove through Alice's narration, in a state of gratified self-satisfaction: 'Jove was lying on his back smiling at me' (*GS* 27); 'Later, admiring his own erection' (*GS* 27). The one exception to this is Alice's single comment: 'Later, inside me' (*GS* 98). Thus, the hetero-sex between Jove and Alice is always orientated towards male gratification. Although Alice handles the narration, she makes no mention of her own pleasure, only Jove's, and he is always portrayed in passive terms, in which he is not submissive but rather the non-active receiver of Alice's attentions. Significantly, one of Alice's statements is juxtaposed with the hetero-sex scenes at this early point in the novel: 'Pleasure = consumption' (*GS* 13), a purportedly patriarchal world-view which is later brought to horrifying reality at the close of the text. Sex between Jove and Stella is likewise shown as an unequal, consumptive act in which Jove is the taker, Stella the giver, of pleasure: 'He gripped me, his prick straight in, the swollen saltiness of it dirty in my dirt. I was dry and cracked, unwashed, closed' (*GS* 185). Once more, it is the woman who handles the narration and through her perspective the heterosexual act is an act of male power. This scene takes place in the final moments of the story, whereas the Jove/Alice couplings occur in the early part of the narrative. Structurally, then, hetero-sex both opens and closes the novel, marking its relegation to the margins of the novel, and the lesbian union takes its place at the narrative centre.

The lesbian sex scene is narrated from Alice's perspective. Winterson's care in her depiction of lesbian sex scenes is well documented. When writing the sex scene for the filmscript of *Oranges*, she noted that she wanted to produce a coupling which 'wouldn't be dirty raincoats or like *Desert Hearts* where the women appeared to have "no hands"'.[11] A similarly sensitive arrangement is achieved in *Gut Symmetries* by depicting the two women on equal terms, in sharp contrast to the dominant/submissive paradigm to which the Jove sex scenes conform. One means by which the power differential shifts, is that although one partner controls the narrative (Alice), both partners participate in the erotic gaze. The male gaze is refused in *Gut Symmetries*, partly through the absence of hetero-sex but also because the lesbian sex scene is self-enclosed: the spectators are both participants, engaged in an endlessly reflective gaze of and at the selfsame, 'she in me, me in she' (*GS* 119).[12] Within a reciprocal coupling, women are both actively desiring agents as well as objects of desire. The emphasis upon sameness also works to reject inequalities: not only is the male gaze absent, but desire is female (not just male) and maleness is neither the norm nor the primary referent.[13] *Gut Symmetries* refuses the categories of male and female by shifting the terms of sexual difference and desire in asserting the attraction of sameness. The Lacanian emphasis upon sexual difference is eschewed in favour of likeness. Stella and Alice don't just *like* one another, they are *alike*. In fact, *Gut Symmetries* subscribes to a view of lesbian sexuality as narcissistic. Alice and Stella's sex is figured in narcissistic terms and Winterson uses the language of narcissism in order to describe Alice and Stella's mutual gaze:

> Her breasts as my breasts, her mouth as my mouth, were more than Narcissus hypnotised by his own likeness. ... I could have rested there beside her, perhaps forever, it felt like forever, a mirror of confusion of bodies and sighs, undifferentiated . . . (*GS* 119)[14]

Likeness/reflection works as a trope of lesbian sexuality in *Gut Symmetries*, and gender likeness becomes a 'governing narrative and aesthetic principle'.[15] Reflection/mirroring in the sex scene between Alice and Stella works to both refuse the male gaze and to destroy the triangular structure of the novel. If, as Virginia Woolf argued in 1929, the historical function of women was to act as mirrors in which men are reflected at twice their natural size, then here Winterson expropriates this image as a means of allowing Stella and Alice to contemplate their likeness rather than their difference, and in so doing the mirror may offer a 'truer' image.[16] If the triangular plot is 'an archetypal setup in fiction and life for opposition to assert its hegemonic cultural position',[17] then the lesbian mirror by contrast offers a paradigm of likeness. Woolf's work is reflected not just through the adoption of images of reflection and mirroring, but also in the way that *Gut Symmetries* recalls Woolf's novel *Night and Day* in its depiction and revision of the triangular love plot, through the developing relationship between Mary Datchet and Katherine Hilbery.[18] In *Gut Symmetries* the triangular/ oppositional logic of hetero-patriarchal relations is described early on: 'In Euclidean geometry the angles of a triangle add up to 180 degrees and parallel lines never meet. Everyone knows the score, and the women are held in tension, away from one another. The shape is beguiling and it could be understood as a new geometry of family life' (*GS* 17). But then it disappears, and heterosexual logic is refused as a description of Stella's and Alice's relationship. The triangle disappears from pages 140-208, in favour of a logic of sameness.

In fact, *Gut Symmetries* uses a logic of sameness as a means of questioning Western binary logic. The early part of the narration adheres to a binary system of representation, as this example describing Jove and Alice shows: 'We made an elegant pair: dark/fair, older/younger, assured/uncertain. The mirror offered us a snapshot of our own desirability' (*GS* 18). However, accompanying the substitution of lesbian sex for hetero-sex is the attempted rejection of an oppositional logic. Toni A. H. McNaron has described this shift:

> We have been told that in sexual matters, opposition is all, but many of us have rejected that message in favour of likeness. If one thing that is supposed to be is not, then why not question all Platonic splits — good/evil, white/black, male/female, right/wrong, order/chaos, mind/body, spirit/matter, light/dark ... Lesbians, by a simple but profound shift in our gaze of attraction, are positioned as thinkers and theorists poised to lead the way within larger spheres of feminist thought toward a rejection of the very notions of either/or-ness.[19]

Winterson's work reflects this shift, and therefore also attempts to offers a possible route away from binary logic. In this sense her work also echoes much French feminist theory, especially Cixous's work upon the rejection of binary logic in 'Sorties' and Irigaray's celebration of self-affirmatory narcissisms in 'When Our Lips Speak Together', particularly in its similarly utopian, visionary tone. Yet the novel's disruption of heteropatriarchal gender relations in the loveplot, does not easily extend to a similar disruption in other areas of the novel. *Gut Symmetries* leaves the science-art opposition undeconstructed; and even within the discourse of science itself, the facile stereotypes of a 'masculine' and 'feminine' science remain. Binary structures are ultimately left untouched where it suits the book's sexual ideology, as the various discourses sit awkwardly side-by-side, asymmetrical rather than symmetrical. But Jove does recover enough from the shock of his two angles-on-the-side meeting to attempt a rescue of the situation by sailing away to sea (many of Winterson's characters seek answers at sea), culminating in his final, consumptive act of eating Stella's nether parts. In a crafty reworking of the age-old survival story (providing further similarities to Atwood's work, as the survival narrative is a recurrent preoccupation in her work too), Jove's last-ditch attempt to regain (sexual) control of the situation involves him in literally consuming his wife. By reading Alice's and Stella's story as a 'coming out narrative', and by representing their coupling as a union of the selfsame, we view Jove's cannibalism at the end of the novel as a final, carnal, consumptive bid to regain possession of Stella, and through her, by association, of Alice too. Although a crude literary gesture, Jove's last bite at the apple of Stella's bottom is a necessary final attempt to reassert a hetero-patriarchal dynamic before the triumphant emergence of Stella's and Alice's sexuality. Alike in their births, Stella and Alice are 're-birthed' together as lesbians at the end of the novel.

NOTES

1. Katy Emck, 'Gut Symmetries', *Times Literary Supplement*, 3 January, 1997, 21.
2. For a brief layperson's guide to 'Superstring Theory', see Simon Anthony, 'Superstrings: A Theory of Everything?', *New Scientist*, 107 (29 August, 1985) 34-36. For a more sophisticated treatment, see Stephen Hawking, *A Brief History of Time: From the Big Bang to Black Holes* (Toronto: Bantam, 1988).
3. Michel Serres, 'Lucretius: Science and Religion', in *Hermes: Literature, Science, Philosophy*, ed. by Josué V.Harari and David F.Bell (Baltimore: Johns Hopkins University Press, 1982) 103.
4. Ginny Dougary, 'Truth or dare', *The Times*, 4 January, 1997, 9-11; 10.
5. Ibid., 11.
6. For a discussion of woman-to-woman attachments, both lesbian and feminist, see Paulina Palmer, *Contemporary Lesbian Writing: Dreams, Desire, Difference* (Buckingham: Open University Press, 1993) 14-22.
7. See Radicalesbians, 'The Woman Identified Woman', in *Radical Feminism*, ed. by Anne Koedt, Ellen Levine and Anita Rapone (New York: Quadrangle, 1973) 242. This argument suggests that the lesbian is defined by her primary commitment to women, and therefore her primary identification is with other woman, in contrast to heterosexual women, whose primary referent is male. We are aware of a blurring of lesbian and feminist identities here, a characteristic of much early lesbian theory, particularly evident in Adrienne Rich's 1980 essay, 'Compulsory Heterosexuality and Lesbian Existence'. The conflation of lesbian and feminist identifications has since been extensively critiqued; however in *Gut Symmetries*, Winterson does seem to be subscribing to this early proto-lesbian/feminist position.
8. More recent lesbian theory has sought to separate lesbian (sexual) relationships from female-support (Platonic) relationships. See, for example, Ann Snitow, Christine Stansell and Sharon Thompson, eds., *Desire: The Politics of Sexuality* (London: Virago, 1984). Another useful, and more recent, discussion may be found in the introduction to *Sexual Practice, Textual Theory: Lesbian Cultural Criticism*, ed. by Susan J. Wolfe and Julia Penelope (Cambridge, MA, and Oxford: Blackwell, 1993) 6-7.
9. See *Contemporary Lesbian Writing*, 41-45.
10. Palmer describes the coming-out novel/novel of self-discovery as one which depicts the protagonist's 'discovery of her lesbian orientation, which is the focal point', *Contemporary Lesbian Writing*, 41.
11. Jeanette Winterson, 'Interview', *Spare Rib* 209 (1990) 26-9.
12. For a discussion of lesbian use of the gaze, particularly in relation to the cinema, see Penny Florence, 'Lesbian Cinema, Women's Cinema', in *Outwrite: Lesbianism and Popular Culture*, ed. by Gabrielle

Griffin (London: Pluto. 1993) 126-147. Florence's essay has been especially useful here in our thinking about Winterson's use of the gaze. Also see Reina Lewis and Katrina Rolley. 'Ad(dressing) the Dyke: Lesbian Looks and Lesbians Looking'. in *Outlooks: Lesbian and Gay Sexualities and Visual Cultures*, ed. by Peter Horne and Reina Lewis (London: Routledge. 1996) 178-190.

13. See Florence. 130.
14. Despite Winterson's subscription to such a view. the idea of lesbian sexuality as a form of narcissism is. however, highly problematic in lesbian theory. See Carolyn J. Allen's discussion of narcissism in *Following Djuna: Women Lovers and the Erotics of Loss* (Bloomington: Indiana University Press. 1996) 21-46. Allen links her discussion of narcissism to Winterson's work too. in relation to *Written on the Body*. Also see Jackie Stacey. 'Desperately Seeking Difference'. *Screen* 28. 1 (Winter. 1987) 48-61; and Teresa De Lauretis. *The Practice of Love: Lesbian Sexuality and Perverse Desire* (Bloomington: Indiana University Press. 1994) 116-123. Both of the above link discussions of narcissism and 'intra-feminine fascination'.
15. Toni A. H. McNaron. 'Mirrors and Likeness: A Lesbian Aesthetic in the Making'. in *Sexual Practice, Textual Theory*. op.cit., 293.
16. Ibid.
17. Ibid., 291-295.
18. Ibid., 296.
19. Ibid. The problems of transcending Platonic logic are also usefully discussed by Teresa De Lauretis in 'Sexual Indifference/Lesbian Representation'. in *The Lesbian and Gay Studies Reader*. ed. by Henry Abelove. Michele Aina Barale and David M. Halperin (New York and London: Routledge, 1993) 141-158; 152.

NOTES ON CONTRIBUTORS

Tess Cosslett is Senior Lecturer in English and Women's Studies at Lancaster University. She is author of *The 'Scientific Movement' and Victorian Literature* (Harvester, 1982), *Woman to Woman: Female Friendship in Victorian Fiction* (Harvester, 1988), *Women Writing Childbirth: Modern Discourses of Motherhood* (Manchester University Press, 1994) and *Victorian Women Poets* (Longman, 1996). She has edited *Science and Religion in the Nineteenth Century* (Cambridge University Press, 1984) and co-edited *Women, Power and Resistance: An Introduction to Women's Studies* (Open University Press, 1996).

Patricia Duncker is Senior Lecturer in English at the University of Wales, Aberystwyth, where she teaches writing, literary theory and nineteenth century literature. Her critical work includes *Sisters and Strangers: An Introduction to Contemporary Feminist Fiction* (Blackwell, 1992). She is editor of *In and Out of Time: Lesbian Feminist Fiction* (Onlywomen, 1990), and co-editor, with Vicky Wilson, of *Cancer through the eyes of ten women* (Pandora Press, 1996) to which she is also a contributor. Her first novel, *Hallucinating Foucault* (Serpent's Tail, 1995), has been translated into Dutch, French and German and her collection of short stories, *Monsieur Shoushana's Lemon Trees* will be published by Serpent's Tail in 1997.

Helena Grice is currently completing her doctorate on the negotiation of identity in Asian American women's writing at the University of Wales, Aberystwyth, where she also teaches courses on women writers and the history of feminism. She has published articles in *Hitting Critical Mass, Borderlines* and *Melus*.

Ute Kauer teaches at the Philipps-University Marburg, Germany. She is author of *Didaktische Intention und Romankonzeption bei D. H. Lawrence* (Heidelberg: C. Winter Universitaetsverlag, 1993) and has published in *Anglia* and in the *Canadian Review of Comparative Literature*.

Paulina Palmer lectures in English Literature and Women's Studies at the University of Warwick. She is author of *Contemporary Women's Fiction: Narrative Practice and Feminist Theory* (Hemel Hampstead: Harvester Wheatsheaf, 1989) and *Contemporary Lesbian Writing: Dreams, Desire, Difference* (Buckingham: Open University Press, 1993). She has published essays on the fiction of Angela Carter and on the lesbian thriller and has a story in *Girls Next Door* (Women's Press, 1985).

Lynne Pearce is Senior Lecturer in English and Women's Studies at Lancaster University. She is author of *Woman Image Text: Readings in Pre-Raphaelite Art and Literature* (Harvester, 1991), *Reading Dialogics* (Edward Arnold, 1994), *Romance Revisited* (Lawrence and Wishart, 1995) and co-author with Sara Mills of *Feminist Readings Feminists Reading* (Harvester, 1996), as well as numerous articles. Her latest book, *Feminism and the Politics of Reading* (Edward Arnold) will be published in 1997.

Lyn Pykett is Professor of English and head of department at the University of Wales, Aberystwyth. She is author of *Emily Bronte* (Macmillan, 1989), *The Improper Feminine* (Routledge, 1992), *The Sensation Novel: From 'The Woman in White' to 'The Moonstone'* (Northcote House, 1994) and *Engendering Fictions: The English Novel in the Early Twentieth Century* (Edward Arnold, 1995). She is also the editor of *Reading Fin de Siècle Fictions* (Longman, 1996).

Cath Stowers is writing her doctorate on contemporary women's writing at the Centre of Women's Studies, University of York. She teaches adult education courses in women's studies and women's creative writing, and also runs the International Academic Network on Contemporary Women's Writing. She has had articles published in *Heterosexual Politics* (Taylor Francis, 1995), *Kicking Daffodils: Essays on Twentieth Century Women's Poetry* (Edinburgh University Press, forthcoming), and *Critical Survey*.

Scott Wilson lectures in English at Lancaster University. He is author of *Cultural Materialism: Theory and Practice* (Blackwell, 1995), and has also published in numerous journals, including *Textual Practice*.

Tim Woods lectures in English and American Studies at the University of Wales, Aberystwyth. He is co-author with Peter Middleton of a monograph exploring new histories in literature (forthcoming Edward Arnold, 1998) and *Beginning Postmodernism* (Manchester University Press, 1998). He is co-editor with Dominic Rainsford of *Critical Ethics: Text, Theory and Responsibility* (forthcoming Macmillan, 1998), and co-editor with Andrew Hadfield and Dominic Rainsford of *The Ethics in Literature* (forthcoming Macmillan, 1998). He has published articles in several journals on contemporary fiction and poetry, including *English*, *Textual Practice* and *Parataxis*.

SELECT BIBLIOGRAPHY

I. Primary Texts

Jeanette Winterson, *Oranges Are Not the Only Fruit* (first published 1985; London: Vintage, 1991)

—, *Boating for Beginners* (first published 1985; London: Minerva, 1990)

—, *The Passion* (first published 1987; London: Penguin, 1988)

—, 'One Friday Not a Million Miles Past', in *Young Playwrights Festival 1988* (BBC, 1988)

—, *Sexing the Cherry* (first published 1989; London: Vintage, 1990)

—, 'The Lives of the Saints', in *Indiscreet Journeys: Stories of Women on the Road*, ed. by Lisa St. Aubin de Teran (Boston: Faber and Faber, 1990)

—, 'First Rites: Rewriting the Book of Love', *The Guardian*, 7 August 1991, 28

—, 'The Cells, Tissues, Systems and Cavities of the Body', in *The Body* (New York: Granta, 1992)

—, 'Newton', in *The New Gothic: A Collection of Contemporary Gothic Fiction*, ed. by Patrick McGrath and Bradford Morrow (London: Picador, 1992)

—, *Written on the Body* (London: Jonathan Cape, 1992)

—, 'The Poetics of Sex', in *The Penguin Book of Lesbian Short Stories*, ed. by Margaret Reynolds (London and New York: Viking, 1993)

—, 'The Queen of Spades', in *Venice*, ed. by John Miller and Kirsten Miller (San Francisco: Chronicle Books, 1994)

—, *Great Moments in Aviation, and Oranges Are Not the Only Fruit: Two Filmscripts* (London: Vintage, 1994)

—, *Art and Lies* (first published 1994; London: Vintage, 1995)

—, *Art Objects: Essays on Ecstasy and Effrontery* (first published 1995; London: Vintage, 1996)

—, *Gut Symmetries* (London: Granta, 1997)

II. Secondary Texts

A. Reviews

Annan, G., 'Written on the Body', *New York Review of Books*, 40, 5 (1993) 22-23

Barnet, A., 'Art-Objects — Essays on Ecstasy and Effrontery', *New York Times Book Review* (1996) 20

Boaz, A., 'Art-Objects — Essays on Ecstasy and Effrontery', *Library Journal*, 121, 3 (1996) 153

Bowcott, Owen, 'Coming out in the pantry', *The Guardian*, 4 January 1997

Burchill, Julie, 'Art and Lies', *The Spectator*, 25 June 1994, 26

Clark, A., 'Art-Objects — Essays on Ecstasy and Effrontery', *TLS*, 4810 (1995) 40

Cumming, Laura, 'Romantic Quips and Quiddities', *The Guardian*, 3 September 1992, 22

Duchene, A., 'The Passion', *TLS*, 4395 (1987) 697
Emck, Katy, 'Gut Symmetries', *TLS*, 3 January 1997, 21
Fisher, E., 'Boating for Beginners', *TLS*, 4309 (1985) 1228
Foden, Giles, 'GS', *The Guardian*, 16 January 1997
Gerrard, Nicci, 'Winterson, Jeanette, The Novelist Who Says If It Doesn't Shock It Isn't Art', *New Statesman & Society*, 2, 65 (1989) 12-13
Gill, A.A., 'All Spit and No Polish', *Sunday Times*, 16 July 1995, 10
Gorra, M., 'Sexing the Cherry', *New York Times Book Review*, April (1990) 24
Hegi, U., 'Oranges Are Not the Only Fruit', *New York Times Book Review*, November (1987) 26
Heller, Z., 'Storia 3, Consequences', *TLS*, 4548 (1990) 586
Hensher, Philip, 'Sappho's Mate', *The Guardian*, 5 July 1994, 13
Indiana, Gary, 'Art Objects — Essays of Ecstasia and Effrontery', *Artforum* (1996) 5
Johnson, Daniel, 'A Death Greatly Exaggerated', *The Times*, 20 May 1995, 14
Kaveney, R., 'Oranges Are Not the Only Fruit', *TLS*, 4277 (1985) 326
Lodge, David, 'The Passion', *New York Review of Books*, 35, 14 (1988) 25-26
MacCarthy, Fiona, 'Taking Up An Old Battle Cry', *The Observer*, 28 May 1995, 13
Mackay, S., 'Sexing the Cherry', *TLS*, 4511 (1989) 1006
Mars-Jones, Adam, 'From oranges to a lemon', *The Observer*, 5 January 1997
Messud, Claire, 'Written on the Body', *The Guardian*, 7 September 1993, 11
Pages, A., 'Written on the Body', *American Book Review*, 16, 6 (1995) 19
Pritchard, W.H., 'Art and Lies, A Piece For Three Voices And A Bawd', *New York Times Book Review* (1995) 14-15
Sage, Lorna, 'Art and Lies', *TLS*, 4759 (1994) 22
Turner, Jenny, 'Novels Are Not the Only Voice', *The Guardian*, 26 May 1995, 9
Wood, James, 'Art and Lies by Jeanette Winterson', *The London Review of Books*, 16, 13 (7 July 1994) 9
—, 'The Three Jeanettes', *The Guardian*, 2 January 1997

B. Articles and Books

Allen, Carolyn, *Following Djuna: Women Lovers and the Erotics of Loss* (Bloomington: Indiana University Press, 1996)
Barr, Helen, 'Face to Face: A Conversation Between Jeanette Winterson and Helen Barr', *The English Review*, 2, 1 (September 1991) 31
Bollinger, Laura, 'Models for Female Loyalty: The Biblical Ruth in Jeanette Winterson's "Oranges Are Not the Only Fruit"', *Tulsa Studies in Women's Literature*, 13, 2 (Fall 1994) 363-80
Burns, C.L., 'Fantastic Language: Jeanette Winterson's Recovery of the Postmodern World', *Contemporary Literature*, 37, 2 (1996) 278-306
Connor, Steven, *The English Novel in History, 1950-1995* (London: Routledge, 1996)
Gerrard, Nicci, 'The Ultimate Self-Produced Woman', *The Observer*, 5 June 1994, 7
—, 'Cold Blast of Winterson At the Door', *The Observer*, 3 July 1994, 11
Griffin, Gabrielle, *Heavenly Love?: Lesbian Images in Twentieth-Century Women's Writing* (Manchester University Press, 1993)
Hinds, Hilary, '"Oranges Are Not the Only Fruit": Reaching Audiences Other Lesbian Texts Cannot Reach', in *The New Lesbian Criticism: Literary and Cultural Readings*, ed. by Sally Munt (Hemel Hampstead: Harvester Wheatsheaf, 1992) 153-73

Langland, E, 'Sexing the Text: Narrative Drag as Feminist Poetics and Politics in Jeanette Winterson's "Sexing the Cherry"', *Narrative*, 5, 1 (1997) 99-107

Longrigg, Clare, 'Get Out of My Life — Get One of Your Own', *The Guardian*, 8 July 1994, 24

Messud, Claire, 'The Body Politic', *The Guardian*, 26 August 1992, 29

Moore, Jane, 'Theorizing the Body's Fictions', in *Theorizing Culture: An Interdisciplinary Critique after Postmodernism*, ed. by Barbara Adam and Stuart Allan (New York University Press, 1995) 70-86

Moore, Lisa, 'Teledildonics: Virtual Lesbians in the Fiction of Jeanette Winterson', in *Sexy Bodies: The Strange Carnalities of Feminism*, ed. by Elizabeth Grosz and Elspeth Probyn (London: Routledge, 1995)

Palmer, Paulina, 'Postmodern Trends in Contemporary Fiction: Margaret Atwood, Angela Carter, Jeanette Winterson', in *Postmodern Subjects, Postmodern Texts*, ed. by Jane Dowson and Stephen Earnshaw (Amsterdam: Rodopi, 1995) 181-199

Pearce, Lynne, *Reading Dialogics* (London: Edward Arnold, 1994)

—, '"Written on Tablets of Stone?": Roland Barthes, Jeanette Winterson and the Discourse of Romantic Love', in *Volcanoes and Pearl Divers: Essays in Lesbian Feminist Studies*, ed. by S. Raitt (London: Onlywomen Press, 1995)

—, *Feminism and the Politics of Reading* (London: Edward Arnold, 1997)

Picardie, Ruth, 'Feuds Corner: Jeanette Winterson v Julian Barnes', *The Guardian*, 3 September 1992, 21

Reynier, C, 'The Paradoxical of Jeanette Winterson', *Etudes Anglaises*, 50, 2 (1997) 183-194

Singer, Bennett L., *Growing Up Gay Growing Up Lesbian: A Literary Anthology* (New York: New Press, 1994)

Stowers, Cath, 'Journeying with Jeanette: Transgressive Travels in Winterson's Fiction', in *Heterosexual Politics*, ed. by Mary Maynard and Jane Purvis (London: Taylor and Francis, 1995) 139-159

Turner, Jenny, 'Preacher Woman', *The Guardian*, 18 June 1994, 18

Woods, Tim and Peter Middleton, *New Histories in Literature* (forthcoming London: Edward Arnold)

INDEX

Printed in the United Kingdom
by Lightning Source UK Ltd.
100225UKS00001B/55-56